# DAVIDSON'S INTRODUCTORY
# HEBREW GRAMMAR

# DAVIDSON'S
# INTRODUCTORY
# HEBREW GRAMMAR

Twenty-Seventh Edition

James D. Martin

t & t clark

T&T Clark Ltd

*A Continuum imprint*

The Tower Building,
11 York Road,
London, SE1 7NX

80 Maiden Lane,
Suite 704
New York, NY 10038

www.continuumbooks.com

Copyright © T&T Clark Ltd, 1993

First published 1993
Reprinted 1998, 2003, 2004, 2006

ISBN 0 567 09642 4

British Library Cataloguing-in-Publication Data
A catalogue record for this book is available from the British Library

# CONTENTS

# PREFACE

Changed and changing circumstances in University education and in the educational background of students have made it clear for some years that a new edition of this long-established Hebrew Grammar was essential. Through the good offices of my colleague Professor J. C. L. Gibson of New College, Edinburgh – the same college where the original author held the Hebrew chair when the Grammar first saw the light of day in 1874 – and at the request of the publisher, I was invited, as long ago as the summer of 1981, to undertake this revision and given a completely free hand in the task.

When I was a student of Hebrew over thirty years ago and working with the 24th edition of this same Grammar, we spent a whole session learning basic Hebrew grammar before beginning the study of our set texts from the Hebrew Bible. Nowadays, for the most part, we have one term in which to learn the grammar before completing the session with a limited number of set texts. This complete revision of the Grammar is, therefore, much more condensed than previous editions, though it is interesting to note that the Grammar has progressively grown in length from a 1st edition of 166 pages to a 26th edition of 319. There are here now none of the exceptions and minutiae which filled the pages even of the 26th edition. Much of that last edition, too, still presupposed an education in the classics on the part of students, and often the grammatical terminology used was that of Greek and Latin. Now students are often not conversant with the grammar of English, and I have endeavoured to explain grammatical terms as I have gone along. There have been attempts in the recent past to present Hebrew grammar in terms not of traditional terminology but of that of modern linguistics. I am not convinced that students are any more familiar with the jargon of the latter than they are with the former, and since it is traditional terminology that they will encounter in every other Grammar, Dictionary and Commentary that they will use, it seems perverse not to introduce them to it from the beginning. This, then, in many ways, is a 'traditional' Grammar. In view of the reduced time factor for the learning of the basic grammar, English–Hebrew translation exercises have been omitted. The primary aim of the Grammar is to bring students as soon as possible to an ability to read the Hebrew Bible, and the emphasis is on reading and understanding and translating from Hebrew into English. Those familiar with earlier editions of the Grammar will see from the Contents page where this edition differs from its predecessors. The introductory material has been pruned and simplified; the order in which the grammar is dealt with is different, mainly in the treatment of the verb; I have added a section at the end to assist students in progressing to the next stage, namely the reading of the Hebrew Bible. In view of the very explicitly introductory nature of this new edition, I have also, in that final section, made a point of directing students to more detailed and reference Grammars, for inevitably not all grammatical points which they will find in the Hebrew Bible are dealt with in the pages that follow. With the same primary aim in mind I have introduced as exercises in the later chapters passages from the Hebrew Bible itself, and from time to time even in earlier sections Biblical phrases and sentences have been introduced where appropriate.

I have not followed that path chosen by a number of recent Hebrew Grammars of avoiding all but phrases and sentences actually attested in the Hebrew Bible. It does not seem to me to be possible, without constant explanation - or, often, non-explanation! - of constructions not yet covered at this or at that point in the Grammar, to limit oneself in that way. I therefore make no apologies for providing, for practice in forms and constructions, 'composed' Hebrew. This is particularly the case in dealing with the verb, since the total verbal system of Biblical Hebrew cannot be introduced at a stroke. Actual phrases and sentences from the Hebrew Bible - to begin with sometimes simplified - are introduced progressively more frequently.

In the preparation of this edition I have been indebted to a number of people. I am grateful to a succession of St Andrews students who have used earlier drafts of the Grammar in their first year class. Many of them have commented on structure and content over the years and have had their influence on the final version. I am most especially indebted to one of their number, Miss Anna C. Parsons of New Hampshire, USA, who volunteered over the summer of 1989 to prepare the Hebrew-English word-list and the Index and who did so in her usual efficient manner. Professor John Gibson of Edinburgh read and thoroughly criticised successive drafts and made many helpful suggestions. I hope that the eventual appearance of the revised Grammar will encourage him to complete his projected revision of Davidson's *Syntax*. Perhaps my greatest thanks goes to one of my St Andrews colleagues - not a fellow Hebraist but a New Testament scholar - Dr R. A. Piper. Thanks to his stimulus, his patient teaching and constant availability when problems arose - as arise they did! - I was introduced to the world of word-processing. Anyone familiar with that world will know how greatly facilitated the production of successive revisions of this book has been. Without Ron's help this revision of Davidson would have been even longer in the making than it has been.

In so far as John Mauchline, the reviser of the 25th and 26th editions, was my own teacher of Hebrew in Glasgow, it is to be hoped that the production of the 27th edition in St Andrews has not severed a chain of tradition that goes back through McFadyen (Mauchline's predecessor in the - originally Free Church College - chair in Glasgow) to Davidson himself (who was in the New - Free Church

– College in Edinburgh ). I trust too that John Mauchline would have been not unsympathetic to this very radical revision to suit the needs of times so very different from those in which he worked on earlier editions in the late 50s and early 60s. I can but echo what he himself said in his Preface to the 25th Edition: 'To write a Hebrew Grammar is to essay a difficult task; to revise a Hebrew Grammar which has been in use for many years is an unenviable one... It is hoped that the changes and modifications which have now been made will not detract from the worth of the Grammar and that it will continue to find acceptance and to be used widely in days to come as it has in the past.'

St Mary's College,
St Andrews

# INTRODUCTION

Contrary to popular opinion, Hebrew is not a difficult language to learn. It has the obvious initial impediment of a strange script and a direction of writing - from right to left - which is unfamiliar to us. But once these difficulties have been surmounted, Hebrew is no more difficult than any other language and is, indeed, a good deal simpler in its structure than most. There are, admittedly, no familiar pegs on which to hang new vocabulary. Words from Latin and, to a lesser extent, Greek have found their way into English and French, and there is a close relationship between English and German. The result is that when we try to learn Greek or Latin or French or German we find that there is much that is familiar. This is not the case with Hebrew, and students sometimes find it difficult to imprint Hebrew vocabulary on their minds. This again is a problem that gradually disappears with familiarity, and, in any case, Biblical Hebrew has a comparatively small working vocabulary. I quote from the Introduction to the 26th edition: To know thoroughly a dozen chapters is to acquire a vocabulary which has a wide usefulness.

Hebrew, the language in which the bulk of the Christian Old Testament is written, is a Semitic language. Languages are for the most part groupable in families. For example, French, Italian, Spanish and Portuguese are all directly descended from Latin and are known collectively as the Romance languages. The Semitic languages are a family of languages spoken throughout the Middle East. The most prominent members of that family are Hebrew and Arabic, but it also includes other ancient languages such as Akkadian (the language in ancient times of the Tigris-Euphrates valley) and Ethiopic, Syriac and Aramaic (in which parts of Ezra and Daniel are written).

This Grammar is concerned exclusively with Biblical Hebrew. Modern Israeli Hebrew is largely a linguistic revival, a rebirth, though Hebrew in some form or other has continued to be written and spoken since the Biblical period and has indeed flourished in some places and circumstances. Although this Grammar deals with what is essentially a *written* language, it is a language that in the context of worship has continued to be read aloud. There are various divergent traditions of such reading, but such complexities are beyond the scope of this book or the needs of the majority of its users. Written though the language may be, it is of help to be able to read it aloud intelligently and intelligibly, and I have recommended, broadly, the pronunciation of an educated speaker of Israeli Hebrew, since this is one which students may well encounter or already have encountered in the context of a visit to Israel. It cannot be promised that a grasp of Biblical Hebrew will be of much assistance in modern Israel. No one, having learned the language of Chaucer's *Canterbury Tales*, would hope thereby to make himself or herself understood in late 20th century Britain. But a familiarity with Biblical Hebrew is, of course, not a *dis*advantage to any who wish to proceed to learn modern Hebrew.

The learning of any language takes time and patience and a considerable amount of application. It may seem to many that, in the initial stages, the time is disproportionate, but with a determination to learn and a motivation in that the end result will be an ability to come to grips with the Hebrew Bible/Christian Old Testament in its original language, the learning of this ancient and beautiful language will be within the grasp of most. I have tried to smooth the path and give helpful pointers along the way, and it is my hope that with the assistance of the following pages, many will be brought to an appreciation of what the Hebrew Bible has to say to us across the centuries of those things which are of abiding value.

# HEBREW ALPHABET

| Form | | Sound and Sign | Name | Pronunciation | Numeri-cal Value |
|---|---|---|---|---|---|
| | Final | | | | |
| א | | ʾ | Aleph | Silent. Cf. *h* in 'hour' | 1 |
| ב בּ | | b, ḇ | Bēt | *b* as in 'book; *v* as in 'village' | 2 |
| ג גּ | | g, ḡ | Gimel | *g* as in 'good' | 3 |
| ד דּ | | d, ḏ | Dalet | *d* as in 'dark' | 4 |
| ה | | h | Hē | *h* as in 'hot' | 5 |
| ו | | v | Vav | *v* as in 'village' | 6 |
| ז | | z | Zayin | *z* as in 'zoo' | 7 |
| ח | | ḥ | Ḥēt | *ch* as in Scottish 'loch' | 8 |
| ט | | ṭ | Ṭēt | *t* as in 'ten' | 9 |
| י | | y | Yod | *y* as in 'yes | 10 |
| כ כּ | ך | k, ḵ | Kaph | *k* as in 'king'; *ch* as in 'loch' | 20 |
| ל | | l | Lamed | *l* as in 'long' | 30 |
| מ | ם | m | Mēm | *m* as in 'make' | 40 |
| נ | ן | n | Nūn | *n* as in 'now' | 50 |
| ס | | s | Samekh | *s* as in 'sing' | 60 |
| ע | | ʿ | Ayin | Silent | 70 |
| פ פּ | ף | p, p̄ | Pē | *p* as in 'pill'; *ph* as in philosophy | 80 |
| צ | ץ | ṣ | Ṣade | *ts* as in 'Watson' | 90 |
| ק | | q | Qoph | *k* as in 'king' | 100 |
| ר | | r | Rēsh | *r* as in 'run' | 200 |
| שׂ שׁ | | ś, š | Sin/Shin | *s* as in 'sing' *sh* as in 'shoe' | 300 |
| ת תּ | | t, ṯ | Tav | *t* as in 'ten' | 400 |

# HOW TO WRITE HEBREW

| *Printed Characters* | ← *Written Form* |
| --- | --- |
| א | א |
| ב | ב |
| ג | ג |
| ד | ד |
| ה | ה |
| ו | ו |
| ז | ז |
| ח | ח |
| ט | ט |
| י | י |
| כ | כ |
| ך | ך |
| ל | ל |
| מ | מ |

| Printed Characters | ← Written Form |
|---|---|
| ם | ־ ר ב ם |
| ן | י ו ו ן |
| ן | ־ ו ן |
| ך | ־ ר כ ס |
| ע | ` י ע |
| ף | . c ף פ |
| ף | ־ c ף ף |
| ץ | ' ו ע ץ |
| ץ | ' ו ץ |
| ק | ן ן ף ף |
| ר | ־ ר |
| ש | \ ∪ ש ש |
| שׁ | ' ∪ ש ש |
| ת | ᵕ ן ת ת |

## ALPHABET

Note that five letters modify their forms when they appear in final position in a word:

כ - ך; מ - ם; נ - ן; פ - ף; צ - ץ.

In both reading and writing Hebrew, the following letters should be carefully compared and distinguished.

1. ב and כ: כ is rounded, while ב is more angular and, above all, has the 'tittle' (cf. Matt. 5 :18) at the bottom right hand corner.

2. נ and כ: נ comes back on itself at the foot, while כ is square-cornered (usually rounded in the written form). Note, too, that נ is a narrow letter, while כ is broader.

3. ד and ך and ר: ד is square (with a tittle) at the top right-hand corner. ך (the final form of כ) is like ד but has its leg extending below the line. ר, on the other hand, is round at the top right-hand corner.

4. ה and ח and ת: ה is open at the top left-hand corner, ח is closed, while ת has, in addition, the hook at the bottom left-hand corner.

5. ו and ן and ז: ו and ן (the final form of נ) are the same, except that the latter extends below the line. ז is distinguished by its diagonal cross-bar which, in writing, should be kept fairly small.

6. מ and ט: מ is open at the *bottom* left-hand corner, while ט is open at the *top* left-hand corner. Both have tittles. ט should also be distinguished from ס which is completely closed.

7. ם and ס: ם (the final form of מ) is square, while ס is rounded.

8. ע and צ (ץ): ע is less curvaceous than צ. The latter's final form ( ץ) has its leg extending *below* the line, and this should distinguish it from ע which sits *on* the line. It should be carefully noted and remembered that ע is a (voiced) glottal stop, which should on no account be confused with the English consonantal sound 'y' (as in 'you'). The latter is represented in Hebrew by י.

Hebrew is written from right to left. That means that words are read from the right, pages from the top right hand corner and books from what we would consider to be the back.

# THE SOUNDS OF HEBREW – I

## THE CONSONANTS

In the Alphabet Table a rough and ready guide to the pronunciation of the Hebrew consonants has already been given. It might be helpful here to attempt a slightly more scientific description and classification, though we must always remember that Biblical Hebrew is a literary language which has been transmitted through the centuries by sometimes very different reading traditions in Jewish communities in different parts of the world. The pronunciation which we have indicated in the Alphabet Table approximates to that of the educated modern Israeli speaker of Hebrew. The variety of pronunciation recommended in traditional grammars of Biblical Hebrew (see, e.g., the 26th edition of Davidson) has no very firm scientific basis and is a Christian academic one which is based on the Sephardic (i.e. oriental, non-Yemenite, Jewish) pronunciation of Hebrew but departs from it in a number of particulars. The advantage of the modern Israeli pronunciation is that it is that of a living language which the student may encounter personally, or may indeed have already encountered, in Israel.

The consonants of Hebrew may be classified in the following way.

(a) *Labials* (those which use both lips in pronunciation):

These are 'p' ( פ ), 'b' ( ב ), and 'm' ( מ ) ; 'b' is the voiced version of voiceless 'p'. In the traditional pronunciation, 'w' ( ו ) was also included here, but in modern Israeli pronunciation (IH = Israeli Hebrew) it is pronounced as the voiced labio-dental fricative 'v' (see below).

(b) *Labio-dentals* (those which use the top teeth and lower lip):

These are the fricative consonants p ( פ ) and ḇ ( ב ), the latter being the voiced version of voiceless p (= f) and pronounced as 'v' in 'village'. Included here, too, is the fricative ו, also pronounced as 'v' in 'village'.

(c) *Dentals* (those which are produced by means of the tongue between the teeth):

This class comprises the fricatives, voiceless ṯ ('th' of 'thin') and voiced ḏ ('th' of 'this'), the traditional academic pronunciation of ת and ד in post-vocalic position (i.e. immediately following a vowel). However, in IH no distinction is made between ת and ת, and both are pronounced 't'. Similarly, no distinction is made between ד and ד, and both are pronounced 'd'.

However, the Jewish scholars who handed down to us the text of the Hebrew Bible (the Masoretes, from Hebrew 'Masorah' = 'tradition') seem to have intended that a distinction should be made, and the forms without the dot (*dagesh*; see below pp. 20-21) have traditionally been pronounced as ṯ and ḏ respectively. In this Grammar, in accordance with IH practice, the plosive pronunciation (t/d) will be used.

(d) *Alveolars* (those which are produced by contact between the tongue and the alveolar ridge, i.e. the ridge behind the top teeth). These are:

(i)   the lateral 'l' ( ל ).

(ii)  the nasal 'n' ( נ ).

(iii) the sibilants 's' ( ס ) and 'ś' ( שׂ ), which are essentially indistinguishable in pronunciation, and their voiced equivalent 'z' ( ז ).

(iv)  the rolled 'r' ( ר ). This has at least one trill, as is common in most dialects of Scots.

(v) the plosives 't' (voiceless) and 'd' (voiced), represented by ת/תּ and ד/דּ in Hebrew (see the note on the Dentals above).

(e) *Palatals* (those pronounced by contact between the tongue and the palate):

   (i) the plosive ṭ, the sound traditionally represented by ט. In IH this is not differentiated from the alveolar plosive t (ת/תּ), see above.

   (ii) the sibilants ṣ (צ) and š (שׁ), though the latter is pronounced slightly further forward and may perhaps be more accurately described as palato-alveolar or post-alveolar.

   (iii) the lateral 'y' (י).

(f) *Velars* (those pronounced by contact between the back of the tongue and the soft palate):

   (i) the plosives, voiceless 'k' (כּ) and voiced 'g' (ג/גּ).

   (ii) the fricative ḵ (כ in post-vocalic position), pronounced like the 'ch' in Scottish 'loch' (or German 'Bach'). In the traditional pronunciation, a voiced version g was represented by post-vocalic ג, but in IH no distinction is made between ג and גּ.

(g) *Uvulars* (those produced by contact between the uvula and the back of the tongue):

The only example of such a sound in Hebrew is the traditional pronunciation of 'q' (ק). In IH, however, the pronunciation of ק is not differentiated from that of the velar plosive כּ (k), see above.

(h) *Pharyngals* (those produced by the very back of the tongue being pulled back so far as almost to touch the wall of the pharynx):

These are the voiceless fricative ḥ (ח) and its voiced partner ḥ (ח). The former is pronounced much like the 'h' in 'house', though when it occurs in final position in a word in Hebrew, it is usually silent unless written ה (see below p. 21) The latter ( ח ) is, in IH, not differentiated from the velar fricative ‫כ‬ (see above).

(i) *Glottal stops* (where the passage of air through the space between the vocal chords ['the glottis'] is stopped):

This phonetic phenomenon occurs, e.g., in some British English pronunciations of 'water', where there is a 'stop' instead of the 't' sound: wo'er. In Hebrew there are two glottal stops, א and ע. In IH these are not differentiated, though originally the latter probably had quite a distinct 'consonantal' effect. Students must, however, be careful to distinguish א and ע in spelling. They are distinguished in transliteration and are represented by ' ( א ) and ' ( ע ).

In most Hebrew Grammars, and therefore in most works of reference, the pharyngals ( ה and ח ) and the glottals ( א and ע) have been somewhat inaccurately known as 'gutturals'. In the body of this Grammar, too, the term 'guttural' will be used, but always with single quotation marks or prefaced with the word 'so-called'.

For this whole descriptive approach to the phonetics of the consonants, students might like to consult, for example, J. D. O'Connor, *Phonetics* (Penguin Books, 1973), especially ch. 2, 'Articulatory Phonetics: How Speech Sounds are Produced' (pp. 22-70).

The classification of consonants may be laid out as follows in tabular form. The forms in square brackets are found in the traditional pronunciation but no longer occur in IH.

| | Labial | Labio-dental | Dental | Alveolar | Palatal | Velar | Uvular | Pharyngal | Glottal |
|---|---|---|---|---|---|---|---|---|---|
| Plosive | p,b, [w] | | | t,d | [ṭ] | k,g | [q] | | ' |
| Fricative | | p̱,ḇ,v | [ṯ,ḏ] | | | ḵ[g̱] | | h,ḥ | ' |
| Sibilant | | | | s/ś,z | ṣ,š | | | | |
| Lateral | | | | l | y | | | | |
| Rolled | | | | r | | | | | |
| Nasal | m | | | n | | | | | |

## EXERCISE

Transliterate, using the symbols from the 'Sound and Sign' column of the Alphabet Table on p. 3, the following groups of consonants (**remember that Hebrew is read from right to left and that all exercises begin at the right hand end of a line**):

דבר, ירד, גבר, זקן, דרך, טעם, מעט, עצה, עשׂה,
החשׁך, מים, קצף, אזן, כנען:

# THE SOUNDS OF HEBREW – II

## THE VOWELS

It will be observed that so far we have spoken only of the consonantal sounds and have said nothing about vowel sounds. This is because the Hebrew alphabet comprises only consonants, and Hebrew is therefore basically written without vowels. This is the case with modern Hebrew and with Arabic. If we were to write English in this way, for example, we might have a sentence such as

Th brwn br lpt vr th fnc.

It should not take us too long to realise that this can be read as

The brown bear leapt over the fence.

The third word is ambiguous and could be read as 'boar', but, assuming that such a sentence occurs not in isolation but in a wider narrative context, that context would almost certainly resolve the ambiguity.

In that we use English as our spoken *and* our literary language, it would not be too difficult to become accustomed to reading it in a purely consonantal script, and so it would be (and, indeed, is today in modern Israel) when Hebrew was the spoken *and* the literary language. Even from an early period in the written representation of Hebrew - the earliest Hebrew inscription, the so-called Gezer Calendar, dates from the 10th century BC/BCE - use was made of some consonants ( ה, ו and י ) to indicate vowel sounds. Difficulties increased, however, when Hebrew ceased to be the commonly spoken language of ancient Israel and was replaced by Aramaic, a related Semitic language which, from the time of the return from exile in Babylon (that is towards the end of the 6th century BC/BCE), progressively replaced Hebrew as the spoken language of Palestine. So, over this lengthy period, there was change and evolution in the use of these consonants, but by the end of the Old Testament period the following scheme was in use:

ה represented ā in final position.
  [e.g. מה = mā (when the ה itself is not pronounced and ā = 'a' as in 'father')]

ו represented both ō and ū in both final and internal positions.
  [e.g. לו = lō or lū (ō = 'o' as in 'bone' and ū = 'oo' as in 'zoo')]

י represented both ī and ē in both final and internal positions.
  [e.g. לי = lī or lē (ī = 'i' as in 'ravine' and ē = 'ay' as in the Scottish pronunciation of 'day' ('é' in French 'été')]

Not only did such a scheme still leave unresolved ambiguities, but there was a very strong desire that the Biblical text should be preserved as faithfully as possible. Such considerations impelled Jewish textual scholars to develop a more refined and sophisticated system of vowel-sound representation. What these scholars were endeavouring to do was to preserve and hand on the *tradition* of the pronunciation of the biblical text. The word for 'tradition' in Hebrew is *Masora*; the scholars who transmitted it are known as the *Masoretes*, and what they have transmitted is the *Masoretic Text* which includes not only the consonants but also the Masoretic system of vocalisation.

This last is a system of dots and dashes which are placed, for the most part, below the consonants and are thus not an integral part of the words themselves. This system of vocalisation arose out of a fairly long process of trial and error, in the course of which other, less comprehensive systems failed to hold their ground. This Masoretic system emerged in Tiberias (and is sometimes, therefore, known as the Tiberian system) and probably became dominant in the 6th/7th centuries AD (CE).

The vowel signs are mostly written below the consonants, and the order of pronunciation is consonant + vowel. Thus, for example, the sign ֗ is used to indicate a, and the combination לַ is pronounced la.

The following table indicates the signs used for the vowel sounds.

|   |   | *Short* |   |   | *Long* |   |   |
|---|---|---------|---|---|--------|---|---|
| a | (pataḥ) | ֗ | לַ (la) | ('hat') | (qāmeṣ) ֗ | לָ (lā) | ('calf') |
| e | (segōl) | ֯ | לֶ (le) | ('pen') | (sērē) ֗ | לֵ (lē) | ('pain') |
| i | (ḥīreq) | ֗ | לִ (li) | ('pin') | (ḥīreq) ֗ | לִי (lī) | ('ravine') |
| o | (qāmeṣ ḥaṭūp) ֗ | | לֹ (lo) | ('on') | (ḥōlem) וֹ | לֹ (lō) | ('bone') |
| u | (qibbūṣ) | ֗ | לֻ (lu) | ('put') | (šūreq) וּ | לוּ (lū) | ('true') |

*Notes*

1. The above division into 'long' and 'short' vowels is one that is convenient and practical for teaching and learning purposes rather than a scientific classification. The length or otherwise of vowels was probably determined by whether they occurred in a stressed or an unstressed syllable. On Syllable and Stress see below pp. 22 ff.

2. It will be obvious from the above table that the Masoretes pronounced what have been described above as a and o in exactly the same way (probably o), since they use the same vowel sign for both. However, both traditional pronunciation and IH distinguish two vowel sounds. These two sounds, o and a can be distinguished only with a knowledge of syllable structure and of accentuation within the Hebrew word (see below p. 23). The o-sound is by far the less common of the two, and to begin with in this Grammar the sign ֗ will always represent a.

3. Ṣērē sometimes appears with a vowel-letter written:
לֵי.

4. In IH no distinction is made, for the most part, between e (segōl) and ē (ṣērē). However, students may find it useful to distinguish them since they are represented in the Masoretic vocalisation system by two distinct vowel signs.

5. Note the position of the dot in relation to the vowel-letter in the cases of ō and ū. In these situations the ו has no consonantal value and simply acts as the stand or container for the vowel point: לֹו = lō ; לוּ = lū. In the case of ō when there is no ו as vowel letter, the dot is written at the top left-hand corner of the consonant: לֹא (lō'). If the ō-vowel precedes שׁ (š) or follows שׂ (ś), the sign for the vowel usually coincides with the point on the leg of שׁ/שׂ; for example מֹשֶׁה (mōše); שֹׂנֵא (śōnē'). In some print types, for example that used in Biblia Hebraica Stuttgartensia (the current critical edition of the Hebrew Bible), this coalescence does not happen, and two dia-critical points appear: מֹשֶׁה and שֹׂנֵא.

6. Grammarians have usually distinguished two different types of long vowels, pure long and tone long, and have tended to associate this distinction with the presence (pure long) or absence (tone long) of the vowel letters. This association can almost certainly not be consistently maintained, but the distinction itself is nevertheless important.

> (i) *Pure long* vowels are long by their nature and do not change, no matter what modifications take place in the word of which they are part.

> (ii) *Tone long* vowels, on the other hand, are long by virtue of their relationship to the stress (or 'tone') in a word; when that relationship varies as a result of modifications made to the word, so the length of these vowels can vary.

On the significance of 'stress' in Hebrew, see below pp. 22ff.

So far we have looked at full vowels - 'long' (pure long and tone long) and 'short'. But not all vowels are full vowels. In the English word 'potato', for example, the second and third vowels are both full vowels and both long, ē and ŏ respectively, but the first vowel is pronounced in a hurried and indistinct way. The term used in phonetics for such an indistinct vowel-sound is 'schwa', and this is the Hebrew term for such a vowel-sound: šəvā (שְׁוָא). In Hebrew it is represented thus: ְ . So לְ is read as lə, where ə represents the indistinct (or 'neutral') vowel. In the Grammar, instead of using scientific transliteration for this term, the form *sheva* will be used throughout.

The *sheva* sign occurs under every consonant in a Hebrew word which does not have a full vowel of its own, unless that consonant be the final consonant of a word. There are a very small number of forms (e.g. the 2nd f. s. of the Perfect of the verb: שָׁמַרְתְּ - see below p. 45) where the final consonant has a *sheva*. Only the final form of כ (ך) regularly has the *sheva* sign, and the latter is placed inside the consonant rather than under it: ךְ.

(a) The *sheva* is a *vocal sheva* (i.e. ə) if it occurs under the first consonant of a syllable, either at the beginning (e.g. קְטֹל [qəṭōl]) or in the middle (e.g. קָטְלוּ [qāṭəlū]) of a word. A syllable in a Hebrew word comprises consonant + vowel [cv] or consonant + vowel + consonant [cvc]. For a full discussion of the syllable see below, pp. 22ff.

(b) When it *closes* a syllable in the middle of a word it is a silent *sheva*, e.g. אַרְצָה 'arṣā ).

The *sheva* which follows a *long* vowel is generally a vocal *sheva* (as in קָטְלוּ above ), while the one which follows a *short* vowel is generally a silent *sheva* (as in אַרְצָה above).

If two *shevas* occur together in a word, the first is a silent *sheva* and the second a vocal one, e.g. יִשְׁמְרוּ ( yišmərū ). Two vocal *shevas* can never occur together. If, in the course of modifications made to the length of the vowels in a word as a result of a shift in the stress, such a situation were to arise, the first of these vocal *shevas* becomes the short vowel i.

There are three other vowel-sounds which are at a midway point between the *sheva* and the short vowels a, e and o. They are represented by a combination of the sign for *sheva* and the signs for these short vowels.

| | | | |
|---|---|---|---|
| ḥaṭep pāṭaḥ | ֲ | הֲ | ( hă ) |
| ḥaṭep segōl | ֱ | הֱ | ( hĕ ) |
| ḥaṭep qāmeṣ ḥaṭūp | ֳ | הֳ | ( hŏ ) |

These semi-distinct vowels occur in place of the simple *sheva* with the 'gutturals' ( א, ה, ח, ע - see above p. 11 ).

The vowels of Hebrew are mostly pure, but in some combinations of vowels and consonants, what appear to be diphthongs arise. These occur when a vowel-letter is preceded by a vowel which is not homogeneous with it. In such cases the vowel-letter assumes its consonantal value, and the resultant combination of vowel and consonant tends to become a diphthong.

For example :

- יַ  ay  pronounced like the word 'eye'
- וַ  āv  pronounced like the 'ow' in 'cow' traditionally but in IH as 'av' as in 'halve'
- וִ  īv  pronounced like 'ee' in 'see' traditionally but in IH like the word 'eve'

There are two other factors, connected with 'the sounds of Hebrew', which need to be noted to enable us to read the language correctly.

1. The Israelites seem to have been incapable of pronouncing a *final* 'guttural' unless it were preceded by a vowel of the a-type. If a vowel of a different type precedes the 'guttural', an 'a'-sound is intruded between

the vowel and the final 'guttural'. This is known as pātaḥ
furtive, and though it is often written *beneath* the
'guttural', it is pronounced before it and not after it,
e.g. רוּחַ (rūaḥ).

2. A number of letters are silent (quiescent) when they
occur at the end of a syllable. This is particularly the
case with א, e.g. רָאשִׁים (rāšīm) and with ה when, as we
have already seen (above pp. 10f.), it occurs at the end
of a word.

## EXERCISE

Transliterate the following Hebrew words:

יָד, גֵּר, חֵן, חֹק, גַּם, עַל, שׁוֹם, אִם, אַף, עֶבֶד, בְּךָ,
דֹּב, צַר, צָרָה, עִיר, אֹכֶל, רָץ, רוּץ, הֲנֵם, דִּבֵּר, אֱמֶת,
חָזַק, אֲשֶׁר, רֶפֶשׁ, שְׁפֶט, קָם:

# DAGESH

In the Alphabet Table (above, p. 3), we noted that six letters ( ב, ג, ד, כ, פ, ת ) were written either with a dot in them or without a dot. Traditional pronunciation distinguished between a plosive pronunciation (*with* the dot) and a fricative one (*without* the dot), though we noted that IH no longer makes this distinction in the cases of ג, ד and ת and simply uses the plosive pronunciation in every case. The plosive/fricative distinction is still made, however, in the cases of ב, כ and פ. This dot is known as *dagesh lene* (or 'soft *dagesh*'; *lene* [pronounced 'laynay'] is the Latin word for 'soft'; many terms traditionally used in Hebrew grammatical descriptions are Latin or of Latin origin, since Latin was once the international language of scholarship), and this type of *dagesh* occurs only with these six letters. The latter are often strung together to form an artificial word : bəgadkəpat ( בְּגַדְכְּפַת ), and these letters are known as the 'begadkephat letters'.

But *dagesh* is also used in Hebrew to indicate the doubling of a letter. Instead of writing the same letter twice (as, e.g., the 't' in English 'letter'), Hebrew writes it once and puts a dot inside it: עַמִּים ('ammīm). This *dagesh* is known as *dagesh forte* ('strong *dagesh*'; *forte* [pronounced 'fortay'] is the Latin word for 'strong'). In IH this doubling is not usually reproduced in pronunciation, and עַמִּים would be pronounced as 'amīm.

*Dagesh lene* is found in the 'begadkephat letters' at the beginning of a word (e.g. דָּבָר ) and at the beginning of a syllable if the immediately preceding syllable is closed (e.g. מִדְבָּר [midbār]; on open/closed syllables see below p. 22 ). One could express this in a different way by saying that in IH ג, ד and ת always have the plosive pronunciation, whether or not they contain *dagesh lene* and that ב, כ

and פ have the plosive pronunciation unless they are immediately preceded by a vowel sound. [In the traditional pronunciation this last formulation ('have the plosive pronunciation unless they are immediately preceded by a vowel sound') applies to all the 'begadkephat letters'.] This second way of formulating the rule allows for the possibility that if two words are felt to belong very closely together and if the first ends in a vowel sound and the second begins with ב, כ or פ (or, traditionally, any one of the 'begadkephat letters'), the latter, even at the beginning of a word, will not necessarily have the plosive pronunciation. Its closeness to the preceding word, which ends in a vowel, is such that it is felt to be 'immediately preceded by a vowel sound': cf. וַיְהִי כֵן (vayhīḵēn) = 'and it was so' (Gen 1:7).

If one of the 'begadkephat letters' is preceded by a vowel sound and has a *dagesh*, then it is *dagesh forte*, and it indicates doubling. In such a case it is always the plosive pronunciation that is 'doubled', e.g. דִּבֶּר (dibber or, in IH, diber).

It is a characteristic of the 'guttural' letters (א, ה, ח, ע - pp. 10-11) and of ר that they never take *dagesh forte*. In the cases of א, ע and ר, the immediately preceding vowel is often lengthened by way of compensation. That compensatory lengthening does not usually, however, take place with ה and ח.

There is one further usage of a dot inside a letter, in this case ה. When ה occurs as the final letter in a word, it is most often being used as a vowel-letter, mostly indicating a long a-sound. In such cases it is silent. There are a number of words, however, where ה is a consonant in its own right, and, where such is the case, final ה has a dot within it ( הּ ) to indicate its consonantal value as opposed to its use as a vowel-letter. The dot in this instance is known as mappīq.

# SYLLABLE AND STRESS

All Hebrew words and all syllables within a word begin with a consonant. A syllable in a Hebrew word comprises consonant + vowel (cv) or consonant + vowel + consonant (cvc). The former is known as an *open* syllable and the latter as a *closed* syllable.

In the word יָלַד (yālad ), we have two syllables: יָ ( yā ), an open syllable and לַד ( lad ), a closed syllable. Keeping in mind the rule that all syllables must begin with a consonant, there is no other way in which the word יָלַד can be divided.

A consonant followed by a simple ( vocal ) or a composite *sheva* is not considered to be a syllable in its own right. It is regarded as a kind of 'upbeat' before the following cv (c). In דְּבָרִים , for example, there are only two syllables, dəḇā and rīm. In IH some speakers still pronounce the vocal *sheva* as the neutral vowel, but an increasing number of speakers no longer distinguish the vocal *sheva* from the silent *sheva*, especially at the beginning of a word and after a long vowel. Such speakers would pronounce דְּבָרִים as dḇārīm. This, of course, emphasises the point just made, namely that in דְּבָרִים there are only two syllables. The syllabic structure of דְּבָרִים could, therefore, be described as ccv + cvc.

In terms of the long vowel/short vowel classification described above pp. 15f. - though keeping in mind that that was a classification helpful for teaching and learning purposes rather than a scientific description - we can say that an open syllable usually contains a 'long' vowel (as in the יָ of יָלַד ). The vowels of closed syllables may be either 'long' or 'short', though such a distinction does not seem to be determined by the stress in a word. In דָּבָר , for example, the stress falls on the final syllable, and the vowel of that syllable ( בָר ) is 'long', while in

יֶלֶד the stress also falls on the final syllable, but the vowel in that instance (לֶד) is traditionally classified as 'short'. It may, however, be more accurate to describe the vowel as 'long patah', but for our purposes, it may, for the time being, be thought of as 'short', even though it is in the accented syllable. This difficulty in classification and description serves to point to the problem of trying to classify what is ultimately unclassifiable. What pass for 'rules' in the grammar of any language have to be regarded as 'general guides' which do not cover every situation.

A syllable which is closed and *un*accented must, however, have a short vowel. It is by means of this rule that we can distinguish between ָ = ā and ָ = o. If ָ occurs in a closed and unaccented syllable, the vowel of such a syllable must be short and therefore ָ = o. If ָ occurs in an open syllable, the vowel of such a syllable must be long and therefore ָ = ā. In the word חָכְמָה, for example, the accent falls on the final syllable. The final ה is a vowel-letter so that the final syllable is regarded as open, and the vowel of that open syllable must be long and is therefore ā. The first syllable is closed and is unaccented; its vowel must therefore be short, so ָ here represents o. The word, then, reads ḥokmā ('wisdom'). In דָּבָר, the second syllable is closed, but it is accented, and its vowel is most probably long and therefore ā ; the first syllable is open, and the vowel is therefore also ā, hence dābār ('word').

It will be clear from what has already been said in this section that the accent in a Hebrew word generally falls on the final syllable of a word. The vowel of the accented syllable is generally a long vowel. Cf. again דָּבָר, where the vowel of the final (closed) syllable is long because of its position in relation to the stress in the word (sometimes known, as we have already seen, as the *accent* and sometimes also as the *tone* ). The ā-vowel of the בָר of דָּבָר is often therefore described as 'tone-long' (see the foot of p. 16).

In the case of דָּבָר, the vowel of the penultimate (in this case 'first') syllable of the word, i.e. the vowel of the open, 'pre-tonic' syllable, is also considered to be 'tone-long', i.e. long because of its position immediately before the main accent (or 'tone') in the word. In the form דְּבָרִים, on the other hand, the accent is now on the ים_ ending, it is the vowel of בָ that is now pre-tonic and tone-long, while the vowel of the ד is now two places from the accent and has reduced to *sheva*. If the pre-tonic syllable is closed, however, as, for example, in מִדְבָּר (midbăr), then its short vowel is 'protected' by the consonant which follows it, and the position of the accent within the word has no effect on it, hence מִדְבָּרִים (midbărīm).

There is, however, another stress pattern in Hebrew where the vowel of the pre-tonic syllable reduces to *sheva*. In a noun of the type קוֹטֵל, the form קוֹטְלִים has its accent, as usual, on the final syllable, but the pre-tonic vowel, originally ε ( קוֹטֵל ), reduces to *sheva*. We find the same structure in verb forms also, where a singular form יִשְׁמֹר becomes plural יִשְׁמְרוּ, where again the accent is on the final syllable ( רוּ ) and the original ŏ of יִשְׁמֹר has reduced to *sheva*.

There is no need at the moment for the student to do other than observe that two different stress patterns occur in Hebrew. As we encounter them in context in the chapters that follow, we shall refer back to whichever of these two patterns is the relevant one.

Not all Hebrew words are accented on the final syllable, and a considerable number of words, including an important class of nouns, have the accent on the penultimate syllable, e.g. מֶלֶךְ ( mélek ), נַעַר ( ná'ar ). Penultimate stress will be noted in the body of the Grammar (but not in the phrases and sentences in the

Exercises), otherwise it should be assumed that the stress is on the final syllable of a word.

Two other symbols, both having to do with stress, are essential for the correct reading of Hebrew.

1. There is a sign which resembles the hyphen in English and which serves to join two basically separate entities into a single stress or accentual unit. For example, in the Hebrew expression אֵת הַשָּׁמַיִם ( = 'the heavens', the object of 'God created' in Gen 1:1) the two component parts can stand, as in the text of the Hebrew Bible in this particular verse, as two separate units each with its own accent. The expression is, however, also found, in other texts in the Bible (cf., e.g., Ex 20:11), as אֵת־הַשָּׁמַיִם, where the sign ־ (called maqqēp) joins them into a single unit where there is only *one* accent (on the penultimate syllable of הַשָּׁמַיִם) and where אֵת has lost its own accent and has had its long *ē* -vowel reduced to short e . On the significance of אֵת ( אֵת־) see below p. 46.

2. There is also a sign which comprises a small upright stroke to the left of the vowel sign (or under the consonant in the case of ō and ū ). This is known as *meteg* (usually found as *metheg*) and serves to preserve a full vowel two places from the tone. In the first of the stress patterns noted above, the vowel in such a position reduces to *sheva* (e.g. דְּבָרִים ). Where a full vowel *is* found in such a position, it is to some extent anomalous, and its status is preserved by means of *meteg*, e.g. אָנֹכִי, הָאָדָם. In the second of the two stress patterns we have seen that the pre-tonic vowel reduces to (vocal) *sheva*, and the preceding vowel, now in an open syllable and therefore usually long, is again preserved by means of *meteg*. Hence אָכְלָה ( 'āḵəlā ). The same form without *meteg* would be אָכְלָה ( 'oḵlā ), with a silent *sheva* and therefore an unaccented, closed syllable with a short vowel. This is one important way of differentiating ָ = ā and ָ = o ; see above p. 23.

**3.** Two other signs (called *atnah* [ ˄ ] and *silluq* [ ˌ ]
- the latter not to be confused with *meteg*) are found in
the connected text of the Hebrew Bible. They indicate
stress and pause in the verses of the Bible, but they can
be usefully understood only in the context of a complete
verse. We shall, therefore, explain their significance in
such a context in due course (see below, pp. 106f.).

## EXERCISE

Read aloud, and write in their English form, the following
proper names:

אַבְרָהָם, יִצְחָק, יַעֲקֹב, יִשְׂרָאֵל, יְהוּדָה, בִּנְיָמִין, מֹשֶׁה,
מִרְיָם, דְּבוֹרָה, שְׁמוּאֵל, דָּוִד, עָמוֹס, יִרְמְיָהוּ, בֵּית לֶחֶם:

# LESSON ONE

## NOUNS

### I

There is no special way of expressing 'a' (the indefinite article) in Hebrew. מֶלֶךְ can mean either simply 'king' or 'a king'. Hebrew expresses 'the' (the definite article) by prefixing to a noun or adjective the consonant ה with the vowel-sound a and, where possible, doubling the first letter of the word which is being defined. This doubling is shown by means of a *dagesh*.

הַמֶּלֶךְ - the king

When the ה is prefixed to a word which begins with one of the so-called 'gutturals' ( ע, ח, ה, א ) or ר - a type of consonant which is never doubled (see above p. 21) - it *usually* compensates for this lack of doubling by taking a *long* ā-vowel.

| | | | |
|---|---|---|---|
| הָאִישׁ | - the man | הָהָר | - the mountain |
| הָעֶבֶד | - the slave | הָראשׁ | - the head |

In a few cases (usually involving ה and ח ), even where this non-doubling does not take place, the short vowel is still retained.

הַהֵיכָל - the temple  הַחֶרֶב - the sword

In still fewer cases (usually involving ה, ח and ע ), the vowel of the ה is e.

הֶחָכָם - the wise [man](adj)  הֶעָמָל - the trouble

The reasons for these two rarer cases have to do with where the accent falls in the word and need not detain us here. The vocalisation of the article is fully described in tabular form on p. 165.

### II

The conjunction 'and' is expressed in Hebrew by ו (with the indistinct vowel-sound ə - *sheva*) and is prefixed to the word which follows it.

מֶלֶךְ וְכֹהֵן - king and priest

הַמֶּלֶךְ וְהַכֹּהֵן - the king and the priest

It is normally vocalised with *sheva*, but when the word to which it is prefixed itself begins with *sheva* (e.g. the proper name שְׁמוּאֵל 'Samuel') or with one of the consonants ב, מ, פ (the labial consonants, so-called because they are formed by bringing the *lips* [Latin 'labia'] together, see above p. 8), then ו is vocalised with an *ū*- sound.

הַמֶּלֶךְ וּשְׁמוּאֵל - the king and Samuel

כֹּהֵן וּמֶלֶךְ - priest and king

But in הַכֹּהֵן וְהַמֶּלֶךְ 'the priest and the king', the definite article has intervened between the ו and the labial consonant, so the vowel of the ו is, as usual, *sheva*.

If the ו comes immediately before the accent, it is often vocalised with qāmeṣ ( ָ ). This is particularly the case with words which belong together as a pair.

יוֹם וָלַיְלָה - day and night

זָהָב וָכֶסֶף - gold and silver

In כֶּסֶף וְזָהָב, however, the ו is no longer pre-tonic and is vocalised with *sheva*.

### III

Nouns in Hebrew are either masculine or feminine in gender. Where they refer to living beings, the gender corresponds to the sex of the person (or animal) referred to.

אִישׁ ('man') is masculine

אִשָּׁה ('woman') is feminine

But when nouns refer to inanimate objects, there is no fixed way of knowing what their gender may be. All *feminine* nouns in this Grammar will be marked as such: *f.*

אֶרֶץ *f* - land, earth

(note the form of this particular noun with the definite

article: הָאָרֶץ ‎)

עִיר ‎*f* - city, town

If no gender indication is noted, the noun in question is masculine.

## EXERCISE ONE

Vocabulary (in addition to words used in Lesson):

| | | | |
|---|---|---|---|
| אוֹר ‎ | - light | חֹשֶׁךְ ‎ | - darkness |
| בֹּקֶר ‎ | - morning | עֶרֶב ‎ | - evening |

Translate:

1. אִישׁ וְאִשָּׁה: 2. הָאִישׁ וְהָאִשָּׁה: 3. הָאוֹר וְהַחֹשֶׁךְ:

4. יוֹם וָלַיְלָה: 5. הַכֶּסֶף וְהַזָּהָב: 6. הָעֶרֶב וְהַבֹּקֶר:

7. הָעֶבֶד וְהֶחָכָם: 8. הַחֶרֶב וְהַהֵיכָל: 9. כֹּהֵן וּמֶלֶךְ:

10. הָעִיר וְהָהָר:

## Note

Students are strongly advised to begin now making their own personal Hebrew-English 'dictionary' either by means of an indexed notebook (suitably adapted for the Hebrew alphabet!) or of index cards. All words occuring in the Grammar will be given - for the most part - only once, either in the body of the Lesson or in the supplementary Vocabulary with the Exercise. All appear in the Hebrew-English word-list at the end of the Grammar (pp. 200ff.) with a page reference indicating their first and/or first *significant* occurrence, but it cannot be stressed too much that the building up of a working vocabulary for a student must be cumulative. For guidance on the systematic building up of a vocabulary see p. 160 (IV).

# LESSON TWO

## ADJECTIVES – VERBLESS SENTENCES

### I

An adjective may be used in two different ways.

1.  It may be used to *qualify* a noun, as in 'a great king' or 'the good man'. When used in this way in Hebrew it usually comes *after* the noun it qualifies.

מֶלֶךְ גָּדוֹל - a great king

אִישׁ טוֹב - a good man

If the noun has the definite article ('the'), then the adjective must also have it.

הַמֶּלֶךְ הַגָּדוֹל - the great king
(lit. 'the king, the great [one]')

הָאִישׁ הַטּוֹב - the good man

If a noun is qualified by two adjectives, then both follow the noun.

מֶלֶךְ גָּדוֹל וְטוֹב - a great and good king

Again, if the noun has the definite article, both adjectives will also have the definite article.

הַמֶּלֶךְ הַגָּדוֹל וְהַטּוֹב - the great and good king

When an adjective qualifies a noun in this way, it must be in agreement with it, not only, as we have just seen, with regard to its definiteness, but also with regard to its *gender*. The usual indicator of feminine gender is the ending ה ָ - (cf. the noun אִשָּׁה - woman).

הָאִשָּׁה הַטּוֹבָה - the good woman

In the case of many adjectives, the addition of the feminine ending ה ָ - involves a change in the vowel pattern of the adjective. The feminine form of גָּדוֹל , e.g., is גְּדוֹלָה .

הָעִיר הַגְּדוֹלָה - the great city

We shall return to this phenomenon when we deal with the different patterns of nouns, but it may be noted

- 30 -

now that this is an example of the first stress pattern in Hebrew, referred to above pp. 23f.

2. But an adjective may also be used as the *complement* of the verb 'to be', as in 'the king is great'. In Hebrew in this usage the verb 'to be' is not expressed, and the adjective usually comes first. In sentences of this kind in Hebrew ('nominal' *or* 'verbless' sentences), the adjective does *not* take the article even when the noun has it.

נָּדוֹל הַמֶּלֶךְ – The king is great
(lit. 'Great [is] the king')

טוֹב הָאִישׁ – The man is good
(lit. 'Good [is] the man')

In this type of sentence the two elements are called *subject* ('the king') and *predicate* ('[is] great'). When an adjective, then, is the predicate of a verbless sentence, there is, as we have seen, no agreement with regard to definiteness, but there is gender agreement between subject and predicate.

טוֹבָה הָאִשָּׁה – The woman is good
גְּדוֹלָה הָעִיר – The city is great

There are a number of instances where the word order would be noun + adjective (i.e. subject + predicate), but the circumstances under which this order would occur involve a more detailed examination of the structure of the Hebrew sentence than is possible in an elementary treatment of the language such as this.

## II

The common negative in Hebrew is לֹא 'not', and it usually precedes the word which it negates.

לֹא צַדִּיק הַמֶּלֶךְ – The king is not righteous

## III

Although וֹ is mostly translated by 'and', when a

contrast is implied between the two elements which it
joins, then it may more suitably be translated by 'but'.

קְדוֹשָׁה הָעִיר וְלֹא קְדוֹשָׁה הָאָרֶץ - The city is holy but
the land is not holy

## EXERCISE TWO

Vocabulary (in addition to words already used):

Nouns:

עַם ( הָעָם ) - people
(cf. also הַר ( הָהָר ) - mountain )
רָעָב - famine

Adjectives:

רַע ( הָרָע ) - bad, evil     כָּבֵד - heavy, serious
עָצוּם - powerful

Translate:

1. הַמֶּלֶךְ הַצַּדִּיק:
2. הָהָר הַגָּדוֹל וְהָאָרֶץ הַטּוֹבָה:
3. הָעִיר הַקְּדוֹשָׁה:
4. הַהֵיכָל הַגָּדוֹל:
5. הָעָם הֶעָצוּם וְהַגָּדוֹל:
6. הָאִישׁ הַטּוֹב וְהֶחָכָם:
7. טוֹב הָעֶרֶב וְטוֹב הַבֹּקֶר:
8. קְדוֹשָׁה הָעִיר:
9. צַדִּיק הַכֹּהֵן וְלֹא צַדִּיק הָעָם:
10. כָּבֵד הָרָעָב:
11. רַע הַכֶּסֶף וְרַע הַזָּהָב:
12. רַע הַחֹשֶׁךְ וְטוֹב הָאוֹר:

# LESSON THREE

## NUMBER

Nouns are said to be 'singular' when they refer to only one person or thing, e.g. boy, book, etc. They are 'plural' when they refer to more than one, e.g. boys, books, etc. The Hebrew noun has three ways of expressing *number*: singular, plural and dual. The 'dual' form is used to refer to 'two' of the category.

## Singular

We have already met the singular. The *masculine* singular has no special form.

אִישׁ – (a) man     דָּבָר – (a) word     מֶלֶךְ – (a) king

The characteristic ending of the *feminine* singular is הָ . This is the way in which the feminine is indicated in the adjective (see above Lesson Two I,1), and many feminine nouns also end in הָ as we have already seen in the case of אִשָּׁה 'woman'. But many nouns which are feminine have, like the masculine, no special ending in the singular.

אֶרֶץ *f* – land     עִיר *f* – city     בַּת *f* – daughter

Gender, in these instances, has to be learned, if it is not implied by the sex of the person (or animal) designated, as it is, for example, in בַּת – 'daughter'.

## Plural

The plural ending for masculine nouns is ים_ .

סוּס – horse     סוּסִים – horses

The same operates in the case of the adjective.

טוֹב – good (m.s.) טוֹבִים – good (m.pl.)

The accent in a Hebrew word usually falls on the last syllable, and the addition of the masculine plural ending to a word of more than one syllable often has an effect on the length of the vowels in the word to which

– 33 –

it is added. In דָּבָר , for example, the accent is on the second syllable (bār), and its vowel is long. The vowel of the syllable immediately before the accent (dā) is also long (tone-long). This is the first stress pattern referred to above pp. 23f. In the plural דְּבָרִים, the stress is on rīm; bā is tone-long immediately before the accent, but the vowel of the original first syllable is two places from the accent and has been reduced to *sheva*. We shall deal with the classification of nouns in due course. For the moment it will be sufficient to remember that the addition of both plural (and dual) endings affects the vowel pattern of many nouns of more than one syllable.

In the case of feminine nouns, where they have the characteristic feminine ending ָה , that ending is changed to וֹת.

סוּסָה – mare          סוּסוֹת – mares

Again, the same operates in the case of the adjective.

טוֹבָה – good (f.s.)   טוֹבוֹת – good (f.pl.)

When the feminine noun has no special ending, the וֹת is often simply added to the singular form.

כּוֹס *f* – cup          כּוֹסוֹת – cups

## Dual

The dual ending is ַיִם , and this termination is added to the singular form (sometimes with vowel modification) if that has no specific ending. If the noun has the ending ה in the singular, the ה is modified to ת before the dual ending.

יָד *f* – hand          יָדַיִם – (two) hands
שָׂפָה *f* – lip          שְׂפָתַיִם – (two) lips

In Hebrew, the use of the dual is largely confined to things which go in pairs, e.g. parts of the body such as 'hand', 'lip', etc. and to one or two other common expressions such as the numbers '2', '200' and the like. It is worth

– 34 –

noting that those things which *do* occur 'in pairs' in this way are usually feminine in gender.

We can now add to our earlier rule that qualifying adjectives follow the noun and agree with it in definiteness and in gender, the fact that they also agree in number. There is no dual form of the adjective. With dual nouns it is the plural form of the adjective that is used.

סוּס טוֹב - a good horse
הַסּוּס הַטּוֹב - the good horse
טוֹב הַסּוּס - the horse is good

סוּסָה טוֹבָה - a good mare
הַסּוּסָה הַטּוֹבָה - the good mare
טוֹבָה הַסּוּסָה - the mare is good

סוּסִים טוֹבִים - good horses
הַסּוּסִים הַטּוֹבִים - the good horses
טוֹבִים הַסּוּסִים - the horses are good

סוּסוֹת טוֹבוֹת - good mares
הַסּוּסוֹת הַטּוֹבוֹת - the good mares
טוֹבוֹת הַסּוּסוֹת - the mares are good

שְׂפָתַיִם צַדִּיקוֹת - righteous lips
הַשְּׂפָתַיִם הַצַּדִּיקוֹת - the righteous lips
צַדִּיקוֹת הַשְּׂפָתַיִם - the lips are righteous

# EXERCISE THREE

Vocabulary (additional):

Nouns:

שִׁיר - song        נָבִיא - prophet

שָׁמַיִם (pl.) - heaven(s), sky

(This noun is plural in its form in Hebrew, as is also the word מַיִם - water. The meaning of both nouns is, however singular, and they are translated by singular nouns in English.)

פַּר ( הַפַּר ) - ox        פָּרָה *f* - cow

שַׂר ( הַשַּׂר ) - prince, officer   שָׂרָה *f* - princess

Adjectives:

חָדָשׁ - new        רָם - high, lofty

Translate:

1. הַדְּבָרִים הַטּוֹבִים:
2. הַפָּרוֹת הָרָעוֹת:
3. הַשָּׂרוֹת הַטּוֹבוֹת:
4. הַשִּׁירִים הַחֲדָשִׁים:
5. הַנְּבִיאִים הַקְּדוֹשִׁים:
6. טוֹבִים הַסּוּסִים וְטוֹבוֹת הַסּוּסוֹת:
7. צַדִּיקִים הַנְּבִיאִים וְלֹא צַדִּיקִים הַשָּׂרִים:
8. רָעִים הַפָּרִים וְטוֹבוֹת הַפָּרוֹת:
9. רָמִים הֶהָרִים וְרָמִים הַשָּׁמַיִם:
10. קָדוֹשׁ הָעָם וְלֹא קְדוֹשִׁים הַשָּׂרִים וְהַנְּבִיאִים:

# LESSON FOUR

## PRONOUNS

A 'pronoun' is a word which stands 'in place of' (Latin 'pro') a noun. There are several different kinds of pronouns, of which the most important are the personal pronouns and the interrogative pronouns.

## I

## PERSONAL PRONOUNS

It is important that the student should *memorise* these personal pronouns. Fragments of them are used in the verb to distinguish person, gender and number, and familiarity with them in their full form as given here will greatly help an understanding of the verb forms. The fact that they are given in the order of 3rd - 2nd -1st (whereas in English grammar we tend to find them in the order 1st - 2nd - 3rd) will become clear when we come to the verb.

|  |  | Singular |  | Plural |  |
|---|---|---|---|---|---|
| 3rd person | m. | הוּא | – he/it | הֵמָּה / הֵם | – they |
|  | f. | הִיא | – she/it | הֵנָּה | – they |
| 2nd person | m. | אַתָּה | – you | אַתֶּם | – you |
|  | f. | אַתְּ | – you | אַתֵּן | – you |
| 1st person | c. | אֲנִי/אָנֹכִי | – I | אֲנַחְנוּ | – we |

Notice that Hebrew has different ways of speaking *to* someone (2nd person) depending on how many people are being addressed (singular/plural) and of what sex they are (masculine/feminine), whereas in English the same word ('you') is used for all situations (though in religious contexts the archaic 'thou'/'thee' are still sometimes used when addressing God). The same distinction occurs when speaking *about* someone (3rd person), though English here also makes a gender distinction in the singular ('he'/'she'). No such gender distinction is made in the 1st person, and it is therefore described as being 'of *common* (c.) gender'.

These forms of the pronoun in Hebrew are used only when they are the subject of a sentence.

הוּא הַמֶּלֶךְ - He (is) the king

אַתָּה הָאִישׁ - You are the man (2 Sam 12:7)

This order, subject (personal pronoun) + predicate (noun), occurs when the sentence is *identifying* the subject. In such cases the predicate is definite. In a sentence of this kind which is *classifying* (or defining) the subject, the predicate is normally indefinite and comes first.

צַדִּיק אַתָּה - You are righteous (O Lord) (Jer 12:1)

כֵּנִים אֲנַחְנוּ - We are honest (Gen 42:11)

לֹא אָדָם הוּא - He is not a man (1 Sam 15:29)

In the type of verbless sentence discussed in Lesson Two I,2 there is found a characteristic usage of the personal pronoun. When the adjective (predicate) comes first, the sentence is as already described.

גָּדוֹל הַמֶּלֶךְ - Great (is) the king.

When, however, the subject comes first, the sentence is often modified by the use of the 3rd person personal pronoun, in the appropriate gender and number, as a connective word.

הַמֶּלֶךְ הוּא גָּדוֹל - The king, he (is) great.

הָאִשָּׁה הִיא טוֹבָה - The woman, she (is) good

These Hebrew sentences may be translated quite simply as 'The king is great' and 'The woman is good' respectively. The fact that the subject comes first, however, may imply an emphasis on the subject which might be rendered in English as 'It is the king (as opposed to anyone else) who is great' and 'It is the woman who is good'.

## II

## INTERROGATIVE PRONOUNS

These are question words.

1.                     מִי - who?

is used for persons and does not change its form for

gender or number.

(a) מִי הַמֶּלֶךְ הַגָּדוֹל - Who is the great king?

To which the answer might be

שְׁלֹמֹה הוּא הַמֶּלֶךְ הַגָּדוֹל - Solomon is the great king.

(b) מִי הָאִשָּׁה הַצַּדִּיקָה - Who is the righteous woman?

To which the answer might be

דְּבוֹרָה הִיא הָאִשָּׁה הַצַּדִּיקָה - Deborah is the righteous woman.

2. (a) מָה - what?

is used for things. Like מִי , this does not change its form for gender or number, but its vowel varies in a way which is not unlike the way in which the vowel of the definite article varies.

The vowel is a, with the doubling of the first consonant of the word to which מָה is immediately prefixed.

מַה־זֶּה - What is this?

For זֶה = 'this' see below p. 40. Note that מָה and זֶה are joined by maqqeph, for which see above p. 25.

In the case of א and ר the vowel is ā

מָה־אֲנִי - What am I?

מָה־אֱנוֹשׁ - What is man? (Ps 8:5)

אֱנוֹשׁ means 'mankind' and occurs only in poetry in Biblical Hebrew. The verse number here is that of the Hebrew Bible. Because the English versions [EVV] do not give a verse number to the psalm headings, the number of the verse in the EVV of the Psalms is usually one less than that of the corresponding number in the Hebrew.

מָה־אֵלֶּה - What are these? (Zech 2:2,4)

The context is that of Zechariah's vision of four horns and four smiths; for אֵלֶּה = 'these', see below.

In the case of ה and ח it is a

מַה־הוּא - What is he/it?

Sometimes, as was the case with the definite article, the vowel is e and this is often, though not exclusively, the case when an initial 'guttural' in the following word is vocalised with long ā.

מֶה־עָשָׂה – What has he done?

(עָשָׂה – he has done)

(b) When מַה is prefixed to an *adjective*, it is often being used not as an interrogative but as an exclamation and is sometimes, then, best translated into English by 'How...!'

מַה־טּוֹב הַמֶּלֶךְ – How good the king is!

מַה־צַּדִּיק הַנָּבִיא – How righteous the prophet is!

# III

## DEMONSTRATIVES

Although these are often described as pronouns (and often appear to function as such [e.g. This is a book ]), they are best thought of as adjectives, since in Hebrew they behave exactly like adjectives. There are two types of demonstrative: (1) the demonstrative of nearer reference ('this/these') and (2) the demonstrative of further reference ('that/those').

(1)    זֶה m. – this      אֵלֶּה m./f. – these

        זֹאת f. – this

(2)    הוּא m. – that      הֵם m. – those

        הִיא f. – that      הֵנָּה f. – those

Notice that the forms in (2) are identical with those of the 3rd person personal pronouns, m. and f., sing. and pl.

(a) Just as the adjective is used to *qualify* a noun ('a great king' or 'the good man') and, when used in this way in Hebrew, follows the noun and agrees with it in definiteness, gender and number, so too is the case with the demonstratives. The demonstratives are, of course, in this usage always definite, since, in using an expression like 'this boy' or 'that woman', we are referring not to *any* boy or *any* woman but to a particular boy and a particular woman.

הַיֶּלֶד הַזֶּה – this boy (lit. 'the boy, this one')

הָאִשָּׁה הַהִיא - that woman (lit. 'the woman, that one')

הַסּוּסִים הָאֵלֶּה - these horses (lit. 'the horses, these ones')

The demonstratives, then, *used as qualifying adjectives* follow the noun which they qualify, are *always* definite (i.e. have the definite article) and agree with the noun in gender and number.

(b) But an adjective may also be used as the predicate of a verbless sentence:

נָּדוֹל הַמֶּלֶךְ - The king is great
(lit. 'Great [is] the king')

and the demonstratives may also be used in this way:

זֶה הַמֶּלֶךְ - This (is) the king.

זֶה הַיּוֹם - This (is) the day (Judg 4:14).

אֵלֶּה הַדְּבָרִים - These (are) the words.

הִיא הַבַּת - That (or 'she') (is) the daughter.

Notice that the last example could be translated either as 'That is the daughter' or 'She is the daughter'.

Similarly:

הוּא הַיֶּלֶד - He is the boy *or* That is the boy

A wider context would help to decide which is the more appropriate translation.

So the demonstratives, *used as predicative adjectives in verbless sentences*, come first in the sentence, are always *indefinite* and agree with the noun (the subject of the verbless sentence) in gender and in number.

# EXERCISE FOUR

Vocabulary:

עֶבֶד (pl. עֲבָדִים) – slave      אִיזֶבֶל – Jezebel

נְבִיאָה – prophetess

Translate:

1. הוּא הַנָּבִיא הַקָּדוֹשׁ:

2. אַתָּה הָאִישׁ הָרָע:

3. אֲנִי הַמֶּלֶךְ הַגָּדוֹל:

4. אֲנַחְנוּ עֲבָדִים:

5. אַתֶּן נְבִיאוֹת צַדִּיקוֹת:

6. הֵם מְלָכִים עֲצוּמִים:

7. מִי אַתֶּם: אֲנַחְנוּ כֹּהֲנִים קְדוֹשִׁים:

8. מַה־זֶּה: זֶה הַהֵיכָל הֶחָדָשׁ:

9. הָאִשָּׁה הַטּוֹבָה הַזֹּאת:

10. הָהָר הָרָם הַהוּא:

11. הַיּוֹם הַזֶּה וְהַלַּיְלָה הַהוּא:

12. אֵלֶּה הַדְּבָרִים הַקְּדוֹשִׁים:

13. הֵם הֶהָרִים: מָה־רָמִים הֶהָרִים:

14. זֶה הַיֶּלֶד הַטּוֹב וְאֵלֶּה הַיְלָדִים הָרָעִים:

15. מִי הַשָּׂרָה הַזֹּאת: הִיא אִיזֶבֶל:

# LESSON FIVE

## THE VERB - THE PERFECT

### I

In English, different forms of a verb are used to indicate whether what is being described is linked to the past or the present or the future. For example, 'I guard' is the *present tense* of the verb '(to) guard', while 'I guarded' is the *past tense*. In an English verb further variety is achieved largely by using helping (auxiliary) verbs along with the infinitive or past participle, e.g. I shall guard, I have guarded, I had guarded, etc., where 'shall' (or 'will'), 'have', 'had', etc. are auxiliary verbs. In English, the differences in the *subject* of the verb are shown mostly by the use of the personal pronouns, e.g. *I* guard, *you* guard, *he* guards (in this last there is also a slight modification of the form of the verb), etc.

Also in English, when we refer to a verb, we usually refer to it in its *infinitive* form. We speak of 'the verb "to guard"', and 'to guard' is the infinitive. That part of the Hebrew verb which is usually cited as the simplest form of the verb (the citation form) is the 3rd person masculine singular of the perfect, since this is a form which is unencumbered by suffixes or prefixes. So we speak of 'the verb שָׁמַר' (note the short a in the final, stressed syllable; see above pp. 22 f.). In Hebrew-English word-lists or vocabularies we might well find the following:

שָׁמַר - to guard

where the two forms do not actually correspond in sense. The Hebrew form שָׁמַר could be translated by 'he has guarded', but it is simpler to cite the verbs in this way, using the normal citation forms of the two languages שָׁמַר for Hebrew and 'to guard' for English. Another common way of speaking of the Hebrew verb is to refer to שָׁמַר as the *root* of the verb. It is to the *root* that various elements will be added and various modifications made in order to indicate variety of person, number, gender and, sometimes, of meaning.

The words *tense* and *aspect* are used to describe ways in which verbs function in a sentence. 'Tense' denotes a form of the verb where the 'time' of an action is indicated. 'Aspect' is used when the main idea expressed by the verb is that of completeness or incompleteness of the activity. In the main, the Hebrew verbal system is an 'aspectual' one rather than a 'tense' one, that is, the main emphasis is on the completeness (Perfect) or incompleteness (Imperfect) of the activity being described. That is not to say that the Hebrew verb form does not or cannot express time ('tense'), and in an elementary treatment of grammar such as this it will be the tense usage that will predominate. It is, however, probably best to avoid the use of the terms 'tense' and 'aspect' and simply refer to the two conjugations as 'Perfect' and 'Imperfect'. For practical purposes for the moment, the meaning of the Perfect may be taken as 'past' - 'he has guarded' (the present perfect) or 'he guarded' (the simple past).

The *Perfect* of the Hebrew verb is formed by the addition of suffixes to the simplest form of the verb, which is itself already part of the Perfect, the 3rd person masculine singular, e.g. שָׁמַר - he has guarded. The added suffixes are mostly related in form to the personal pronouns which we have already learned (see above p. 37).

(A paradigm using the verb קָטַל may be found on p. 176.)

# THE PERFECT

| | | | |
|---|---|---|---|
| 3 s.m. | שָׁמַר | | he has guarded |
| 3 s.f. | שָׁמְרָה | | she has guarded |

Cf. the characteristic הָ feminine
ending in noun and adjective

| | | | |
|---|---|---|---|
| 2 s.m. | שָׁמַרְתָּ | Cf. אַתָּה | you have guarded |
| 2 s.f. | שָׁמַרְתְּ | Cf. אַתְּ | you have guarded |
| 1 s.c. | שָׁמַרְתִּי | | I have guarded |

Cf. the יָ ending of אָנֹכִי/אֲנִי

| | | | |
|---|---|---|---|
| 3 pl.c. | שָׁמְרוּ | | they have guarded |
| 2 pl.m. | שְׁמַרְתֶּם | Cf. אַתֶּם | you have guarded |
| 2 pl.f. | שְׁמַרְתֶּן | Cf. אַתֶּן | you have guarded |
| 1 pl.c. | שָׁמַרְנוּ | | we have guarded |

Cf. the נוּ - ending of אֲנַחְנוּ

This scheme of endings is the same for the Perfect of all forms of all verbs. If once the Perfect endings of the 'regular' verb are known, they will be easily recognisable in all other verbs. The same will hold true for the Imperfect in due course.

## II

The normal vowel-pattern of the 3rd masculine singular of the Perfect is ā-a (as in, e.g., שָׁמַר). Sometimes the vowel-pattern is ā-ā (cf. עָשָׂה - he has done, above p. 40). Verbs with these vowel-patterns (ā-a/ā-ā) describe *actions* (guarding, doing, ruling, killing) and are therefore known as *active verbs*. Another type of verb describes states (e.g. to *be* heavy, to *be* old, to *be* able, to *be* small) and are known as *stative verbs*. The vowel-pattern of the 3rd masculine singular of the Perfect of such verbs is either ā-ē or ā-ŏ.

כָּבֵד - to be heavy
זָקֵן - to be old
יָכֹל - to be able
קָטֹן - to be small

- 45 -

As with all rules, there are occasional exceptions. The vowel pattern ā-a is found, e.g., in חָכַם - to be wise.

The verbs with ē are inflected exactly like the verbs with a - כָּבַדְתָּ etc. (cf. שָׁמַרְתָּ). Those with ō retain the ō (קָטֹנְתָּ) except in the 2nd plural forms, where, in the unaccented, closed syllable the ō becomes a short o - קְטָנְתֶּם (qətontem). The Perfect of stative verbs corresponds to the English present tense.

כָּבַדְתִּי - I am heavy
קָטֹנְתִּי - I am small

## III

We have already observed the structure of the *verbless sentence* in Hebrew (see above p. 31). The other main type of sentence structure is the *verbal sentence*.

שָׁמַר הַכֹּהֵן אֶת־הַמִּזְבֵּחַ - The priest has guarded the altar.

The person who is the 'doer' of the action which the verb describes is known as the *subject* of the verb. The person (or, in this case, the thing) 'to whom' the action is done is the *object*. In the English sentence 'The priest has guarded the altar', 'the priest' is the subject, 'has guarded' is the verb and 'the altar' is the object. In the Hebrew sentence, two things should be noted. The verb usually comes first in the sentence (unlike English, where the subject is usually in first position). Secondly, the object, if it is definite (i.e., for the moment, if it has the definite article or is a proper name) is often, in prose (but not necessarily always there, and rarely in poetry), preceded by the particle אֵת (or אֶת־ with a short e-vowel, if it is joined to the following word by *maqqeph*, see above p. 25) which serves simply as the *object marker*, has no meaning as such and is therefore unrepresented in the English translation. The order *Perfect* + subject is quite regular in speech, but, as we shall see in due course (Lesson 12, pp. 85 ff.), in narrative the verb form is a different one.

- 46 -

Although the normal word-order of a Hebrew verbal sentence is verb - subject - object, the subject does sometimes precede the verb (as could also even the object!). When it does so, this is usually for reasons of emphasis.

שָׁמַר הַמֶּלֶךְ אֶת־הָעִיר וְהַכֹּהֵן שָׁמַר אֶת־הַמִּזְבֵּחַ - The king has guarded the city and (or but) the priest (by contrast) has guarded the altar (i.e. but it was the priest who guarded the altar).

# IV

In the previous chapter we examined the pronouns. To these may now be added the 'relative'. The 'relative' is a kind of pronoun in that it stands in place of a noun and serves to join together sentences which are 'related'. For example:

The man spoke. He was my brother.
The man *who* spoke was my brother.

'Who' in this instance is the 'relative pronoun'. In English there are various forms of this, depending on whether the thing referred to is animate (who, etc.) or inanimate (which). The form used for animate beings varies according to its function in its own part of the sentence (who, whom, whose). In Hebrew the word אֲשֶׁר may serve in all these different ways, referring to either animate or inanimate and with no change, whatever its function in its own part of the sentence.

זֶה הַכֹּהֵן אֲשֶׁר שָׁמַר אֶת־הַמִּזְבֵּחַ - This is the priest *who* has guarded the altar.

זֶה הַמִּזְבֵּחַ אֲשֶׁר שָׁמַר הַכֹּהֵן - This is the altar *which* the priest has guarded.

זֶה הַנָּבִיא אֲשֶׁר שָׁמַר הַמֶּלֶךְ - This is the prophet *whom* the king has guarded.

This last sentence is, admittedly, potentially ambiguous. It *could* mean 'This is the prophet who has guarded the king'. If that *were* its meaning, we might expect the object of שָׁמַר to be signalled as such by the use of אֵת־ immediately preceding it.

זֶה הַנָּבִיא אֲשֶׁר שָׁמַר אֶת־הַמֶּלֶךְ

This is not, however, universal usage in Hebrew, and total ambiguity would be removed only when the sentence is seen in a wider narrative context.

## EXERCISE FIVE

Vocabulary:

Verbs:

| | | | |
|---|---|---|---|
| כָּתַב | _ to write | זָכַר | _ to remember |
| שָׁפַט | _ to judge | קָרָא | _ to call, read |
| הָרַג | _ to kill, slay | בָּרָא | - to create |

Nouns:

הַכֹּהֵן הַגָּדוֹל – the high priest

סֵפֶר – book

דָּבָר – as well as meaning 'word', דָּבָר is also used in the sense of 'thing, affair, matter'.

תּוֹרָה *f* - law

In later Hebrew, תּוֹרָה is used as a collective name for the first five books of the Hebrew Bible. The term used for these books in non-Jewish scholarship is 'Pentateuch', meaning 'consisting of five books'.

אֱלֹהִים - God       בְּרֵאשִׁית - in the beginning

Translate:

1. שָׁמַר הַמֶּלֶךְ אֶת־הָעִיר הַגְּדוֹלָה:

2. כָּתַב הַכֹּהֵן הַגָּדוֹל אֶת־הַדְּבָרִים הָאֵלֶּה:

3. זָכַרְתָּ אֶת־הַשִּׁיר הַהוּא:

4. שָׁמְרָה הָאִשָּׁה הַצַּדִּיקָה אֶת־הַיֶּלֶד הַטּוֹב:

5. כָּתַבְתִּי אֶת־הַסֵּפֶר הַזֶּה:

6. שָׁפַטְנוּ אֶת־הָעָם הֶעָצוּם הַהוּא:

7. זְכַרְתֶּן אֶת־הַדְּבָרִים הַחֲכָמִים הָאֵלֶּה:

8. שָׁמְרוּ הַכֹּהֲנִים וְהַנְּבִיאִים אֶת־הַהֵיכָל הַקָּדוֹשׁ:

9. ‏הוּא הַכֹּהֵן הֶחָכָם אֲשֶׁר קָרָא אֶת־הַתּוֹרָה הַזֹּאת:

10. ‏קְדוֹשִׁים הַנְּבִיאִים אֲשֶׁר הָרַג הָעָם הָרַע הַהוּא:

From the Hebrew Bible:

‏בְּרֵאשִׁית בָּרָא אֱלֹהִים אֵת הַשָּׁמַיִם וְאֵת הָאָרֶץ: (Gen. 1:1)

‏מִי עָשָׂה הַדָּבָר הַזֶּה: (Judg. 6:29)

# LESSON SIX

## PREPOSITIONS

A preposition is a word which is 'placed before' ('pre-posed') a noun or pronoun in order to show the relation of the noun or pronoun to some other word in the sentence. Words such as 'to', 'on', 'in', etc. are prepositions.

> The prophet went *to* the city.
> The king sat *on* the throne.
> Joseph lived *in* Egypt.

### I

The following are some common prepositions in Hebrew and are used exactly as in English, standing immediately in front of a noun.

אֶל - to, towards

אֵת - with (in the sense of 'together with'; not to be confused with the object marker)

בֵּין - between

עַד - until, as far as

עַל - upon, beside, on account of, against

עִם - with (in the sense of 'together with')

תַּחַת - beneath; in place of

Here are some sentences containing these prepositions:

הָלַךְ שְׁמוּאֵל אֶל־הָעִיר - Samuel has gone to the city.

יָשַׁב דָּוִד עַל־הַכִּסֵּא - David has sat on the throne.

עָמַד הָעֶבֶד עַל־הַכִּסֵּא - The servant has stood beside the throne.

עָמַד הַמַּלְאָךְ בֵּין הָעֵצִים - The angel has stood between the trees.

יָשְׁבָה דְּבוֹרָה תַּחַת הָעֵץ - Deborah has sat beneath the tree.

יָרְדָה הָאִשָּׁה עַד־מִצְרַיִם - The woman has gone down as far as Egypt.

הָלַךְ הַנָּבִיא אֶת־הַכֹּהֵן - The prophet has gone with the priest.

אָכַל שָׁאוּל עִם־שְׁמוּאֵל - Saul has eaten with Samuel.

These prepositions are independent words, though notice that some of them are closely linked to the noun they precede by means of *maqqeph* (see above p. 25).

## II

There are three prepositions where this linking of preposition and noun has taken place to such an extent that the prepositions no longer stand alone but are immediately prefixed to the noun itself and are *inseparable* from it. The prepositions are:

> בְּ - in, with ( in the sense of 'by means of' )
>
> כְּ - as, like
>
> לְ - to, at, for

i) Their normal vocalisation is with vocal *sheva*:

לֹא יָשַׁבְתִּי בְּבַיִת - I have not dwelt in a house.
(II Sam 7:6)

ii) If the word to which it is prefixed already has a *sheva* under its first consonant (e.g. the proper name שְׁמוּאֵל- Samuel), instead of two *shevas* coming together, the first of them becomes the full short vowel i (hireq).

אֵין אִישׁ בְּיִשְׂרָאֵל כִּשְׁמוּאֵל - There is not a man in Israel like Samuel.

(For אֵין = 'there is not' see below p. 65)

If the first consonant in such a case is י, the י becomes silent and merges with the i-vowel of the preposition to produce the long ī-vowel ( בְּיִ > בִּי > בִּי' ).

יְרוּשָׁלַיִם - Jerusalem    בִּירוּשָׁלַיִם - in Jerusalem
יְהוּדָה - Judah    בִּיהוּדָה - in Judah

iii) If the sheva is a composite one, as in, e.g., אֱדוֹם - 'Edom' or אֲרִי - 'lion', then the preposition takes the corresponding short vowel:

לֶאֱדוֹם - for Edom    לַאֲרִי - for a lion

In the case of the word אֱלֹהִים, the א always becomes silent and the preposition takes the long ē-vowel:

אֱלֹהִים - God (gods)　כֵּאלֹהִים - like God (like gods)

Only the context will make clear whether אֱלֹהִים is being used in a monotheistic or a polytheistic sense.

If the preposition immediately precedes the accent (i.e. is prefixed to words stressed on the first syllable or to monosyllables), it is occasionally - but not invariably - vocalised with ā.

iv) When these prepositions are prefixed to a noun which has the definite article, the ה of the article drops out and the preposition adopts its vowel.

הַיּוֹם הַהוּא - that day

בַּיּוֹם הַהוּא - on that day

הָאָרֶץ הַזֹּאת - this land

לָאָרֶץ הַזֹּאת - for this land

הַנָּבִיא הַגָּדוֹל - the great prophet

כַּנָּבִיא הַגָּדוֹל - like the great prophet

Here are some phrases from the Hebrew Bible, some of them slightly modified, which contain these prepositions with a definite noun.

וְהָעִיר שָׂרְפוּ בָאֵשׁ - And the city they burned with fire. (Josh 6:24)

שָׁבַת אֱלֹהִים בַּיּוֹם הַשְּׁבִיעִי - God rested on the seventh day. (Gen 2:2)

קָרָא אֱלֹהִים לָאוֹר יוֹם - God called the light 'day'. (Gen 1:5)

שָׁפְכוּ דָם כַּמַּיִם - They shed blood like water. (Ps 79:3)

## III

There is, finally, a common preposition which may either stand independently of the noun (like עַל and אֶל) or be prefixed directly to it (similar to, though not exactly in the same way as, בְּ, כְּ and לְ).

מִן - 'from' is usually prefixed directly to a noun. The letter נ is a weak letter, and when it occurs as the second consonant of a closed syllable it invariably assimilates with the first consonant of the immediately following syllable:

מִמֶּלֶךְ > מִמְמֶלֶךְ * > מִנְמֶלֶךְ * > מִן מֶלֶךְ

An asterisk [*] indicates a form which is not extant in the language but which represents a supposed stage of, in this instance phonetic, development.

Prefixed מִן , then, retains its own vowel, assimilates to the following consonant which is thus doubled and is written with *dagesh forte*. Should the first consonant of the word to which מִן is prefixed be a consonant which does not show doubling, i.e. one of the 'gutturals' or ר, the short vowel of the מִן is lengthened to ε.

מֵעִיר > מִן עִיר

If the noun which follows מִן has the definite article, then either מִן remains separate:

מִן הָאָרֶץ הַזֹּאת

or it is prefixed directly with the long ε-vowel before the non-doubling ה of the article. Note that, unlike the situation with ב, כ and ל, the ה of the article is *not* displaced in this instance:

מֵהָאָרֶץ הַזֹּאת

One very characteristic and idiomatic usage of the preposition מִן is worth noting. מִן is used in Hebrew, in the sense of '(distinct) from', to express what is conveyed in English by the 'comparative' form of the adjective, as in 'David is smaller than Goliath'. In such a context Hebrew uses the adjective ( קָטֹן - 'small') followed by מִן preceding the noun with which the comparison is made ( גָּלְיַח [golyat] - Goliath; notice that the vowel sign ָ here represents the short o-vowel - see above p.23).

קָטֹן דָּוִד מִגָּלְיַח (מִן גָּלְיַח) - David is small as distinct from Goliath, i.e., is smaller than Goliath.

- 53 -

This same sentence could also be translated as

'David is too small for Goliath.'

Generally the context will make it clear which of these two senses is intended.

Here is an example from the Hebrew Bible of this construction in question form.

מַה־מָּתוֹק מִדְּבַשׁ וּמֶה עַז מֵאֲרִי - What is sweeter than honey and what is stronger than a lion? (Judg 14:18).

On the 'comparative', see further below p. 120.

## EXERCISE SIX

Vocabulary:

כִּי - (a) for, because (cf. sentence 4)
(b) that (after verbs of seeing, saying, etc.; cf. sentence 6)

בָּרוּךְ - Baruch (Jeremiah's secretary)

עֲבֹדָה f - work; service (in late BH [Biblical Hebrew] in the sense of 'worship')

יָשַׁב - to sit, dwell

Translate:

1. הָלַכְתִּי אֶל־הָעִיר הַגְּדוֹלָה:

2. כָּתַב בָּרוּךְ בְּסֵפֶר אֶת־הַדְּבָרִים הָאֵלֶּה:

3. בַּיּוֹם הַהוּא הָרַג הַמֶּלֶךְ אֶת־הָעֲצוּם אֶת־הַנְּבִיאִים אֲשֶׁר שָׁפְטוּ בִּיהוּדָה:

4. יָרַדְתָּ מִיִּשְׂרָאֵל עַד־מִצְרַיִם כִּי כָבֵד הָרָעָב בָּאָרֶץ הַהִיא:

5. חָכָם שְׁמוּאֵל הַנָּבִיא מִשָּׁאוּל הַמֶּלֶךְ הָרָע:

6. זָכַרְתִּי בַבֹּקֶר כִּי טוֹבִים הַדְּבָרִים אֲשֶׁר קָרָא הַכֹּהֵן לָעָם הַצַּדִּיק הַזֶּה:

7. יָשַׁבְתֶּם בַּלַּיְלָה הַהוּא תַּחַת הָעֵץ אֲשֶׁר עַל־הַבַּיִת בִּירוּשָׁלַיִם:

8. בָּעֶרֶב שָׁבַת הָעֶבֶד מֵהָעֲבֹדָה אֲשֶׁר עָשָׂה:

# LESSON SEVEN
## THE PERFECT - II

### I

The verb which we have taken as the paradigm in Lesson Five, שָׁמַר - 'to guard', consists of three perfectly normal consonants. We have already seen in the case of the definite article that some consonants, chiefly the so-called 'gutturals', cause modifications in the vocalisation of the article.

These same 'gutturals' also cause slight modifications of the שָׁמַר paradigm in the vocalisation of the Perfect of the verb.

1. In early Jewish grammars, the verb פעל was used as the universal paradigm. When the grammarian wished to refer to the first letter of a normal three-letter (triliteral) root, he called it the פ-letter; the second was called the ע-letter, and the third the ל-letter. 'Gutturals' may occur in any of the three positions, so we have three types of verbs with 'gutturals':

| | | |
|---|---|---|
| פ-gutturals - e.g. | עָמַד | - to stand |
| ע-gutturals - e.g. | בָּחַר | - to choose |
| ל-gutturals - e.g. | שָׁלַח | - to stretch out, send |

The student will never have any difficulty, in the case of these verbs, in discovering the form of the verb to be looked for in the dictionary. The main point to observe in the case of the Perfect of these verbs is that where the normal verb has a simple *sheva*, in the verbs with 'gutturals' we find a *composite sheva*. 'Gutturals' on the whole tend to prefer vowels of the 'a'-type, so it is ḥatep pataḥ ( ⟨ ◌ֲ ⟩ ) that is most commonly found in such positions.

    (1)   Regular verb: שָׁמַר   2nd m.pl. - שְׁמַרְתֶּם

          פ-guttural   : עָמַד   2nd m.pl. - עֲמַדְתֶּם

(2)   Regular verb: שָׁמַר      3rd pl. - שָׁמְרוּ

    ע-guttural   : בָּחַר      3rd pl. - בָּחֲרוּ

(3) The only variation in the ל-guttural verb is in the 2nd f.s.: שָׁלַחְתְּ. This is, in fact, a peculiar form, possibly an attempt to combine

שָׁלַחְתְּ•   and   •שָׁלַחַת.

2. There are two sub-classes of the 'guttural' verbs, those with א as their first letter (פ''א verbs; e.g. אָמַר - to say) and those with א as their third letter (ל''א verbs; e.g. מָצָא - to find). In the Perfect, פ''א verbs are no different from the other פ-guttural verbs, and the same observations apply:

2nd m.pl. - אֲמַרְתֶּם   (see 1,(1), above)

In the case of ל''א verbs, the א is silent at the end of a syllable, and the immediately preceding vowel (a in the normal verb) becomes long (ā).

Regular verb: שָׁמַר      1 s. - שָׁמַרְתִּי

ל''א verb   : מָצָא      1 s. - מָצָאתִי

## II

Just as the 'guttural' consonants occasion modification in the vocalisation of words, so too there are certain letters which are 'weak'. The letters in question are ו, י and נ, and these have a tendency to drop out or become assimilated to the following consonant. ו and י may occur in any position in the root and, as is the case with the 'guttural' verbs, this produces three distinct classes of verb.

1.   פ''ו and פ''י

Those verbs which, strictly speaking, have ו as their פ-letter have lost the ו in the Perfect of the simple form of the verb, and it has been replaced with י. The result is that both these classes of verb appear with an initial י in the Perfect of the simple form. There are very few

genuine פ״י verbs, and most verbs with an initial י are
in fact פ״ו. For example:

    a) פ״י : יָנַק - to suck
    b) פ״ו : יָשַׁב - to sit, dwell

These verbs are no different in the Perfect from שָׁמַר.

    2. ע״ו and ע״י

These two classes of verb are also identical in the Perfect
of the simple form. The 3rd m. sing. has become a mono-
syllable, with the middle ו or י having dropped out
completely. קָם - 'to arise' is usually taken as the paradigm
of this verb-class.

| | Singular | Plural |
|------|------|------|
| 3rd m. | קָם | קָמוּ |
| 3rd f. | קָמָה | קָמוּ |
| 2nd m. | קַמְתָּ | קַמְתֶּם |
| 2nd f. | קַמְתְּ | קַמְתֶּן |
| 1st c. | קַמְתִּי | קַמְנוּ |

Note the shift of the stress in some of these forms as
compared with the שָׁמַר type.

Against normal practice (above, p. 43), the dictionary lists
verbs of this type under the form קוּם, which is the
infinitive ('to arise'), a form which shows, more clearly
than does the Perfect in this verb-class, the original
triliteral form of the verb. Similarly the verb שָׂם - 'to put,
place' appears in the dictionary under its infinitive form
שִׂים.

Some verbs are what we might call 'doubly weak' in
that *two* out of the three letters of their root are such as
to cause modification of the normal verb pattern. One
very common one may be mentioned here since it is ע״ו,
though it is also ל״א, namely בָּא - to come. This differs
from קָם to the extent that when the א is at the end of a
syllable, the ל״א phenomenon occurs of the א becoming
silent and being preceded by a long a-vowel. For example:

קַמְתִּי    but    בָּאתִי

**3.** לִ"ה (לִ"י)

In the case of verbs whose third letter is, strictly speaking, י, when that third letter is not followed by any suffix, e.g. in the 3rd m.s. of the Perfect, the י appears as a ה. (The ה here is a vowel letter representing the sound ā which developed from an original diphthong ay.) It is for this reason that this class of verbs is more commonly known as לִ"ה verbs. Their original third letter, י, can be seen in those forms of the Perfect which have suffixes, e.g. the 1st s.c. Here is the full paradigm of נָלָה - to reveal, uncover.

|  | Singular | Plural |
|---|---|---|
| 3rd m. | נָלָה | נָלוּ |
| 3rd f. | נָלְתָה | נָלוּ |
| 2nd m. | נָלִיתָ | נְלִיתֶם |
| 2nd f. | נָלִית | נְלִיתֶן |
| 1st c. | נָלִיתִי | נָלִינוּ |

Note the forms where the י appears and note, too, the 3rd f.s., where the ה of the 3rd m.s. becomes ת before the addition of the characteristic הָ feminine ending. Contrast, from the point of view of stress, קָמוּ (p. 57) and נָלוּ. Original לִ"ו verbs have, for the most part, been accommodated to the לִ"י type.

### III

Two other classes of verbs remain to be noted.

1. The first has נ as its first letter (פ"ן verbs; e.g. נָפַל - to fall). These too are, in the Perfect of the simple verb, no different from שָׁמַר. There is, however, one very common verb in this class whose deviation from the normal is caused by the fact that נ is also its *third* letter (though there is no recognised לִ"ן class of verbs). The verb in question is נָתַן - to give. The letter נ, when it closes a syllable and has no vowel sound of its own, assimilates with the immediately following consonant (cf. the way in which the נ of the preposition

מִן is assimilated to the first consonant of the noun to which it is immediately prefixed: מִמֶּלֶךְ ; see above p. 53), causing doubling in that consonant, a doubling that is shown by means of *dagesh forte*. The form that is found is thus, for example, נָתַתִּי < ‎**נָתַנְתִּי .

The Perfect of נָתַן is as follows:

|  | Singular | Plural |
|---|---|---|
| 3rd m. | נָתַן | נָתְנוּ |
| 3rd f. | נָתְנָה | נָתְנוּ |
| 2nd m. | נָתַתָּ | נְתַתֶּם |
| 2nd f. | נָתַתְּ | נְתַתֶּן |
| 1st c. | נָתַתִּי | נָתַנּוּ |

Other verbs whose third root letter is נ do not have this assimilation, e.g. שָׁכַן - to dwell, 1st s.c. שָׁכַנְתִּי.

2. The second of these two final classes of verbs comprises those where the second and the third letters of the root are identical ( ע״ע or 'double ayin' verbs; e.g. סָבַב - to turn about, surround). The Perfect is fairly straightforward, but note that the doubled consonant is mostly written only once, with *dagesh forte* again showing its doubled nature. Note also the use of וֹ (ŏ) as a helping vowel before those suffixes which begin with a consonant, namely all 2nd and 1st person forms, singular and plural.

The Perfect of סָבַב is as follows:

|  | Singular | Plural |
|---|---|---|
| 3rd m. | סָבַב | סָבְבוּ |
| 3rd f. | סָבְבָה | סָבְבוּ |
| 2nd m. | סַבּוֹתָ | סַבּוֹתָם |
| 2nd f. | סַבּוֹת | סַבּוֹתֶן |
| 1st c. | סַבּוֹתִי | סַבּוֹנוּ |

For all these verb forms, especially those for which the Perfect has not been set out in full here, reference should be made to the Paradigms on pp. 176 ff.

# EXERCISE SEVEN

Vocabulary:

Verbs:

רָאָה – to see        עָשָׂה – to do, make

בָּחַר בְּ – to choose

קוּם עַל – to rise (up) against

Nouns:

מָקוֹם – place      אֹיֵב (pl. אֹיְבִים) – enemy

Other:

לָמָה (lit. 'for what?') – why?

Translate:

1. אָמַרְתִּי אֶל־הַכֹּהֵן הַגָּדוֹל זֶה הַהֵיכָל הַקָּדוֹשׁ:

2. בָּאתִי אֶל־הָעִיר הַגְּדוֹלָה:

3. עֲמַדְתֶּם עַל־הָהָר הָרָם:

4. רָאִיתָ כִּי שְׁלֹמֹה הוּא מֶלֶךְ חָכָם:

5. נָתַתִּי אֶת־הַסֵּפֶר הַקָּדוֹשׁ אֶל־הַמֶּלֶךְ הַטּוֹב:

6. קָמוּ הָאֹיְבִים הָרָעִים עַל־הָעָם הַצַּדִּיק:

7. בָּחֲרוּ הַנְּבִיאִים הַקְּדוֹשִׁים בַּמָּקוֹם הַהוּא:

8. לָמָה עֲשִׂיתֶם אֶת־הַדָּבָר הָרָע הַזֶּה:

# LESSON EIGHT

## POSSESSION - I

In English we express possession in two ways. The first is by means of the preposition 'of', as in 'the horse of the king', 'the word of the prophet'. The second is by use of the letter 's', as in 'the king's horse', 'the prophet's word'.

In Hebrew, possession of this kind is expressed by the placing of the two nouns side by side.

1. *Masculine Singular*

סוּס הַמֶּלֶךְ - the horse of the king
(*or* the king's horse)

דְּבַר הַנָּבִיא - the word of the prophet

In both of these examples, the first word (דָּבָר/סוּס) is so closely related to the second word (נָבִיא/מֶלֶךְ) that the two together are counted as a single unit with only one stress. The vowel in סוּס is a pure long vowel (see above p. 16) and is therefore unalterable. The vowels of דָּבָר, however, are tone-long vowels (see above p. 16), and when the stress is removed from it and centred solely on נָבִיא, the vowels of דָּבָר reduce in quantity to give the form דְּבַר.

The relationship exemplified in the two phrases

דְּבַר הַנָּבִיא    and    סוּס הַמֶּלֶךְ

is described as a *construct relationship*. The form דְּבַר is known as the *construct state*, while the form נָבִיא is known as the *absolute state*. דְּבַר is said to be or to stand *in construct relationship* to הַנָּבִיא. So, too, with סוּס and הַמֶּלֶךְ, but in the case of סוּס there is no difference in form between the absolute state and the construct state since the vowel of סוּס is pure long and therefore unalterable.

From these two examples note that the noun in the construct state does not take the definite article. In a construct relationship the definiteness or indefiniteness of the noun in the construct state is determined by the definiteness or indefiniteness of the noun in the absolute.

סוּס הַמֶּלֶךְ is 'the horse of the king'

סוּס מֶלֶךְ is 'a horse of a king' or 'a king's horse'

Hebrew expresses by a different construction the ideas of the English 'a horse of *the* king' ( סוּס לַמֶּלֶךְ - lit. 'a horse [belonging] to the king' or סוּס מִסּוּסֵי הַמֶּלֶךְ - 'one of the king's horses', lit. 'a horse from [among] the horses of the king' [ סוּסֵי is the construct form of the m. pl., see below ]) or *the* horse of a king' ( הַסּוּס לְמֶלֶךְ - lit. 'the horse [belonging] to a king' ).

Proper names are, of course, definite. So

דְּבַר שְׁמוּאֵל is 'the word of Samuel'.

We can now draw up a cumulative list of those features which, as far as we have covered at this stage, make a noun definite:

1.  If it is a proper name: e.g. דָּוִד - David, a specific individual.

2.  If it has the definite article: e.g. הַמֶּלֶךְ - *the* king, a specific king.

3.  If it is in construct relationship to a noun which is itself definite (i.e., for the moment, which is a proper name or which has the definite article ):

e.g.   חֶרֶב דָּוִד - *the* sword of David, a specific sword.

דְּבַר הַנָּבִיא - *the* word of the prophet, a specific word.

Here are the construct forms of masculine plural nouns and of feminine nouns, singular and plural laid out in tabular form.

**2. *Masculine Plural***

|  | Absolute | Construct |
|---|---|---|
| (1) | סוּסִים | סוּסֵי |
| e.g. | | סוּסֵי הַמֶּלֶךְ - the king's horses |
| (2) | דְּבָרִים | דִּבְרֵי |
| e.g. | | דִּבְרֵי הַנָּבִיא - the words of the prophet |

### 3. *Feminine Singular*

|  | *Absolute* | *Construct* |
|---|---|---|
| (1) | סוּסָה | סוּסַת |
| e.g. |  | סוּסַת הַמֶּלֶךְ - the king's mare |
| (2) | צְדָקָה | צִדְקַת |
| e.g. |  | צִדְקַת הָעָם - the righteousness of the people |

### 4. *Feminine Plural*

|  | *Absolute* | *Construct* |
|---|---|---|
| (1) | סוּסוֹת | סוּסוֹת |
| e.g. |  | סוּסוֹת הַמֶּלֶךְ - the king's mares |
| (2) | צְדָקוֹת | צִדְקוֹת |
| e.g. |  | צִדְקוֹת הָעָם - the righteousnesses (i.e. the righteous acts) of the people |

The absolute *dual* ending ◌ַיִם becomes, like the m. pl., ◌ֵי in the construct:

שְׂפָתַיִם - (two) lips    שִׂפְתֵי הַמֶּלֶךְ - the lips of the king

When two construct relationships are joined by 'and', Hebrew is normally less succinct than is possible in English:

סוּסֵי הַמֶּלֶךְ וְסוּסֵי הַמַּלְכָּה - the horses of the king and the queen

(lit. 'the horses of the king and the horses of the queen')

Occasionally with very common phrases we find that this pattern is not strictly followed, and a tighter form of expression occurs:

מַלְכֵי יִשְׂרָאֵל וִיהוּדָה - the kings of Israel and Judah

( מַלְכֵי is the construct form of מְלָכִים, pl. of מֶלֶךְ )

It follows from what has been said that an adjective qualifying a noun in a construct relationship cannot intrude between the noun in the construct and the noun in the absolute but must come at the end of the construct unit. Also, if the construct is definite by virtue of being in construct relationship to a definite noun (e.g. סוּסֵי הַמֶּלֶךְ ), then the qualifying adjective must also be definite, i.e. it must have the definite article.

סוּסֵי הַמֶּלֶךְ הַטּוֹבִים - the king's good horses (lit. the horses of the king, the good ones)

Clearly sometimes this could give rise to ambiguity, if the two nouns were of the same gender and number. In such a case it would not be clear with which of the two nouns the adjective was in agreement. For example,

סוּס הַמֶּלֶךְ הַטּוֹב   could mean either
                           a) the horse of the good king
                        or b) the good horse of the king.

The adjective טוֹב could be qualifying either סוּס or מֶלֶךְ. There is, however, obviously a limit to such ambiguity. The context would normally make it clear which of the two meanings is intended.

Such ambiguity can, in any case, be avoided in one of two ways:

(1)   הַסּוּס הַטּוֹב (אֲשֶׁר) לַמֶּלֶךְ - the good horse (which [belongs]) to the king

(2)   הַסּוּס (אֲשֶׁר) לַמֶּלֶךְ הַטּוֹב - the horse (which [belongs]) to the good king

Two other points are perhaps worth noting.

1. It is possible to have a compound construct relationship:

בְּנֵי נְבִיאֵי אֱלֹהִים - the sons of the prophets of God

דִּבְרֵי נְבִיאֵי יהוה - the words of the prophets of Yahweh

יהוה, which was probably originally pronounced 'Yahweh', is what one might call the 'proper name' of Israel's God. The Israelites considered the name too sacred ever to pronounce, and in the context of reading the Hebrew Bible the word אֲדֹנָי (lit. 'my Lord' but usually translated in the modern EVV as 'the LORD') was usually substituted for it. In the Grammar it will be left unvocalised; it should always be read אֲדֹנָי.

2. Hebrew sometimes expresses by means of a construct relationship what in English would be more commonly expressed by a qualifying adjective and noun:

הַר הַקֹּדֶשׁ - lit. 'the hill of holiness', i.e. 'the holy hill'.

# EXERCISE EIGHT

Vocabulary:

Verb:

סָפַר - to count

Nouns:

כֹּל (כָּל־) - basically a noun meaning 'totality'.
In construct relationship (mostly with *maqqeph*), it is usually rendered in English by the adj. 'all'

אַיִן - non-existence.
In construct relationship (אֵין) it has the sense of 'there is/was not' (cf. sentence 8). There is a positive equivalent יֵשׁ (יֶשׁ־) with the sense of 'there is/was'

כּוֹכָב - star     חוֹל - sand     יָם - sea

בֵּן (pl. בָּנִים) - son

שָׂפָה *f* - as well as meaning 'lip' is also used in the sense of 'edge, shore' (cf. sentence 4)

מַלְאָךְ - messenger, angel (**not** to be confused with מֶלֶךְ)

לֶחֶם - bread (cf. בֵּית לֶחֶם - Bethlehem, lit. 'house of bread')

כְּנַעַן - Canaan     עַיִן (du. עֵינַיִם) *f* - eye

Adjective:

רַב (pl. רַבִּים) - many, numerous

Adverb:

מְאֹד - very (always **follows** the adjective it qualifies)

Translate:

1. אֵלֶּה הַדְּבָרִים אֲשֶׁר קָרְאוּ נְבִיאֵי יִשְׂרָאֵל לָעָם הַזֶּה:
2. לֹא הָלַכְנוּ בְּתוֹרַת יהוה אֱלֹהֵי יִשְׂרָאֵל:
3. שָׁפְטוּ בְּנֵי הַנְּבִיאִים בְּכָל־אֶרֶץ יְהוּדָה:
4. סָפַר יהוה אֶת־כּוֹכְבֵי הַשָּׁמַיִם וְהֵם רַבִּים מְאֹד כַּחוֹל אֲשֶׁר עַל־שְׂפַת הַיָּם:
5. יָשְׁבוּ מַלְכֵי יְהוּדָה בִּירוּשָׁלַיִם עִיר דָּוִד:
6. שְׁלַחְתֶּם אֶת־נְבִיאֵי יִשְׂרָאֵל לְמַלְאָכִים אֶל־מֶלֶךְ אֱדוֹם:
7. טוֹבוֹת צִדְקוֹת הָעָם הַזֶּה בְּעֵינֵי יהוה:

- 65 -

8. מָצָאנוּ לֶחֶם בְּאֶרֶץ מִצְרַיִם כִּי אֵין לֶחֶם בְּכָל־אֶרֶץ
כְּנָעַן :

# LESSON NINE

## POSSESSION - II

### I

In the construct relationship we have seen one way in which Hebrew expresses possession.

סוּס הַמֶּלֶךְ – The horse of the king *or* The king's horse
But if 'the king' has been referred to earlier in the narrative context, we would talk simply of *'his* horse', that is we would use what we call the *possessive adjective*: *his* horse - *your* horse - *my* horse - etc. In Hebrew this is expressed in much the same way as the construct relationship, with a similar close relationship between a noun and, in this instance, a suffix immediately appended to the noun. These suffixes are commonly referred to as the *pronominal suffixes*. Most of them, with the exception of those expressing the 2nd person singular 'your', look like fragments of the independent personal pronouns (see above p. 37 and cf. also the Perfect of the verb, whose suffixes are also related to the personal pronouns).

*Singular Noun*

|  | Singular Suffix | Plural Suffix |
|---|---|---|
| 3rd m. (הוּא) | סוּסוֹ – his horse | סוּסָם (הֵם) – their horse |
| 3rd f. (הִיא) | סוּסָהּ – her horse | סוּסָן (הֵנָּה) – their horse |
| 2nd m. ( - ) | סוּסְךָ – your horse | סוּסְכֶם (אַתֶּם) – your horse |
| 2nd f. ( - ) | סוּסֵךְ – your horse | סוּסְכֶן (אַתֵּן) – your horse |
| 1st c. (אֲנִי) | סוּסִי – my horse | סוּסֵנוּ (אֲנַחְנוּ) – our horse |

*Plural Noun*

| | | |
|---|---|---|
| 3rd m. | סוּסָיו – his horses | סוּסֵיהֶם – their horses |
| 3rd f. | סוּסֶיהָ – her horses | סוּסֵיהֶן – their horses |
| 2nd m. | סוּסֶיךָ – your horses | סוּסֵיכֶם – your horses |
| 2nd f. | סוּסַיִךְ – your horses | סוּסֵיכֶן – your horses |
| 1st c. | סוּסַי – my horses | סוּסֵינוּ – our horses |

These suffixes are basically the same whether added to a singular noun or to a plural noun. In the 3rd person plural, a contracted form ( ם, ן ) is added to the singular noun in place of the fuller form which is added to the plural noun ( הן, הם ). Notice that the י of the masculine plural ending ( ִים/ ֵי ) is always present to indicate that we are dealing with a plural noun. When the 1st singular suffix is added (also י ), there is coalescence, and only one י appears. The distinction is in the vocalisation:

סוּסִי  - my horse        סוּסַי  - my horses

*These two forms should be carefully distinguished both from each other and from the construct masculine plural* סוּסֵי.

It will be clear from the tables on pp. 166 f. that the ה of the feminine singular noun becomes ת before the addition of the suffixes:

סוּסָתוֹ – סוּסָה

In סוּסָתוֹ the stress falls on the suffix, and the vowel of the penultimate syllable is pre-tonic and therefore long ( ā ). In the forms with the suffixes of the 2nd person plural (m. and f.), however, the vowel of the pretonic syllable is short ( a ).

From these tables, too, it will be observed that in the feminine plural nouns not only does the feminine plural ending ( וֹת ) appear in the forms with suffixes, but so too does the י which really belongs to the *masculine* plural noun. It is as if that masculine plural י has become part of the suffix as appended to plural nouns (of whatever gender).

סוּסוֹתֶיךָ > סוּסוֹת + ֶיךָ

The *dual* form of those nouns which have such a form (see above p. 34) takes the suffixes in the same way as does the plural.

עֵינֵי הַמֶּלֶךְ וְאָזְנָיו  - the eyes of the king and his ears

( אֹזֶן f - 'ear'; du. אָזְנַיִם, where the vowel of the first syllable is o- see above p. 23.)

This last is also an example of how Hebrew deals with two construct relationships joined by וּ 'and'. Hebrew cannot express literally what in English would appear as 'the eyes and ears of the king' but has to say, as in the above example, 'the eyes of the king and his ears'. See above p. 63.

We can now add to our cumulative list of features which make a noun definite (above p. 62) and observe that a noun is definite if it has a pronominal suffix or is in construct relationship to a noun with a pronominal suffix. 'My horse' is a specific horse. An adjective qualifying such a noun will therefore also have to be definite and, in *its* case, have the definite article.

סוּסִי הַטּוֹב - my good horse (lit. 'my horse, the good one')

In English we can have a possessive adjective followed by more than one noun, e.g. 'He took his sons and daughters'. In Hebrew, however, the suffix is repeated with each noun.

לָקַח אֶת־בָּנָיו וְאֶת־בְּנוֹתָיו - lit. 'he has taken his sons and his daughters'

(בָּנוֹת is the plur. of בַּת)

## II

*Prepositions with Suffixes*

As will be seen from the tables on p. 174, these same suffixes may be appended to prepositions. When they are, they represent English pronouns (by *me*, for *you*, etc.) and not possessive adjectives, which is the way in which they function with nouns (*my* horse, *your* word, etc.).

1. For the moment we shall note only בְ and לְ, where the forms are identical.

| | Singular Suffixes | | Plural Suffixes | |
|---|---|---|---|---|
| 3rd m. | לוֹ | בּוֹ | לָהֶם | בָּהֶם (בָּם) |
| 3rd f. | לָהּ | בָּהּ | לָהֶן | בָּהֶן |

- 69 -

|  | Singular Suffixes | | Plural Suffixes | |
|---|---|---|---|---|
| 2nd m. | לְךָ | בְּךָ | לָכֶם | בָּכֶם |
| 2nd f. | לָךְ | בָּךְ | לָכֶן | בָּכֶן |
| 1st c. | לִי | בִּי | לָנוּ | בָּנוּ |

With the suffix of the 3rd m. pl. ל has the form לָהֶם while with ב the abbreviated form בָּם is also found.

Prepositions with suffixes are dealt with more fully in Lesson 17 below.

**2.** The pronoun as the direct object of a verb may be expressed by means of these same suffixes appended to the object marker אֵת. The forms are as follows:

|  | Singular Suffixes | | Plural Suffixes | |
|---|---|---|---|---|
| 3rd m. | אֹתוֹ | – him | אֹתָם | – them |
| 3rd f. | אֹתָהּ | – her | אֶתֶן | – them |
| 2nd m. | אֹתְךָ | – you | אֶתְכֶם | – you |
| 2nd f. | אֹתָךְ | – you | אֶתְכֶן | – you |
| 1st c. | אֹתִי | – me | אֹתָנוּ | – us |

Sometimes these forms are also written with the vowel letter in the first syllable: אוֹתוֹ, etc.

In a full expression one might say:

שָׁמַר הַכֹּהֵן אֶת־הַמִּזְבֵּחַ – The priest has guarded the altar. But if 'the altar' had already been referred to in the context, the sentence might read:

שָׁמַר אֹתוֹ הַכֹּהֵן – The priest has guarded *it*. Similarly with any pronominal object of a verb.

זְכַרְתָּ אֹתִי אֱלֹהִים – You have remembered me, God.

For the suffixes directly appended to verb forms, see below Lesson 24.

### III

The preposition ל with the pronominal suffixes is frequently used in Hebrew to express what we express in English by means of the verb 'to have'. Hebrew has no verb corresponding to 'have' but expresses possession in point of time by means of the preposition לְ.

For example:

> יֶשׁ־לִי סוּס - lit. 'There is to me a horse',
> i.e. 'I have a horse'.

> אֵין־לוֹ חֶרֶב - 'There is not to him a sword',
> i.e. 'He has no sword'.

For the meaning of יֵשׁ and אֵין see above p. 65.

This usage is not confined to לְ with suffixes.

> יֶשׁ־לַנָּבִיא סֵפֶר - The prophet has a book.
> אֵין־לַמֶּלֶךְ הֵיכָל - The king does not have a palace.

Here is an example from the Hebrew Bible:

> וְכֹל אֲשֶׁר־יֶשׁ־לוֹ נָתַן בְּיָדִי - And all that he has, he has given into my hand.
> OR He has put me in charge of all that he has. (Gen 39:8)

## EXERCISE NINE

Vocabulary:

Verbs:

> שָׁמַע - to hear      שָׁמַע בְּ - to pay heed to
> יָשַׁב - in sense of 'to settle (in a place)'
> כָּרַת - to cut;     כָּרַת בְּרִית - to *make* a covenant
> (cf. Gen 15:9-11,17; Jer 34:18-20 for a possible explanation of this idiom) In the 2nd m.s., the ת of the root and the ת of the suffix coalesce: כָּרַתָּ > *כָּרַתְתָּ

Nouns:

> בְּרִית *f* - covenant (see above)     קוֹל - voice
> תְּפִלָּה *f* - prayer      מִדְבָּר - desert, wilderness
> עַם (with suffs. עַמִּי etc.) - people

Prepositions:

אֵת ( אֶת־ ) – with  (identical in form to the object marker, but with suffixes the prep. has the forms אִתּוֹ, etc. – see below p. 174)

לִפְנֵי – before  Both of these are really plural

אַחֲרֵי – after  nouns in the construct and take suffixes accordingly.

Other:

כֹּה – thus    גַּם – also, even    הִנֵּה – behold, see

עַתָּה – now  (distinguish from אַתָּה – you [m.s.])

Translate:

1. כֹּה אָמַר יהוה לֹא שָׁמְרוּ אֶת־בְּרִיתִי וְלֹא שָׁמְעוּ בְּקוֹלִי:

2. נָתַתָּ לָהֶם אֶת־הָאָרֶץ הַטּוֹבָה הַזֹּאת אֲשֶׁר עַתָּה יָשְׁבוּ בָהּ:

3. זָכַרְתָּ הַיּוֹם הַזֶּה אֶת־בְּרִיתְךָ אֲשֶׁר כָּרַתָּ אֶת־עַמְּךָ יִשְׂרָאֵל:

4. בַּמִּדְבָּר הָלַךְ יהוה לִפְנֵיכֶם וְגַם אַחֲרֵיכֶם וְעַתָּה נָתַן לָכֶם אֶת־כָּל־אֶרֶץ כְּנָעַן:

5. שָׁמַע יהוה אֱלֹהֵינוּ אֶת־תְּפִלָּתֵנוּ וְגַם זָכַר אֶת־צִדְקוֹתֵינוּ:

6. אֵין לָנוּ לֶחֶם בְּאֶרֶץ־כְּנַעַן וְהִנֵּה שָׁמַעְנוּ כִּי יֶשׁ־לָכֶם לֶחֶם בָּאָרֶץ הַזֹּאת:

7. זָכַרְתָּ אֹתִי יהוה אֱלֹהַי וְעַתָּה קָרָאתִי לְךָ בִּתְפִלָּתִי הַזֹּאת:

8. וְכֹל אֲשֶׁר־יֶשׁ־לִי נָתַתִּי בְיָדוֹ וְהִנֵּה שַׂמְתִּי אֹתוֹ לְרֹאשׁ עַל־כָּל־אֶרֶץ מִצְרַיִם:

# LESSON TEN

## THE VERB – THE IMPERFECT AND RELATED FORMS

### I

We have already looked at the *Perfect* of different types of verbs (above pp. 43-49, 55-60). We turn now to the other conjugation, namely the *Imperfect*, and we look, in the first instance, at the normal verb of the שָׁמַר-type.

In the Imperfect the variation in person, gender and number is shown mainly by means of prefixes (preformatives), though suffixes (afformatives) are also used, chiefly to distinguish number and gender. The relationship of these preformatives to the personal pronouns is not so obvious as is the case with the suffixes (afformatives) of the Perfect.

### THE IMPERFECT

( A paradigm using the verb קָטַל may be found on p.176 )

| | | | |
|---|---|---|---|
| 3 s.m. | יִשְׁמֹר | | he will guard |
| 3 s.f. | תִּשְׁמֹר | | she will guard |
| 2 s.m. | תִּשְׁמֹר } | Cf. the ת of | you will guard |
| 2 s.f. | תִּשְׁמְרִי } | אַתְּ/אַתָּה | you will guard |
| 1 s.c. | אֶשְׁמֹר | Cf. the א of אֲנִי | I shall guard |
| 3 pl.m. | יִשְׁמְרוּ | | they will guard |
| 3 pl.f. | תִּשְׁמֹרְנָה | | they will guard |
| 2 pl.m. | תִּשְׁמְרוּ } | Cf. the ת of | you will guard |
| 2 pl.f. | תִּשְׁמֹרְנָה } | אַתֵּן/אַתֶּם | you will guard |
| 1 pl. c. | נִשְׁמֹר | Cf. the נ of אֲנַחְנוּ | we shall guard |

The preformative of the 3rd person masculine is י and of the 3rd person feminine is ת. ת is also the preformative of the second person (masculine and feminine, singular and plural). The 3rd feminine singular and 2nd masculine singular are identical in form, as are the 3rd and 2nd person feminine plurals. In these cases contexts will make clear which is intended. The 1st person preformatives are א and נ in singular and plural respectively. The masculine plurals (3rd and 2nd) end in וּ_ and the feminines in _נָה. In the singular only the 2nd feminine has an afformative, _ִי. Note that some of these Imperfect forms (תִּשְׁמְרִי, יִשְׁמְרוּ, תִּשְׁמְרוּ) belong to the second stress pattern described above p. 24. As with the Perfect, this scheme of preformatives and afformatives is the same for the Imperfect of all forms of all verbs. If once the Imperfect of the normal שָׁמַר-type verb is known, there will be no difficulty with the Imperfect of any other verb.

As we have already observed (above, p. 44), the Hebrew verb forms can express both time ('tense') and completeness/incompleteness ('aspect'). So the Imperfect, from the aspectual point of view, refers to action as yet incomplete. 'Aspect' is more characteristic of the Imperfect than it is, perhaps, of the Perfect, but, again for the time being, we shall concentrate on the 'time' usage and, for practical purposes, think of the Imperfect as expressing 'future' time (he will guard, etc.) or 'past *continuous*' (he was guarding, etc.).

While the vowel of the second syllable of the Imperfect of *active* verbs is ō (יִשְׁמֹר), in the case of *stative* verbs (see above p. 45), that vowel is a. In the Perfect, these verbs fall into two classes, the ē-types (כָּבֵד) and the ō-types (קָטֹן), but both have the same form in the Imperfect (יִכְבַּד and יִקְטַן). In the occasional stative verbs in a (e.g. חָכַם – to be wise) the Imperfect is also in a, יֶחְכַּם (where the e of the preformative is caused by the 'guttural' ח ).

## II

### Imperatives

Positive commands are expressed in Hebrew by means of forms similar to those of the Imperfect. Such commands are, of course, in the second person (they are *addressed directly to* people) and may be either masculine or feminine,

singular or plural, depending on the gender and number
of the person(s) so addressed. The forms are as follows,
with the corresponding Imperfect forms in brackets.

|  | *Singular* | *Plural* |
|---|---|---|
| m. | שְׁמֹר (cf. תִּשְׁמֹר) | שִׁמְרוּ (cf. תִּשְׁמְרוּ) |
| f. | שִׁמְרִי (cf. תִּשְׁמְרִי) | שְׁמֹרְנָה (cf. תִּשְׁמֹרְנָה) |

Notice that the Imperative forms are identical with
those of the corresponding 2nd person Imperfect forms
but with the removal of the preformative. In the m. pl.
and f. s. the occurrence of two vocal *shevas* side by side
is avoided by the first of them becoming the short vowel i.
Notice particularly the vowel of the first syllable of the
m. pl. Imperative ( i ) and distinguish this form (שִׁמְרוּ )
carefully from the 3rd pl. of the Perfect which has an ā-
vowel in the first syllable ( שָׁמְרוּ).

All of these Imperative forms may be translated
by the single English word 'Guard!', since there is no
distinction in the English imperative to indicate either
gender or number.

Sometimes the particle נָא־ is appended to these Imperative forms with the effect of adding an element of
entreaty to the relevant command. This 'particle of
entreaty', as it is known, attracts to itself the accent of
the composite expression and is joined to the Imperative
form by *maqeph*.

שְׁמֹר - guard! (m.s.)

שְׁמָר־נָא (šəmomā) - please guard!

guard, I beseech you!

## III

*Jussive*

(**a**) In order to express prohibitions (negative commands) Hebrew uses what for the moment may be thought
of simply as the ordinary Imperfect along with one or
other of two negative particles.

(1) The normal prohibition is expressed by the use of the negative particle, אַל.

אַל תִּשְׁמֹר - Do not guard

     (Please refrain from doing so)

(2) But if it is the negative לֹא which is used, the one with which we are already familiar, the sense is that of a very strong prohibition.

לֹא תִּשְׁמֹר - Do not guard

     (On no account are you to guard)

This is the way in which the prohibitions of the Ten Commandments (The Decalogue) are expressed.

לֹא תִּגְנֹב - Thou shalt not steal (Ex 20:15)

     (On no account are you to steal)

(b) In (a)(1) above, the form of the verb is identical with that of the Imperfect, but is technically known as the Jussive. As we shall see, in due course, there are some verb-types and conjugations where Imperfect and Jussive are *not* identical, but in the type of verb which we have seen till now, they are.

The Jussive may be used also in the third person to issue an order or command concerning some third party. For example, יִשְׁמֹר , depending on the context, could be translated as 'he will guard' (ordinary Imperfect sense) or as 'let him guard' (Jussive sense). The negative used with the Imperfect sense is לֹא:

לֹא יִשְׁמֹר - he will not guard.

That used with the Jussive sense is אַל :

אַל יִשְׁמֹר - let him not guard.

This is similar to its use with the 2nd person form to express a prohibition, as we have already seen.

# IV

*Cohortative*

Just as commands may be addressed directly to people by means of the Imperative or be made about some third party by means of the Jussive, so, too, they may be addressed to oneself. Hebrew expresses this by means of another modification of the Imperfect form, the 1st person form with the addition of הָ .

אֶשְׁמֹר - I shall guard

אֶשְׁמְרָה - Let me guard

נִשְׁמֹר - We shall guard

נִשְׁמְרָה - Let us guard

This Imperfect sub-group is known as the *Cohortative* and is found only in 1st person forms.

## EXERCISE TEN

Vocabulary:

Verbs:

רָדַף - to pursue      מָשַׁל בְּ - to rule over

שָׁפַךְ - to pour, shed (blood)      שָׁלַח - to stretch out, send

מָכַר - to sell      קָבַר - to bury

Nouns:

גִּדְעוֹן - Gideon      יֹשֵׁב (pl. יֹשְׁבִים) - inhabitant, dweller

קֶבֶר - grave      אָב (cstr. אֲבִי) - father

Adverb:

שָׁם - there

Translate:

1. נִרְדֹּף אַחֲרֵי הַמְּלָכִים הָהֵם מֵהַמִּדְבָּר אֶל־הָהָר וְשָׁם
נִשְׁפֹּט אֹתָם:

2. שִׁמְרוּ אֶת־תּוֹרַת יהוה אֱלֹהֵיכֶם כִּי קְדוֹשָׁה מְאֹד הִיא:

3. אָמַר גִּדְעוֹן לֹא־אֶמְשֹׁל אֲנִי בָּכֶם וְלֹא יִמְשֹׁל בְּנִי בָּכֶם
יהוה יִמְשֹׁל בָּכֶם:

4. נִכְרֹת בְּרִית אֶת־יהוה אֱלֹהֵינוּ וְהוּא יִזְכֹּר אֹתָנוּ בַּיּוֹם
הַהוּא:

5. אָמַר יהוה אֶל־עַמּוֹ יִשְׂרָאֵל לֹא־תִגְנֹבוּ:

6. אָמַר יַעֲקֹב אֶל־בָּנָיו אַל־תִּשְׁפְּכוּ אֶת־דַּם־יוֹסֵף בְּנִי וְאַל־
תִּשְׁלְחוּ בוֹ אֶת־יֶדְכֶם:

7. אָמַר אַבְרָהָם אֶל־יֹשְׁבֵי הָעִיר מִכְרוּ־לִי קֶבֶר בַּמָּקוֹם
הַזֶּה וְאֶקְבְּרָה שָׁם שָׂרָה:

8. תִּכְתֹּב אֶת־תּוֹרָתִי בְּסֵפֶר הַיּוֹם הַזֶּה כִּי אָנֹכִי אֱלֹהֶיךָ
וֵאלֹהֵי אָבִיךָ:

# LESSON ELEVEN

## THE VERB – INFINITIVES AND PARTICIPLES

We have already looked at the Perfect and the Imperfect of the verb, including in the latter the Imperative, the Jussive and the Cohortative. Now we turn to the remaining parts of the verb – two different infinitives and two participles.

### I

(a) The first of the infinitives is identical in form with the m.s. Imperative

שְׁמֹר

This is known as the *Infinitive Construct* and is used in a variety of ways.

1. As a verbal noun:

שְׁמֹר אֶת־תּוֹרַת יהוה טוֹב בְּעֵינָיו – To keep (or 'Keeping') the law of Yahweh is good in his eyes.

2. With the preposition לְ in order to express purpose:

בָּא הַמֶּלֶךְ עַל־הָעִיר הַזֹּאת לִמְשֹׁל בְּאֶרֶץ יְהוּדָה – The king has attacked (lit. 'come against') this city *in order to* rule over (the land of) Judah.

or after a verb such as 'begin', 'cease', etc.:

חָדַל לִסְפֹּר אֶת־כּוֹכְבֵי הַשָּׁמַיִם – He ceased to count (or 'counting') the stars of (in) the sky.

3. With the prepositions כְּ or בְּ to express a subordinate idea of time. This may be expressed by means of a conjunction (e.g. כַּאֲשֶׁר – 'when') and a finite verb:

כַּאֲשֶׁר שָׁמַר הַמֶּלֶךְ אֶת־הַתּוֹרָה יָשַׁב הָעָם בָּאֶרֶץ בְּשָׁלוֹם – When the king kept the law, the people lived in the land in peace (or 'security').

But the same idea can be expressed more succinctly as follows:

כִּשְׁמֹר הַמֶּלֶךְ אֶת־הַתּוֹרָה יָשַׁב הָעָם בָּאֶרֶץ בְּשָׁלוֹם

with exactly the same meaning. The tense of the finite verb – in this case יָשַׁב, so past – will determine the tense of the English verb which one uses to render the Hebrew infinitive construct – hence 'when the king *kept*'.

Here we see how suitable the term 'Infinitive Construct' is as a description of this part of the verb. It *is* a part of the verb ('Infinitive') and so can take a direct object (אֶת־הַתּוֹרָה ); but it can also stand 'in construct relationship' to a noun (in this case הַמֶּלֶךְ ), i.e. 'in the king's keeping...' or 'when the king kept...'.

If 'the king' has already been referred to in the immediately preceding narrative, the place of הַמֶּלֶךְ may be taken by a suffix, 'in *his* keeping...':

כְּשָׁמְרוֹ אֶת־הַתּוֹרָה יָשַׁב הָעָם בָּאָרֶץ בְּשָׁלוֹם - When *he* kept the law the people lived in the land in security.

In the form כְּשָׁמְרוֹ, the vowel under the שׁ is a short o. In other words, when suffixes are added the long ŏ vowel of שָׁמֹר becomes short o and *moves to the preceding syllable*.

שָׁמֹר + וֹ > שָׁמְרוֹ  (šomrŏ)

The same sense in all of these constructions with the infinitive construct could also have been expressed with בּ in place of כּ. Thus, e.g.:

בְּשָׁמְרוֹ אֶת־הַתּוֹרָה יָשַׁב הָעָם בָּאָרֶץ בְּשָׁלוֹם

(b) The second of the two infinitives in the Hebrew verb is known as the *Infinitive Absolute*. Its form is

שָׁמֹר (or שָׁמוֹר )

The Infinite Absolute may sometimes stand by itself and be used to represent any finite part of the verb. In such a situation it most commonly represents the Imperative:

זָכוֹר אֶת־יוֹם הַשַּׁבָּת - Remember the sabbath day
(Ex 20:8)

But it is most often used alongside a finite verb form which it may either precede or follow.

When it *precedes* a finite verb-form

שָׁמוֹר שָׁמַרְתִּי אֶת־תּוֹרַת יהוה

it emphasises the idea contained in the verb, an emphasis which is best expressed in English by means of an adverb:

I have *diligently* (or *carefully*) kept the law of Yahweh.

When it *follows* a finite verb-form

שָׁמַרְתִּי שָׁמוֹר אֶת־תּוֹרַת יהוה

it gives continuity to the verbal idea:

I have *continually* kept the law of Yahweh.

## II

Just as there are two infinitives in the Hebrew verb, so there are also *two participles* - an *active* and a *passive*.

(a) The form of the active participle is as follows:

|  |  |
|---|---|
| m.s. שֹׁמֵר | m.pl. שֹׁמְרִים |
| f.s. שֹׁמֶרֶת (sometimes שֹׁמְרָה) | f.pl. שֹׁמְרוֹת |

(Note again here, in the forms שֹׁמְרִים and שֹׁמְרוֹת, the second stress pattern of Hebrew as described above on p. 24.)

The active participle may be used in exactly the same way as an adjective, either qualifying a noun or as the predicate of a verbless sentence (see above p. 31).

1. הָאִישׁ הַשֹּׁמֵר (אֶת־הָעִיר) - the guarding man,

i.e. the man who guards (the city).

This is one way in which Hebrew expresses what English expresses by means of a relative clause ('the man who...'). In so far as the active participle is a verb-form, it may take a direct object (in this case הָעִיר - the city).

2. When the active participle is used as the predicate of a sentence

הָאִישׁ שֹׁמֵר (אֶת־הַתּוֹרָה)

it expresses a continuity which is best expressed in English by a present continuous tense or possibly, dependent on context, by some such expression as 'is about to' or 'is going to'. Hence:

The man is keeping/is about to keep (the law).

It is often used in such a way to express an ongoing circumstance or situation, in the course of which something happened. For example, Gen 19:1 describes how two angels arrived in Sodom in the evening

וְלוֹט יֹשֵׁב בְּשַׁעַר־סְדֹם – *as Lot was sitting* in the gate of Sodom.

The active participle may also be used as a noun. It often describes the agent of the action designated by the verb.

| | | | |
|---|---|---|---|
| אָיַב | – to be hostile | אֹיֵב | – enemy |
| יָשַׁב | – to sit, dwell | יֹשֵׁב | – dweller, inhabitant |
| מָשַׁל | – to rule | מֹשֵׁל | – ruler |
| שָׁמַר | – to guard | שֹׁמֵר | – watchman |
| שָׁפַט | – to judge | שֹׁפֵט | – judge |

In the case of stative verbs (see above p. 45), the form of the active participle is identical with the 3rd m.s. of the Perfect. Stative participles may be used participially, as in the above examples, but very often they are used as simple adjectives.

| | | | |
|---|---|---|---|
| קָטֹן | – to be small | קָטֹן | – little, small |
| זָקֵן | – to be old | זָקֵן | – old |
| | | | (as a noun – 'elder') |

Stative verbs do not have passive participles.

(b) The form of the passive participle is:

| | | | |
|---|---|---|---|
| m.s. | שָׁמוּר | m.pl. | שְׁמוּרִים |
| f.s. | שְׁמוּרָה | f.pl. | שְׁמוּרוֹת |

This is used, again adjectivally, to describe a person (or persons or things) on whom the action designated by the verb has been inflicted. As with the active participle, so the passive one may be used either

(1) to qualify a noun:

הַמִּשְׁפָּט הַכָּתוּב - the written judgement,
        i.e. the judgement which has been written.

(2) as the predicate of a nominal sentence:

אִישׁ הָאֱלֹהִים קָבוּר שָׁם - The man of God is (or 'has
        been') buried there.

Here is a slightly modified form of Judg. 4:4-5 where participles are used to designate the ongoing or habitual activity of the prophetess Deborah:

וּדְבוֹרָה אִשָּׁה נְבִיאָה הִיא שֹׁפְטָה אֶת־יִשְׂרָאֵל בָּעֵת הַהִיא: וְהִיא יוֹשֶׁבֶת
תַּחַת־תֹּמֶר דְּבוֹרָה בֵּין הָרָמָה וּבֵין בֵּית־אֵל בְּהַר אֶפְרָיִם:

Now Deborah, a prophetess, *used to judge / was in the habit of judging* Israel at that time. And she *used to sit* under the palm tree of Deborah between Ramah and (between) Bethel in the hill-country of Ephraim.

## EXERCISE ELEVEN

Vocabulary:

Verb:

        בָּא (בּוֹא) – to come, enter (above p. 57)

Noun:

        דֶּרֶךְ (pl. דְּרָכִים) – way, road

Adjective:

        רָשָׁע – wicked

Other:

        אֲשֶׁר ... בּוֹ (No. 7) – in which
            (see pp. 111 f. for a fuller treatment of אֲשֶׁר)

Translate:

1. בָּא יוֹסֵף מֵאֶרֶץ מִצְרַיִם לִקְבֹּר אֶת־יַעֲקֹב בְּקֶבֶר יִצְחָק
אָבִיו אֲשֶׁר בְּאֶרֶץ כְּנַעַן:

2. כִּזְכֹּר הַנָּבִיא אֶת־הַדְּבָרִים הָאֵלֶּה קָרָא אֶל־הָעָם הַזֶּה
לִרְדֹּף אַחֲרֵי יֹשְׁבֵי הָעִיר:

3. בִּשְׁמָרְךָ אֶת־הַתּוֹרָה הַזֹּאת הָלַכְתָּ בְּדֶרֶךְ יהוה אֱלֹהֶיךָ:

4. הָלַךְ הָלוֹךְ אֶל־אֶרֶץ יְהוּדָה:

5. שָׁמוֹר שָׁמַרְתִּי אֶת־עִיר יהוה אֱלֹהֵי יִשְׂרָאֵל:

6. מֹשְׁלֵי הָעָם הַזֶּה רְשָׁעִים מְאֹד בְּעֵינֵי יהוה:

7. קָבְרוּ אֶת־אִישׁ הָאֱלֹהִים בַּקֶּבֶר אֲשֶׁר הַנָּבִיא קָבוּר בּוֹ:

# LESSON TWELVE

## THE VERB – PAST AND FUTURE TIME

We have so far observed that Hebrew can express past time by means of the Perfect:

שָׁמַר – he has guarded

and future time by means of the Imperfect:

יִשְׁמֹר – he will guard

though neither of these forms are to be thought of exclusively as 'tenses' (see above p. 44). But Hebrew also expresses these ideas of time in a different way:

1. Future time is frequently expressed by means of the *Perfect form* with a prefixed וֹ *vocalised in the same way as the conjunction* וֹ (see above pp. 27f.).
Thus:

וְשָׁמַר – (and) he will guard
וּמָלַכְתִּי – (and) I shall rule
וִילַדְתֶּן – (and) you (f.pl.) will bear (children)
וַעֲבַדְתֶּם – (and) you (m.pl.) will serve/
be slaves (to)

The two forms of the Perfect which have penultimate stress ( שָׁמַרְתָּ and שָׁמַרְתִּי ) appear, in these forms with prefixed וֹ, with *final* stress ( וְשָׁמַרְתָּ and וְשָׁמַרְתִּי ).

2. Similarly, past time is frequently expressed by means of the *Imperfect* (or, more accurately, *Jussive* as we shall discover in due course, below p. 104) *form* with a prefixed וֹ *vocalised in the same way as the definite article* (see above p. 27), i.e. with the short vowel a and doubling of the following consonant or, in the case of the 1st person singular, which has as its preformative the non-doubling consonant א, with a long ā-vowel.
Thus:

וַיִּשְׁמֹר – (and) he guarded
וָאֶמְלֹךְ – (and) I ruled

In these forms note that the accent is on the penultimate syllable. As we shall see in due course, this sometimes causes a shortening of the vowel of the final syllable.

These two verb forms are known as *Vav* (traditionally written *Waw* and pronounced 'wow') *Consecutive Perfect* and *Vav Consecutive Imperfect* respectively. The reason for the name Vav *Consecutive* is that these forms often seem to occur in a sequence. Sometimes, too, the scene is set, as it were, with the occurrence at the beginning of such a sequence of the normal Perfect or Imperfect.

(a) Here is an example with an initial Perfect followed by a series of Vav Consecutive (V.C.) Imperfects:

פָּתַח עֶזְרָא אֶת־הַסֵּפֶר וַיִּקְרָא בּוֹ וַיִּשְׁמַע הָעָם כָּל־הַיּוֹם

Ezra opened the book and read from (lit. 'in') it, and the people listened all day.

If, however, anything comes between the ו and the verb form (e.g. the negative לֹא), the sequence is broken, and the verb form reverts to the normal Perfect.

פָּתַח עֶזְרָא אֶת־הַסֵּפֶר וַיִּקְרָא בּוֹ וַיִּשְׁמַע הָעָם כָּל־הַיּוֹם וְלֹא חָדַל עַד־הָעָרֶב

Ezra opened the book and read from it, and the people listened all day, and he did not stop (reading) until the evening.

(b) Similarly, too, an initial Imperfect is sometimes followed by a series of V.C. Perfects:

יִפְתַּח עֶזְרָא אֶת־הַסֵּפֶר וְקָרָא בּוֹ וְשָׁמַע הָעָם כָּל־הַיּוֹם

Ezra will open the book and will read from it, and the people will listen all day.

Again, if anything comes between the ו and the verb form, the sequence is broken, and the verb form reverts to the initial Imperfect.

יִפְתַּח עֶזְרָא אֶת־הַסֵּפֶר וְקָרָא בּוֹ וְשָׁמַע הָעָם כָּל־הַיּוֹם וְלֹא יֶחְדַּל עַד־הָעָרֶב

Ezra will open the book and will read from it and the people will listen all day, and he will not stop (reading) until the evening.

This is the traditional explanation of these verb forms, and it is from this that the name 'Vav Consecutive' derives. Such an explanation does not, however, explain the frequent occurrence of such V.C. forms at the beginnings of sentences without any preceding 'scene setting' verb, or even at the beginning of a number of Biblical books such as Ruth, Jonah and Esther. It is probably best simply to accept that Hebrew has two ways of expressing past time:

(1) Perfect       שָׁמַר

and (2) V.C. Imperfect   וַיִּשְׁמֹר

and two ways of expressing future time

(1) Imperfect      יִשְׁמֹר

and (2) V.C. Perfect    וְשָׁמַר

A possible explanation for such a phenomenon is that the straight Perfect/Imperfect forms are those characteristic of the verbs of the West Semitic group of languages, while the V.C. forms have affinities with the verbs of the East Semitic group. Biblical Hebrew, like the country of which it was the language, stood at the crossroads of the ancient Near East and contains elements taken from different sides of the wider Semitic language family.

The two V.C. forms are in regular use in prose - the V.C. Imperfect is the normal Hebrew way of recounting a narrative in past time (cf. what was said above, p. 46, about the use of the Perfect); the V.C. Perfect is characteristic of the direct speech which occurs so frequently in Hebrew prose style - but they are not so common in poetry which tends, like poetry in other languages, to have its own distinctive sentence-structure.

## EXERCISE TWELVE

Vocabulary

Verbs:

קָרָא – to read      קָרָא לְ – to call, name

Nouns:

עוֹלָם – age, eternity    עַד־עוֹלָם – for ever

(pl. abs. יָמִים; cstr. יְמֵי) יוֹם – day

לַיְלָה – night      חַיִּים pl. – life

Translate:

1. וַנִּרְדֹּף אַחֲרֵי הַמְּלָכִים הָהֵם וַנִּשְׁפֹּט אֹתָם בָּהָר הַהוּא:

2. וְשָׁמַרְתִּי אֶת־תּוֹרַת יהוה אֱלֹהַי וְהָלַכְתִּי בִדְרָכָיו כָּל־הַיָּמִים:

3. וַנִּכְרֹת בְּרִית אֶת־יְהוָה אֱלֹהֵינוּ וְזָכַר אֹתָנוּ יהוה עַד־עוֹלָם:

4. וַיִּמְכְּרוּ לְאַבְרָם יֹשְׁבֵי הָעִיר הַהִיא קֶבֶר וַיִּקְבֹּר שָׁם אַבְרָם אֶת־שָׂרָה:

5. וְכָתַבְתָּ אֶת־תּוֹרָתִי בְּסֵפֶר וְקָרָאתָ בּוֹ כָּל־יְמֵי חַיֶּיךָ:

6. וַיִּקְרָא אֱלֹהִים לָאוֹר יוֹם וְלַחֹשֶׁךְ קָרָא לָיְלָה:

# LESSON THIRTEEN

## CLASSIFICATION OF NOUNS - I

### I

So far we have encountered various types of nouns, and it may perhaps be useful to attempt to classify them into categories. These categories are sometimes known as 'declensions'.

1. The *First Declension* contains nouns which have a long ā-vowel in the pre-tonic syllable (e.g. זָקֵן - old; elder) or in the tone syllable (e.g. לֵבָב - heart) or in both (e.g. דָּבָר - word). The vowel of the *pre-tonic* syllable is long by virtue of its position in relation to the stress or accent, thus when that accent is removed (as in the construct singular) or when it shifts, as, for example, it does in the masculine plural, then the syllable in question is two places or more from the accent, and its vowel is reduced to a *sheva*. This is the first stress pattern in Hebrew referred to above pp. 23f. Thus:

m.s.cstr. - דְּבַר        m.pl. - דְּבָרִים

Feminine nouns of this declension which end in הָ have הַ in the construct with vowel reduction:

שָׂפָה    -    שְׂפַת

צְדָקָה    -    צִדְקַת ( < *צִדְקַת - see above pp. 17f. )

In the feminine plural the הָ of the singular becomes וֹ :

צְדָקָה    -    צְדָקוֹת

שָׂפָה - lip has a dual rather than a plural:

שָׂפָה    -    שְׂפָתַיִם

Sometimes the vowel of the pre-tonic syllable is either pure long (e.g. כּוֹכָב - star) or protected inside a closed syllable (e.g. מִדְבָּר - desert, wilderness), in both of which cases the shift in position of the accent has no effect on them. Sometimes, of course, as in, for example, גָּדוֹל - great, it is the vowel of the tone syllable which is pure long.

The table on pp. 166f. lays out the main types of noun which fall into this declension. Note that a number of monosyllables come into this class of nouns, and these are inflected like the last syllable of דָּבָר (e.g. יָד - hand; דָּם - blood; דָּג - fish ) or of זָקֵן (e.g. עֵץ - tree ). Note also that some of the words listed in the tables are adjectives (e.g. רָשָׁע - wicked; שָׂמֵחַ - joyful ), while others are (mono-syllabic) participles of ע״ו verbs, of which we have already encountered the Perfect, above p. 57, (e.g. קָם - rising; מֵת - dead ).

2.  The *Second Declension* (tables on pp. 168f.) comprises nouns which were probably originally monosyllables. A noun-form like מַלְכִּי ('my king'), for example, is probably from an original מַלְךְּ (malk), but, since Hebrew has a dislike of 'consonantal clusters' (such as 'str' in the English word 'strip'), a helping vowel found its way between the second and the third consonants. In this declension that helping vowel was usually e (*segol*), and so these nouns are some-times described as 'segolate' nouns. In the case of those nouns which originally had a in the *first* syllable, the type which evolved was מֶלֶךְ , with e in *both* syllables.

As well as the a-type ( malk > מֶלֶךְ ), there are two other types in this declension. One had an original i-vowel in the first syllable (sipr) and developed to סֵפֶר, while the other had an o (boqr), developing to בֹּקֶר.

So we have the three sub-groups in this second de-clension:

m.s. (abs. & cstr.) מֶלֶךְ - king   סֵפֶר - book   בֹּקֶר - morning
with 1st s.c. suff. מַלְכִּי        סִפְרִי        בָּקְרִי

In this declension the forms of the absolute and construct singular are identical. Note also that in the forms of the singular with suffixes, the first syllable is closed (hence the *dagesh* in the כ of מַלְכִּי ) and retains the original short vowel (a - i - o ; in other words the ָ in בָּקְרִי is o ).

In the plural, however, this declension seems to follow the pattern of the first declension (cf. דְּבָרִים ), and we have the forms:

| m.pl. abs. | מְלָכִים | סְפָרִים | בְּקָרִים |

However, in the construct plural the short vowel of the supposed original form of the noun reappears (e.g. מַלְכֵי ), but here the *sheva* may be regarded as *vocal* and the first syllable as not closed but open. Thus:

| m.pl. cstr. | מַלְכֵי | סִפְרֵי | בְּקְרֵי |

In those cases where dual forms of the noun exist, the dual ending is appended to the supposed original form of the noun:

| s. abs. | רֶגֶל *f* - foot | אֹזֶן *f* - ear |
| with suff. | רַגְלִי | אָזְנִי |
| du. abs. | רַגְלַיִם | אָזְנַיִם |

In feminine forms, the feminine ending ( ָה ) is added to the original monosyllabic form of the noun:
e.g. malk > מַלְכָּה .

| f.s. abs. | מַלְכָּה – queen | כִּבְשָׂה – ewe lamb | אָכְלָה – food |
| cstr. | מַלְכַּת | כִּבְשַׂת | אָכְלַת |

The feminine plural, like the masculine plural, follows the first declension pattern:

| f.pl. abs. | מְלָכוֹת | כְּבָשׂוֹת | אֲכָלוֹת |
| cstr. | מַלְכוֹת | כְּבָשׂוֹת | אֲכָלוֹת |

Some feminine nouns, whose masculine counterparts (e.g. מִשְׁפָּט - judgment, justice ) belong to the first declension, have 'segolate' forms in the construct, e.g. מַמְלָכָה (abs. ) - kingdom; מַמְלֶכֶת (cstr.). In such cases the 'segolate' element behaves in exactly the same way as a second declension noun:

| with 1st s. suff. | מַמְלַכְתִּי |
| f. pl. abs. | מַמְלָכוֹת |
| f. pl. cstr. | מַמְלְכוֹת |

Some of these feminine nouns have 'segolate' forms even in the absolute. For example, both אַיָּלָה and אַיֶּלֶת ('hind') are found.

The inadequacy of the term 'segolate' to describe nouns of this class is evidenced by those nouns in which one of the consonants is a 'guttural'. We have already had occasion to observe the fact that 'gutturals' have a fondness for a-type vowels (see above p. 55). In those cases where the final consonant is a 'guttural', the second vowel of nouns in this declension is often an a-vowel. For example:

זֶרַע - seed, descendants     רֹמַח - spear

If the second consonant is a 'guttural', sometimes *both* vowels are a-vowels:

פַּחַד - fear     נַעַר - young lad

It is obviously not very helpful to describe a noun such as נַעַר as a 'segolate' noun. So 'second declension' is clearly a more neutral classification.

## II

There is a particular phenomenon in Hebrew which looks like the feminine ending but is in fact an ending appended to nouns to indicate 'direction towards'. The ending in question is הָ and is known as '*He locale*' (the latter, pronounced *lokahlay*, is a Latin adjective meaning 'concerning place'), the '*He*' of place (towards which)'. The difference between it and the feminine ending is that the latter takes the main stress in a word while the *He locale* does not.

הַבַּיְתָה - towards the house, i.e. homewards

הָהָרָה - towards the mountain

It can be appended to plurals:

הַשָּׁמַיְמָה - heavenwards

and even to nouns in the construct state:

אַרְצָה מִצְרַיִם - to(wards) (the land of) Egypt

The latter could also have been expressed by

מִצְרַיְמָה

While it may be appended to place names, it is never used with personal proper names. With them the preposition אֶל־ is used:

אֶל־דָּוִד - to(wards) David

## EXERCISE THIRTEEN

Vocabulary:

Verb:

הָיָה - to be

Nouns:

חֵטְא (pl. חֲטָאִים) - sin

צָבָא (pl. צְבָאוֹת) - army, host

עָלֶה (cstr. sg. עֲלֵה; abs. pl. עָלִים) - leaf, leaves (collective)

נָהָר - stream, river

Adjective:

יָפֶה - beautiful

Translate:

1. וַיִּזְכֹּר הַזָּקֵן צִדְקוֹת נְבִיאֵי אֱלֹהִים:

2. וַיִּכְרֹת יהוה אֱלֹהֵי צְבָאוֹת בְּרִית עִם־עַמּוֹ בַּמִּדְבָּר:

3. עֲלֵי הָעֵצִים הָהֵם אֲשֶׁר עַל־שְׂפַת הַנָּהָר הֵם יָפִים מְאֹד:

4. וַיִּשְׁמְרוּ אֶת־סִפְרֵי הַנְּבִיאִים הַקְּדֹשִׁים בְּבֵית יהוה בִּירוּשָׁלַיִם:

5. מַלְכַּת יִשְׂרָאֵל הִיא רְשָׁעָה מְאֹד:

6. חֲטָאֵי הַמַּמְלָכוֹת הָאֵלֶּה הֵם כְּבֵדִים מְאֹד בְּעֵינֵי יהוה:

7. הָיָה רָעָב בָּאָרֶץ וְאַבְרָם יָרַד מִצְרַיְמָה כִּי כָבֵד הָרָעָב בָּאָרֶץ:

8. שָׁלַח אִישׁ הָאֱלֹהִים אֶת־יָדָיו הַשָּׁמַיְמָה וְהָעָם קָרָא אֶל־יהוה:

- 93 -

# LESSON FOURTEEN

## THE IMPERFECT –
## VERBS WITH A 'GUTTURAL' AS ONE OF THEIR LETTERS

In verbs of this type there are no problems of 'root recognition'. There are minor differences of vocalisation between verbs of this type and the so-called 'regular' verb (e.g. שָׁמַר), and these are mainly occasioned by the general observation which we have already made, namely that 'gutturals' have a fondness for a -type vowels. For example, the Imperfect of שָׁחַט ('slaughter') is יִשְׁחַט, where the presence of the 'guttural' has attracted the a-vowel in place of the ŏ of the regular Imperfect (יִשְׁמֹר). For a complete paradigm of these so-called 'guttural verbs', see the tables on pp. 178-185 (left-hand columns only for the moment). The following general points may be made, some of which we have already observed in the context of the Perfect (see above pp. 55f.).

1. A simple vocal *sheva* in the regular verb is replaced under a 'guttural' by a composite *sheva*.
   For example:

   פ-guttural    עָמַד – to stand    m.s. Imper. עֲמֹד (שְׁמֹר)
   ע-guttural    שָׁחַט – to slaughter    2nd f.s. Imperf. תִּשְׁחֲטִי
                                         (תִּשְׁמְרִי)
   פ״א          אָמַר – to say    m.s. Imper. אֱמֹר (שְׁמֹר)

Notice in this last case that א often has vowels of the e-type (cf. the vowel of the preformative of the 1st s.c. of the Imperfect אֶשְׁמֹר).

2. The short vowel which precedes such a composite *sheva* is of the same type as (homogeneous with) the composite *sheva*.
   For example:

   פ-guttural    עָמַד    3rd m.s. Imperf. יַעֲמֹד (יִשְׁמֹר)
   ע-guttural    שָׁחַט    m.pl. Imper.    שַׁחֲטוּ (שִׁמְרוּ)

'Stative' verbs or verbs with a as the second vowel in

– 94 –

the Imperfect have the following pattern:

חָזַק - to be strong    3rd m.s. Imperf. יֶחֱזַק

3. In the case of ל-guttural verbs, the preference for a-vowels operates in two different ways.

(i) If the vowel preceding the final guttural is *unchangeably long*, then that vowel is retained and an a-vowel (known as *patah furtive*; above, pp. 18f) is inserted between the long vowel and the final guttural.
For example:

שָׁלַח - to send, stretch out    Inf. Abs. שָׁלוֹחַ (שָׁמוֹר)

(ii) If the vowel preceding the final guttural is long but not unchangeably long, we find that often that vowel is *replaced* by an a-vowel. For example:

שָׁלַח    3rd m.s. Imperf. יִשְׁלַח (יִשְׁמֹר)

In the case of the Active Participle (ε) and the Infinitive Construct (δ), it is the '*patah furtive*' phenomenon which operates.
For example:

שָׁלַח    Act. Pt. שֹׁלֵחַ (שֹׁמֵר)    Inf.Cstr. שְׁלֹחַ (שְׁמֹר)

4. The majority of verbs having א as their initial letter are no different from other פ-gutturals. There is however an important sub-set of them, known as פ״א verbs, and they have one characteristic which differentiates them from פ-gutturals, namely that in the Imperfect the א is silent. The forms are:

אָמַר - to say    3rd m.s. Imperf. יֹאמַר
אָכַל - to eat    3rd m.s. Imperf. יֹאכַל

In the 1st singular of the Imperfect, which has א as a preformative, only one א is written, and the forms are:

אֹמַר    and    אֹכַל

There are, in any case, only five verbs of this type:

אָמַר - to say    אָבַד - to perish
אָכַל - to eat    אָבָה - to wish
אָפָה - to bake

Two very common forms of אָמַר should be noted.

(1) The V.C. Imperfect is וַיֹּאמֶר, with an e-vowel in the final syllable as opposed to the a of יֹאמַר. This is due to the shift in the position of the accent in V.C. Imperfect forms referred to above p. 86.

(2) The verb אָמַר almost always implies direct speech, but if a different verb of speaking (e.g. קָרָא - to call; זָעַק - to cry out) is used in the sentence, then the form לֵאמֹר will almost always immediately precede the direct speech proper. The form is the Infinitive Construct אֱמֹר with the preposition ל (*לֶאֱמֹר < לֵאמֹר with the א becoming silent). לֵאמֹר is usually translated 'saying', but it may often be left untranslated and be regarded simply as the indicator that what follows is direct speech, in other words as the Hebrew equivalent of inverted commas.

**5.** ל״א verbs are more distinct as a sub-class of ל-gutturals. The vowel which precedes the א is mostly a, with the א having become simply a vowel-letter:

מָצָא - to find    3rd m.s. Imperf. יִמְצָא (יִשְׁמֹר)

but in the 2nd and 3rd f.pl. Imperf. it is e:

תִּמְצֶאנָה (תִּשְׁמֹרְנָה)

Both the Infinitives (Construct and Absolute) and the two Participles (Active and Passive), however, follow the pattern of the regular verb:

מָצוּא - מָצֵא - מָצוֹא - מְצֹא

## EXERCISE FOURTEEN

Vocabulary:

Verbs:

| | | |
|---|---|---|
| עָזַב | - to leave, forsake, abandon | |
| עָמַד | - to stand | עָבַר - to cross |
| אָכַל | - to eat | אָהֵב - to love |
| בָּטַח בְּ | - to trust in (someone) | זָעַק - to cry out |
| עָבַד | - to serve (as a slave) > to worship (a deity) | |

Nouns:

הַיַּרְדֵּן – the Jordan     אֲדָמָה *f* – ground, soil

קֹדֶשׁ – holiness     מִצְוָה *f* – commandment

לֵבָב – heart     נֶפֶשׁ *f* – breath, soul,

עֵשֶׂב – grass, herbage, plants        life force

כִּסֵּא – throne     אָכְלָה *f* – food

בַּעַל – lord, husband; Baal

Other:

לְמַעַן – in order that, so that    אִם – if

בָּם ... אֲשֶׁר (No. 7) – in which    (see pp. 111 f. for a fuller treatment

of אֲשֶׁר)

Translate:

1. וַיַּעַזְבוּ אֶת־תּוֹרָתִי אֲשֶׁר נָתַתִּי לִפְנֵיהֶם וְלֹא שָׁמְעוּ
בְּקוֹלִי וְלֹא־הָלְכוּ בִדְרָכָי:

2. וַיַּעַבְרוּ בְּנֵי יִשְׂרָאֵל אֶת־הַיַּרְדֵּן וַיַּעַמְדוּ עַל־אַדְמַת
הַקֹּדֶשׁ:

3. וַיֹּאמֶר יהוה אֶל־עֲבָדָיו הַנְּבִיאִים כֹּה־תֹאמְרוּ לְעַמִּי
יִשְׂרָאֵל:

4. אִם־תִּשְׁמְרוּ אֶת־מִצְוֹתַי בְּכָל־לְבַבְכֶם וּבְכָל־נַפְשְׁכֶם
וְנָתַתִּי לָכֶם אֶת־הָעֵשֶׂב לְאָכְלָה וַאֲכַלְתֶּם:

5. נָתַתִּי אֹתוֹ לְמֶלֶךְ עַל־כִּסֵּא דָוִד עַבְדִּי לְמַעַן יִבְטַח־בִּי
עַמִּי יִשְׂרָאֵל:

6. וַיִּזְעֲקוּ בְּנֵי יִשְׂרָאֵל אֶל־יהוה לֵאמֹר עֲזַבְנוּ אֶת־אֱלֹהֵינוּ
וַנַּעֲבֹד אֶת־הַבְּעָלִים:

7. הִנֵּה אָנֹכִי שֹׁלֵחַ מַלְאָךְ לְפָנֶיךָ לִשְׁמֹר אֹתְךָ בְּכָל־דְּרָכֶיךָ
אֲשֶׁר אַתָּה הֹלֵךְ בָּם:

8. תֶּאֱהַב אֶת־יהוה אֱלֹהֶיךָ וְאֹתוֹ תַעֲבֹד כָּל־יְמֵי חַיֶּיךָ:

# LESSON FIFTEEN

## CLASSIFICATION OF NOUNS - II

### I

The third category or declension of nouns comprises those which have a long ē in the final syllable and an unchangeable vowel in the penultimate one. That unchangeable vowel may be unchangeable by nature, i.e. pure long (e.g. שׁוֹמֵר, though usually written 'defectively' שֹׁמֵר) or unchangeable by position, i.e. in a closed syllable (e.g. מִסְפֵּד - mourning). The main type of noun in this declension is the Active Participle: שֹׁמֵר.

Third declension nouns follow the second stress pattern described above p. 24, and in accordance with that pattern the ē -vowel usually becomes a vocal *sheva* before plural endings (e.g. שֹׁמְרִים) and before most pronominal suffixes (e.g. שֹׁמְרִי). When the pronominal suffix begins with a consonant (e.g. ךָ, כֶם ), the ē usually becomes the short vowel e (e.g. שֹׁמֶרְךָ). Sometimes it becomes i (e.g. שֵׁם - name > שִׁמְךָ) and with gutturals often a (e.g. כֹּהֵן - priest > כֹּהַנְךָ). In monosyllables like שֵׁם, the long vowel is retained in the pretonic syllable in the absolute plural ( שֵׁמוֹת ), though not, of course, in the construct ( שְׁמוֹת ).

The usual feminine form of the participle is שֹׁמֶרֶת. Here the long vowel (ō) remains unchangeable, and the remainder of the form behaves like a second declension noun ( שֹׁמַרְתִּי etc. ; see above pp. 90 ff. on second declension nouns ).

For the paradigms of third declension nouns see below p. 170.

### II

Sometimes a fourth class of nouns and adjectives is distinguished. These are, for the most part, biliteral monosyllabic nouns (i.e. with one syllable and two consonants ) which double their second consonant before endings and suffixes. Such nouns are derived from *tri*literal roots where the second and third letters are identical (ע״ע roots; for the Perfect of verbs of this type see above p. 59f.). Rather along the lines of second declension nouns, they fall into three sub-groups, an a–class, an i–class and an u–class.

| עַם - people | חֵץ - arrow | חֹק - statute |
|---|---|---|
| עַמִּי | חִצִּי | חֻקִּי |
| עַמִּים | חִצִּים | חֻקִּים |

The noun הַר - 'mountain' also belongs to this declension, but, because ר is a non-doubling consonant, when suffixes and endings are added, the a becomes ā in compensation for the lack of doubling. Thus: הָרִי (contrast עַמִּי ) and הָרִים ( עַמִּים ). Cf. also the feminine form רָעָה - 'evil', where the plural, e.g., is רָעוֹת.

Note that nouns of the 'a'–class usually have a short a in the absolute form, though some (e.g. עַם and הַר ) lengthen that vowel when the definite article is prefixed ( הָעָם and הָהָר ).

For the paradigms of the fourth declension see below pp. 171f.

Nouns of this declension should not be confused with nouns and adjectives such as דָּן and קָם which have a *long* ā–vowel in their absolute form. This latter type of noun derives from ע״י roots and belongs with the first declension (see above pp. 89f. and table on pp. 166f. ).

### III

There is a final category of nouns, some of which, though not all, can be classified in one or other of the four declensions but which are simply to be regarded as irregular. They are, as is usual in most languages, among the most common words: man (אִישׁ), woman (אִשָּׁה), father (אָב), brother (אָח), son (בֵּן), daughter (בַּת),

house (בַּיִת), water (מַיִם), city (עִיר), etc. These can only be learned. They are here laid out in tabular form for ease of reference.

| Abs.s. | Cstr.s. | With suff. | Abs.pl. | Cstr.pl. | With suff. |
|--------|---------|------------|---------|----------|------------|
| אִישׁ | אִישׁ | אִישְׁךָ | אֲנָשִׁים | אַנְשֵׁי | אֲנָשֶׁיךָ |
| אִשָּׁה | אֵשֶׁת | אִשְׁתְּךָ | נָשִׁים | נְשֵׁי | נָשֶׁיךָ |
| אָב | אֲבִי | אָבִיךָ | אָבוֹת | אֲבוֹת | אֲבוֹתֶיךָ |
| בֵּן | בִּנְךָ | בִּנְךָ | בָּנִים | בְּנֵי | בָּנֶיךָ |
| בַּת | בַּת | בִּתְּךָ | בָּנוֹת | בְּנוֹת | בְּנוֹתֶיךָ |
| בַּיִת | בֵּית | בֵּיתְךָ | בָּתִּים | בָּתֵּי | בָּתֶּיךָ |
| | | | מַיִם | מֵי | מֵימֶיךָ |
| עִיר | עִיר | עִירְךָ | עָרִים | עָרֵי | עָרֶיךָ |

אָח ('brother') behaves in exactly the same way as אָב ('father') in the singular. In the plural the forms are as follows: abs. אַחִים ; cstr. אֲחֵי ; with suff. אַחֶיךָ. Note that the first vowel of בָּתִּים is not, as we would expect in the closed and unaccented syllable, o, but ā (bāttīm). This is quite anomalous and is signalled as such by the *meteg* (see above p. 25).

## EXERCISE FIFTEEN

Vocabulary:

Verbs:

שָׂנֵא – to hate            שָׁאַל – to ask, request

Nouns:

מַקֵּל – staff            אֵם (אִמִּי etc.) *f* – mother

נַחַל – stream, wady            אֶבֶן *f* – stone

Other:

אֲלֵיכֶם (No. 4) – 'to you'

and עָלֵינוּ (No. 8) – 'over us'   (see below, p. 110, para. 7)

Translate:

1. שִׁמְךָ יהוה אֱלֹהֵינוּ גָּדוֹל בַּשָּׁמָיִם:

2. שֹׂנְאֵי טוֹב וְאֹהֲבֵי רַע רְשָׁעִים בְּעֵינֵינוּ:

3. לָקַח דָּוִד אֶת־מַקְלוֹ בְּיָדוֹ וַיִּבְחַר־לוֹ אֲבָנִים מִן־הַנַּחַל:

4. אֵלֶּה הַחֻקִּים אֲשֶׁר נָתַן אֲלֵיכֶם יהוה לִשְׁמֹר אֹתָם בְּאֶרֶץ כְּנָעַן:

5. וַיֹּאמֶר אֱלֹהִים עַמִּי אַתֶּם מֵהַיּוֹם הַזֶּה וְעַד־עוֹלָם:

6. וַיֹּאמֶר הַמֶּלֶךְ אֶל־אִמּוֹ לָמָה שָׁאַלְתְּ אֶת־הַדָּבָר הַזֶּה:

7. אֲנִי יהוה אֱלֹהֵי אֲבֹתֵיכֶם אֱלֹהֵי אַבְרָהָם אֱלֹהֵי יִצְחָק וֵאלֹהֵי יַעֲקֹב:

8. וַיֹּאמְרוּ אַנְשֵׁי יְהוּדָה אֶל־דָּוִד מְלָךְ־נָא עָלֵינוּ:

# LESSON SIXTEEN

## THE IMPERFECT - VERBS WITH ו OR י

### I

We have already seen above (pp. 56f.) that those roots which, in the Perfect, begin with a י fall into two categories, those where the י is the original first consonant (a comparatively small group of verbs) and those where the י has replaced an original ו. The former are correctly designated פ״י verbs, while the latter are more correctly described as פ״ו, even though in the Perfect they, too, begin with י.

1.  פ״י  (p. 187)

These have Imperfects in a, and the form is

יָנַק - to suck  -  Imperf. יִינַק

Here the i-vowel of the 3rd m.s. preformative and the י which is the first root letter have coalesced into the long ī-vowel.

2.  פ״ו  (p. 186)

These fall into two categories:

(i) The majority follow the פ״י pattern in the Imperfect -

Active   יָרַשׁ - to inherit   - יִירַשׁ
Stative  יָרֵא - to be afraid - יִירָא

In this last, the fact that this root is also ל״א (see above p. 96) has occasioned the long ā-vowel in the second syllable. In the active verbs the Imperative is monosyllabic

רַשׁ - m.s.

while the Infinitive Construct resembles second declension nouns

רֶשֶׁת   (with suffs. רִשְׁתִּי etc.)

Because of the nature of the vowels here, such a form

or pattern is often described as being 'segolate' (see on second declension nouns above pp. 90ff.).

(ii) A smaller group of common verbs follows a quite distinct pattern:

יָשַׁב - to sit, dwell - Imperf. יֵשֵׁב

Again the Imper. is monosyllabic

שֵׁב

and the Infinitive Construct 'segolate'

שֶׁבֶת    (with suffs. שִׁבְתִּי etc. )

These 'segolate' Infinitives are, like Second Declension nouns (above, pp. 90ff.), accented on their first syllable. The preposition ל, when prefixed to these Infinitives to express purpose, falls in the pre-tonic position and is vocalised with ā:

לָשֶׁבֶת

See above, p. 52.

There are six very common verbs which follow this pattern, and they are worth noting:

| | | | |
|---|---|---|---|
| יָרַד - to go down | יֵרֵד | רֵד | רֶדֶת |
| יָשַׁב - to sit, dwell | יֵשֵׁב | שֵׁב | שֶׁבֶת |
| יָלַד - to bear ( children ) | יֵלֵד | לֵד | לֶדֶת |
| יָדַע - to know | יֵדַע | דַּע | דַּעַת ( דְּעְתִּי ) |

( Notice here how the final 'guttural' attracts a- vowels in place of ē and e)

| | | | |
|---|---|---|---|
| יָצָא - to go out | יֵצֵא | צֵא | צֵאת ( צֵאתִי ) |

(Here the א has, as usual, become silent )

| | | | |
|---|---|---|---|
| הָלַךְ - to walk | יֵלֵךְ | לֵךְ | לֶכֶת ( לָכְתִּי ) |

(Notice that the *Perfect* in this last instance falls outside the usual pattern. הָלַךְ is a very common verb and should be carefully noted.)

In a class by itself among the פ״י verbs is the stative verb יָכֹל - to be able, where the Imperfect is יוּכַל.

In those verbs where in the Imperfect there are two ē-vowels (e.g. יֵרֵד), in the V.C. Imperfect (where the accent falls on the *penultimate* syllable [see above p. 86]) the vowel of the final syllable is reduced to e: וַיֵּרֶד. So, too, וַיֵּשֶׁב etc. This phenomenon does not, however, occur with וַיֵּצֵא.

## II

ע״ו and ע״י (p. 188)

As we have seen already (p. 57), verbs which are ע״ו or ע״י have become monosyllabic in the Perfect:

קָם – to arise      שָׂם – to put, place

and that it is their Infinitive Construct (קוּם and שִׂים respectively) that is used as the 'citation form', since in that particular part of the verb their true nature is evident. The medial ו and י are also in evidence in the Imperfect:

| | | |
|---|---|---|
| 3rd m.s. Imperf. | יָקוּם | יָשִׂים |
| m.s. Imper. | קוּם | שִׂים |
| Inf. Cstr. | קוּם | שִׂים |
| Pt. | קָם | שָׂם |

Notice that, as in the 'regular' verb, the forms of the m.s. Imperative and of the Inf. Cstr. are identical and that in this class of verb the Pt. is identical in form with the 3rd m.s. Perf.

In this class of verbs, too, the *Jussive* (see above pp. 75 f.) is *different* in form from the ordinary Imperfect. The latter is יָשִׂים/יָקוּם, but the Jussive is

יָקֹם       יָשֵׂם

In what we call 'V.C. *Imperfect*', the ו is actually prefixed to the *Jussive* (see above p. 85), and in the V.C. Imperf. the accent falls on the penultimate syllable, with the subsequent shortening of that final vowel (ō > o; ē > e; see also above p. 86 and above on פ״ו verbs):

Jussive יָקֹם  –  V.C. Imperf.  וַיָּקָם (vayyāqom)

יָשֵׂם             וַיָּשֵׂם (vayyāsem)

# III

ל״ה  (p. 190)

We have already noted how verbs which have י as the *third* letter of their root appear in the 3rd m.s. of the Perfect to be ל״ה ( גָּלָה - to uncover, reveal), and this is the name by which this class of verbs is commonly known (see above p. 58). But the ה is really a vowel-letter and appears only when the third root letter is not followed by any suffix or afformative and has become vocalic (ay > ā), and these verbs are, strictly speaking, ל״י, as may be seen, e.g., from a form such as גָּלִיתִי (1st s. Perf.). The following are the characteristic forms:

| | |
|---|---|
| 3rd m.s. Imperf. | יִגְלֶה |
| m.s. Imper. | גְּלֵה |
| Inf. Cstr. | גְּלוֹת |
| Pt. | גֹּלֶה  (cstr. גֹּלֵה; fem. גֹּלָה ) |

In the Imper. and in the 2nd f.s. and 3rd and 2nd m.pl. of the Imperf., the ה disappears before the vocalic afformatives:

גְּלוּ  (m.pl. Imper.)

תִּגְלִי  (2nd f.s. Imperf.)

יִגְלוּ  (3rd m.pl. Imperf.)

The Jussive of this class of verbs tends to appear in a shortened (or 'apocopated') form, where the ה and its vowel drop away and a helping vowel is inserted between the first and second letters of the root:

(יִגְלֶה < יִגְל* < יִגֶל )

It is this 'apocopated' form that is almost invariably found in the V.C. Imperfect of  ל״ה  verbs:

וַיִּגֶל

again with the accent on the penultimate syllable.

A very common verb which belongs to this class is הָיָה - to be.

Imperf. יִהְיֶה - Imper. הֱיֵה - Inf. Cstr. הֱיוֹת (with ל: לִהְיוֹת)

The 'apocopated' Jussive is יְהִי. With a simple וֹ this becomes וִיהִי ( וַיְהִי ‹ וְיְהִי ‹ ‹ ) while the V.C. Imperfect is וַיְהִי . Notice that the יּ unexpectedly has no *dagesh*. There are a number of consonants in Hebrew ( ו, י, ל, מ, נ, ק ) which, when followed by a vocal *sheva*, very often omit *dagesh* even when one would expect it (cf. also the form מַקְלוֹ – the noun מַקֵּל with pronominal suffix of the 3rd m. sg. – in Exercise 15 No. 3; above, p. 101 ).

Besides meaning simply '(and ) he/it was', וַיְהִי is very frequently used in narrative style in a kind of introductory way. It is what the AV (KJV) translated as 'and it came to pass'. In these circumstances it is often followed by a subordinate expression of time, e.g. כ (or ב ) and the Infinitive Construct (see above pp. 79f.) and then by another V.C. Imperfect representing the main clause of the sentence. In this kind of situation וַיְהִי is often best left untranslated. For example:

וַיְהִי כְּבוֹא אַבְרָם מִצְרָיְמָה וַיִּרְאוּ הַמִּצְרִים אֶת־הָאִשָּׁה כִּי־יָפָה הִיא מְאֹד
(Gen 12:14 )

This could be translated literally: 'And it was (came to pass ), when Abram was entering Egypt and the Egyptians saw (the ל״ה verb רָאָה – to see ) the woman that she was very beautiful'. In English that is less 'Biblical' it might read more simply: 'When Abram was about to enter Egypt, the Egyptians saw (*or* noticed ) that the woman was very beautiful'.

### Note on Accents

We referred above on p. 26 to the two signs *atnah* and *silluq*, and we must now look at these more closely. Most verses of the Hebrew Bible fall into two main parts, and there is a feeling of a pause occurring at the end of the first part, rather like that experienced at a comma in an English sentence, and again at the end of the second, though more final on this occasion as at the full stop at the end of an English sentence. In the Hebrew verse, the end of the first part is marked by the sign ָ (*atnah*) placed to the left of the vowel of the accented syllable of the last word in the first part of the verse (in the cases of ŏ and ū the sign is placed beneath the consonant). The end of the complete verse is marked by ָ (*silluq*) which is similarly placed in the final word in the verse. If the vowel in question is 'short' in terms of the 'long' /'short' distinction indicated (with qualifications) above p. 15, then the *atnah* or the *silluq* will lengthen it. The word in question is then said to be 'in pause', and the form which it takes, with such possible vowel modification, is said to be its 'pausal form'. In Gen 1:1

בְּרֵאשִׁית בָּרָא אֱלֹהִים אֵת הַשָּׁמַיִם וְאֵת הָאָרֶץ׃

*atnah* occurs beside the ִי-vowel of אֱלֹהִים and *silluq* beside the ָ-vowel of הָאָרֶץ. In neither case is the pausal form of these words any different from its usual form. In the second sentence of No. 5 in the following translation exercise, לָיְלָה is the pausal form of לַיְלָה.

## EXERCISE SIXTEEN

Vocabulary:

Verb:

לָקַח - to take (Imperf. יִקַּח; Imper. קַח).

See below p. 116

Nouns:

יוֹנָה *f* - dove    מָנוֹחַ - resting place
                     (< verb נוּחַ - to rest)
כַּף *f* - palm (of hand), sole (of foot).
נֹחַ - Noah    תֵּבָה *f* (Noah's) ark;
the Hebrew for the 'ark (of the covenant)' is אֲרוֹן.
רָחוֹק - far, distant

- 107 -

Other:

עִם – with        בַּמָּה – how?

(lit. 'by-means-of what?')

אֵלֶיךָ and אֲלֵיכֶם – אֵלָיו – 'to you' and 'to him'; see below, p. 110 para. 7

אֶחָד – one

(for the numerals see Lesson 25, below, pp. 151 ff.)

Translate:

1. וַיֵּרֶד אַבְרָם מִצְרַיְמָה עִם־אִשְׁתּוֹ וְלֹא יָדַע מֶלֶךְ מִצְרַיִם
כִּי אִשְׁתּוֹ הִיא:

2. וַיֹּאמֶר אַבְרָם לַיהוה אֱלֹהָיו בַּמָּה אֵדַע כִּי אִירַשׁ אֶת־
הָאָרֶץ הַזֹּאת:

3. וְלֹא מָצְאָה הַיּוֹנָה מָנוֹחַ לְכַף רַגְלָהּ וַתָּשָׁב אֶל־נֹחַ אֶל־
הַתֵּבָה:

4. וַיֹּאמֶר לוֹ יהוה קַח־נָא אֶת־בִּנְךָ אֲשֶׁר אָהַבְתָּ וְלֵךְ אֶל־
אֶרֶץ רְחוֹקָה וַיֵּלֶךְ לְדַרְכּוֹ בַּבֹּקֶר הוּא וּבְנוֹ אֶל־הַמָּקוֹם
אֲשֶׁר אָמַר לוֹ יהוה: וַיֹּאמֶר אֶל־נְעָרָיו שְׁבוּ לָכֶם בַּמָּקוֹם
הַזֶּה וַאֲנִי וּבְנִי נֵלְכָה לְדַרְכֵּנוּ וְנָשׁוּבָה אֲלֵיכֶם: וַיָּבֹאוּ
אַבְרָהָם וּבְנוֹ אֶל־הַמָּקוֹם וַיָּשֶׂם אֶת־בְּנוֹ עַל־הַמִּזְבֵּחַ
וַיִּשְׁלַח אַבְרָהָם אֶת־יָדוֹ לַהֲרֹג אֶת־יִצְחָק: וַיִּקְרָא
אֵלָיו מַלְאַךְ יהוה מִן־הַשָּׁמַיִם וַיֹּאמֶר אַבְרָהָם אַל־
תִּשְׁלַח אֶת־יָדְךָ עַל־הַיֶּלֶד כִּי עַתָּה יָדַעְתִּי כִּי יְרֵא
אֱלֹהִים אָתָּה:

5. וַיֹּאמֶר אֱלֹהִים יְהִי אוֹר וַיְהִי אוֹר: וַיִּקְרָא אֱלֹהִים
לָאוֹר יוֹם וְלַחֹשֶׁךְ קָרָא לָיְלָה וַיְהִי־עֶרֶב וַיְהִי־בֹקֶר
יוֹם אֶחָד:

Sentence No. 4 is loosely based on Gen. 22: 2-12

# LESSON SEVENTEEN
## PREPOSITIONS WITH SUFFIXES

### I

Just as nouns have pronominal suffixes appended to them in order to express possession - e.g. סוּסִי 'my horse', etc. - and where the suffix expresses what we express in English by means of 'possessive adjectives' (my, your, his, her, etc.), so too, these same suffixes are appended to prepositions. We have already noted this in relation to the prepositions בּ and לְ above pp. 69f. For a full set of paradigms see below p. 173. Notice that these suffixes when appended to prepositions express what English expresses by means of the object form of the personal pronoun: me, you, him, her, etc. In other words לִי, e.g., means 'to/for *me*'.

1. In the case of the inseparable prepositions בּ ('in, on, among, by [of instrument]') and לְ ('to, for') the forms are identical (לְךָ/בְּךָ, לִי/בִּי etc.). In the case of בּ, in addition to בָּהֶם, there exists also the contracted form בָּם.

2. With the inseparable preposition כּ ('as, like'), the suffixes are appended, for the most part, to a longer form of that preposition which, on its own, occurs mainly in poetry, כְּמוֹ. Thus we find כָּמוֹנִי, כָּמוֹךָ etc. But note forms like כָּכֶם and כָּהֶם (2nd and 3rd pl., m. and f.).

3. A similar kind of phenomenon occurs in the case of מִן ('from'), where suffixes are appended to a reduplicated form *mimmin*. Here we have מִמֶּנִּי , מִמֶּנּוּ etc. But alongside such forms, we have, again in the case of the 2nd and 3rd pl. suffixes, מִכֶּם and מֵהֶם. In the 2nd s. we find forms which come halfway between full reduplication and the simple מִן , namely מִמֶּךָ/מִמְּךָ .

4. Two biliteral prepositions double their second consonant before adding suffixes, in much the same way as do 'fourth declension' nouns (see above pp. 98f.).

These are אֵת and עִם, both meaning 'with'. The forms here are עִמִי/אִתִּי, etc. Note particularly the difference in forms between אֵת – 'with' and suffixes ( אִתִּי, etc., with a short i-vowel and doubling of the ת ) and אֵת – the sign of the definite direct object and suffixes (אֹתִי, etc., with a long ō-vowel).

5. One preposition at least is really a plural noun in the construct, אַחֲרֵי ('after'), and with this might be included also לִפְנֵי ('before'), which is the preposition לְ and the construct form of the (pl.) noun פָּנִים – 'face' (see already the vocabulary of Exercise Nine above p. 72). The suffixes are appended to these in the form and in the way which is usual with plural nouns: דְּבָרַי, דְּבָרֶיךָ etc., thus לְפָנַי/אַחֲרַי, לְפָנֶיךָ/אַחֲרֶיךָ, etc.

6. Two others in this category, but less obviously so, are תַּחַת ('beneath, instead of') and בֵּין ('between'). In the case of תַּחַת, the suffixes are always appended to the plural form: תַּחְתַּי , תַּחְתֶּיךָ, etc. In the case of בֵּין, suffixes which indicate the singular are appended to בֵּין ( בֵּינְךָ, בֵּינִי etc. ), while suffixes which indicate the plural are appended to the form בֵּינֵי ( בֵּינֵינוּ, בֵּינֵיכֶם, etc. ). Students should carefully distinguish the preposition בֵּין, which is written with a י, from the noun בֵּן ('son'),which has no י.

7. Three prepositions – אֶל ('to, towards'; see already the vocabulary of Exercise Sixteen above p. 108 ), עַל ('upon, beside, on account of') and עַד ('until, as far as') – look as if they also come into the category of plural nouns, in that in their cases the resultant form would lead us to think so: אֵלַי/עָלַי/עָדַי, אֵלֶיךָ/עָלֶיךָ/עָדֶיךָ etc. But the presence of the י in the forms with suffixes here is attributable not to a basic 'plurality' but to the fact that these three prepositions are derived from ל"י roots (see above p. 58), the final י not being present in their simple, unsuffixed form.

8. Finally, it is to be noted that Hebrew has a fondness for combining prepositions, especially with מִן.

For example:

מֵעִם (< עִם + מִן ) - from, away from
(lit. 'away from with')

מִלְּפְנֵי (< לִפְנֵי + מִן ) - away from
(lit. 'away from before')

## II

As we have already seen (above pp. 47f. ), אֲשֶׁר is used in Hebrew to link two independent clauses.

הוּא הַמֶּלֶךְ הַגָּדוֹל - He (or That) is the great king.

מָשַׁל הַמֶּלֶךְ הַגָּדוֹל בִּירוּשָׁלַיִם - The great king ruled in Jerusalem.

These two sentences may be combined as follows:

הוּא הַמֶּלֶךְ הַגָּדוֹל אֲשֶׁר מָשַׁל בִּירוּשָׁלַיִם - That is the great king *who* ruled in Jerusalem.

The form of the 'relative pronoun' in English varies according to whether it is the subject or the object of the following verb or whether it bears some possessive relationship to the noun which precedes it. In the above sentence 'who' is the *subject* of 'ruled'. In the following one:

הוּא הַמֶּלֶךְ הַגָּדוֹל אֲשֶׁר רָאִינוּ בִּירוּשָׁלַיִם - That is the great king *whom* we have seen in Jerusalem,

'whom' is the *object* of the verb 'have seen'.

In this one:

הוּא הַמֶּלֶךְ הַגָּדוֹל אֲשֶׁר שָׁמַעְנוּ אֶת־דְּבָרוֹ בִּירוּשָׁלַיִם - That is the great king *whose* word we have heard in Jerusalem

(lit. 'That is the great king with-respect-to-whom we have heard his word in Jerusalem'),

'whose' expresses the *possessive relationship* between 'king' and 'word'. In this last sentence, the relationship of אֲשֶׁר to the clause which it introduces is more closely defined by means of the suffix in דְּבָרוֹ.

In Hebrew, however, the form of אֲשֶׁר never changes. It remains the same whether it functions as subject or object, whether it refers to persons (who/whom) or to things (which/that). It is best thought of, therefore, not as a 'relative *pronoun*', as are 'who', 'whom' etc. in English, but as a *relative particle* with a sense something like 'with-respect-to-whom'/'with-respect-to-which'.

For example:

1.  זֶה הַבַּיִת אֲשֶׁר יָשַׁבְנוּ בּוֹ  - Lit. 'This is the house with-respect-to-which we lived in it', i.e. This is the house *in which* we lived.

2.  זֶה הַדֶּרֶךְ אֲשֶׁר הָלַכְתִּי שָׁם  - Lit. 'This is the road with-respect-to-which I walked there', i.e. This is the road *where* I walked.

In these two sentences, בּוֹ and שָׁם make the sense of אֲשֶׁר more precise.

## III

A number of *prepositions* (which introduce nouns) may be combined with אֲשֶׁר to form *conjunctions* (which introduce subordinate clauses). For example:

עָשָׂה הָאִישׁ כְּנָבִיא  - The man did (acted) *as* (like) a prophet

עָשָׂה הָאִישׁ כַּאֲשֶׁר אָמַר  - The man did (acted) *as* he (had) said (promised).

Similarly

אַחֲרֵי and אַחֲרֵי אֲשֶׁר  ('after...');

בְּ and בַּאֲשֶׁר  ('because...');

לְמַעַן  ('for the sake of...')

and לְמַעַן אֲשֶׁר  ('in order that...').

## EXERCISE SEVENTEEN

We are now in a position to begin reading short portions from the Hebrew Bible itself. The student should now acquire a copy; details of editions may be found on pp. 157f. below. No other aids will be required for the time being, since vocabulary and any necessary notes on the text will be given here. Students should resist the temptation to work with an English translation open beside them. They should work through the Hebrew text with the help of the Grammar (using the Index where necessary), their own personal dictionary (see above p. 29) or the Word-list on pp. 200ff. and the notes given here. Only as a last resort should a translation be consulted at this stage. Once students have worked out their own translation it should then prove rewarding to compare the various English translations with their own and to try to understand how and why differences in translation occur.

Translate : **Genesis 1:1-5**

Vocabulary:

רֵאשִׁית *f* - beginning (here with prep. בְּ)

תֹּהוּ וָבֹהוּ - תֹּהוּ = formlessness

בֹּהוּ = emptiness

The latter never occurs on its own but always alongside תֹּהוּ.

תְּהוֹם - the primæval ocean

רוּחַ *f* - wind; spirit

Notes (the numbers refer to the verses):

2.  רוּחַ אֱלֹהִים - for a discussion of the possible meanings of this expression see below p. 121.

מְרַחֶפֶת - the fem. of the participle (see above pp. 81 and 98) of a verb form which will not be dealt with until Lesson 22 (pp. 136ff.).
The verb in question means 'to hover'.

4.                 וַיַּרְא – V.C. Imperf. of רָאָה.
                             On this form in ל״ה verbs see above p. 105.

           וַיַּבְדֵּל – V.C. Imperf. of a verb form which will not be dealt with until Lesson 23 (pp. 142 ff.).    The verb in question means 'to divide'.

      בֵּין...וּבֵין – Note how Hebrew repeats the prep. בֵּין (lit. 'between...and between') with each of the categories referred to.

# LESSON EIGHTEEN

## THE IMPERFECT –
## VERBS WITH INITIAL נ AND REDUPLICATED VERBS

### I

פ״נ  (pp. 192 f. )

We have already observed above ( pp. 58 f. ) that verbs whose first letter is נ ( פ״נ verbs ) are no different in the Perfect from the 'regular' verb. In that context, however, we noted what happened to the *final* נ of נָתַן at the end of a syllable. Exactly the same phenomenon occurs in the Imperfects of פ״נ verbs.

In a verb like נָפַל – 'to fall' and on the analogy of יִשְׁמֹר, we would expect *יִנְפֹּל, but here the נ closes a syllable and has no vowel of its own. It therefore assimilates with the immediately following consonant, which is thus doubled, a doubling which is shown in writing by means of *dagesh forte* – יִפֹּל ( yippōl ). In verbs such as נָפַל , whose Imperfect is in ō, the Imperative, Infinitive Construct and Participle are all perfectly normal.

| | |
|---|---|
| 3rd m.s. Imperf. | יִפֹּל |
| m.s. Imper. | נְפֹל |
| Inf. Cstr. | נְפֹל |
| Pt. | נֹפֵל |

Verbs whose Imperfect is in a (e.g. נגשׁ – to draw near; the Perfect of this verb is not found in Biblical Hebrew, and it has therefore been left unvocalised ), have a mono-syllabic Imperative and a 'segolate' Infinitive Construct. They are similar, in other words, to the second type of פ״י verbs (e.g. יָשַׁב [see above p. 103 ]).

| | |
|---|---|
| 3rd m.s. Imperf. | יִגַּשׁ |
| m.s. Imper. | גַּשׁ |
| Inf. Cstr. | גֶּשֶׁת |
| | ( with ל - לָגֶשֶׁת; see above, p. 103 ) |
| Pt. | נֹגֵשׁ |

We noted (above, pp. 58f.) the Perfect of the verb נָתַן (to give, grant; to place, put; to allow, permit), where the fact that it had נ as its final letter caused modifications to the normal pattern. Its Imperfect is like that of נגשׁ but with an *e*-vowel rather than a:

|  |  |  |
|---|---|---|
| 3rd m.s. Imperf. | יִתֵּן | |
| m.s. Imper. | תֵּן | |
| Inf. Cstr. | תֵּת | (with suffs. תִּתִּי etc) |
| Pt. | נֹתֵן | |

We should also note the very common verb לָקַח - 'to take' (which has already occurred in the vocabulary of Exercise Sixteen, above p. 107). Again, this is a perfectly normal verb in the Perfect, but the Imperfect and related forms are as if they were from •נקח.

|  |  |  |
|---|---|---|
| 3rd m.s. Imperf. | יִקַּח | |
| m.s. Imper. | קַח | |
| Inf. Cstr. | קַחַת | (note the a-vowels here because of the guttural) |
| Pt. | לֹקֵחַ | (note the *patah* furtive because of the guttural) |

This verb (לָקַח), along with הָלַךְ (see above p. 103), are the only two really *irregular* verbs in Hebrew, in that their Perfects and their Imperfects are as if from different, though not unrelated, roots.

## II

ע״ע  (p. 194)

The last verb-type to be dealt with is that in which the second and third letters of the root are identical, and these verbs are usually known as ע״ע ('double ayin') verbs.

In those Imperfect forms where the doubled letter is in final position, the letter is written only once and doubling is not indicated (e.g. from סָבַב - to turn, turn away, we have 3rd m.s. Imperf. יָסֹב ). When afformatives are added, however, and the doubled letter is no longer in final position, its doubled nature is shown by means of *dagesh forte* (e.g. 2nd f.s. Imperf. תְּסֹבִּי ). In the feminine plural forms, both 3rd and 2nd persons, the long ŏ-vowel bècomes an u (תְּסֻבֶּינָה ).

Both the Imperative and the Infinitive Construct are monosyllabic: סֹב (Inf. Cstr. with לְ: לָסֹב; cf. above, p. 103 ). As was the case with ע״ו (and ע״י ) verbs (see above p. 104 ), the long ŏ of the Imperfect (and Jussive ) becomes a short o in the V.C. Imperfect, with the retraction of the accent in the V.C. forms to the penultimate syllable:

Imperf. and Juss.　　יָסֹב  
V.C. Imperf.　　וַיָּסָב ( vayyāsob )

In some verbs of this type (ע״ע), the influence of Aramaic (a related Semitic language, which, from the time of the return from exile in Babylon, gradually replaced Hebrew as the spoken language of Palestine) has caused the doubling to shift to the *first* consonant of the root in the Imperfect. סָבַב has both types of Imperfect:

יָסֹב　　but also　　יִסֹּב

This variation applies only to the Imperfect and has no effect on the Imperative or Infinitive Construct. In this form of the Imperfect, of course, it is the ס which is doubled and not the ב. When afformatives are added, therefore, the ב does not show doubling as well (e.g. 3rd m.pl. יִסֹּבוּ ).

## EXERCISE EIGHTEEN

Vocabulary:

Verbs:

נָפַל – to fall　　　　נָכָה – to strike, smite  
נָשָׂא – to lift up, raise; bear, carry  
נָסַע – to set out (on a journey ); lit. 'to pull up  
　　　　　　　　　　　　　　　　(tent pegs )'

מוּת (3rd m.s. Perf. מֵת) - to die

שׁוּב (שָׁב) - to return

מָדַד - to measure     חָטָא - to sin

עָנָה - to answer, reply

Nouns:

הַנֶּגֶב - the Negeb     חֶבֶל מִדָּה - a measuring line

כֹּל - totality, all (of) (with suffs. כָּלִי, etc.)

שְׁאֵלָה f - request

רֹחַב - breadth     אֹרֶךְ - length

מִלְחָמָה f - war, battle     עֵלִי - Eli

Other:

אָנָה - to where?, whither?

כַּמָּה - (according to) what?

מֵעִמּוֹ - see above pp. 110f., para. 8

Translate:

1. וַיֹּאמֶר יְהוָה אֶל־אַבְרָם לְךָ אֶתֵּן אֶת־הָאָרֶץ הַזֹּאת וַיִּפֹּל אַבְרָם עַל־פָּנָיו:

2. וַיְהִי בַבֹּקֶר וַיִּסַּע אַבְרָהָם מֵהַמָּקוֹם הַהוּא וַיֵּלֶךְ לְדַרְכּוֹ אַרְצָה הַנֶּגֶב:

3. וַיִּגֹּף יְהוָה אֶת־כָּל־הָעָם וַיָּמֻתוּ כֻלָּם בַּיּוֹם הַהוּא:

4. וָאֶשָּׂא עֵינַי וָאֵרֶא וְהִנֵּה אִישׁ וּבְיָדוֹ חֶבֶל מִדָּה: וָאֹמַר אֵלָיו אָנָה אַתָּה הֹלֵךְ וַיֹּאמֶר אֵלַי לָמֹד אֶת־יְרוּשָׁלַיִם לִרְאוֹת כַּמָּה־רָחְבָּהּ וְכַמָּה־אָרְכָּהּ:

5. וַיָּשָׁב הָעָם מֵהַמִּלְחָמָה וַיֵּשֶׁב בָּעִיר הַזֹּאת:

6. וַיֹּאמְרוּ בְנֵי־יִשְׂרָאֵל אֶל־יְהוָה חָטָאנוּ עֲשֵׂה־אַתָּה לָנוּ כְּכָל־הַטּוֹב בְּעֵינֶיךָ:

7. וַיַּעַן עֵלִי וַיֹּאמֶר לְכִי לְשָׁלוֹם וֵאלֹהֵי יִשְׂרָאֵל יִתֵּן שְׁאֵלָתֵךְ אֲשֶׁר שָׁאַלְתְּ מֵעִמּוֹ:

# LESSON NINETEEN

## THE ADJECTIVE – COMPARATIVE AND SUPERLATIVE

### I

We have already dealt with the adjective in general terms, both in its predicative use and in its qualifying use, where it agrees with the noun it qualifies in definiteness, gender and number.

Adjectives as such have no special form, and we have seen in the lessons on the various declensions of nouns (above pp. 89-93, 98-101; cf. also the tables on pp. 166-173) that adjectival forms are to be found in the first, third and fourth declensions. There is one particular type of adjective, however, of which we have had an example in the quotation of Gen. 12:14 cited above on p. 106. There, alongside the place name מִצְרַיִם ('Egypt'), there occurred the noun/adjective form הַמִּצְרִים. This is the (definite) plural form of מִצְרִי – 'Egyptian'. What is technically known, then, as the *gentilic* adjective, i.e. the adjective which describes the nationality or ethnic origin of a person, ends in ‑ִי in the masculine singular, ‑ִית in the feminine singular and ‑ִים and ‑ִיוֹת in the masculine and feminine plurals respectively.

For example, יְהוּדִי describes a man from the territory of Judah ( יְהוּדָה ), while יְהוּדִית is a woman from the same geographical area. Both of these forms have subsequently become the proper names Yehudi and Judith respectively.

The use of the construct relationship as illustrated above on p.64, where an expression like הַר הַקֹּדֶשׁ – lit. 'hill of holiness' is used to mean what we would more naturally express in English with 'holy hill', is of fairly common occurrence in Hebrew and is often explained as having arisen to compensate for the often claimed rarity of the adjective as a language phenomenon in Hebrew.

– 119 –

Whether this supposed rarity is quite so certain as is often claimed may be open to question.

## II

In English we can express a *comparative* element (e.g. 'The king is *greater than* the prophet') by means of the -er ending to the adjective (or the use of the word 'more' if the adjective of comparison has two syllables with the accent on the first of them [e.g. 'hopeful'] or has more than two syllables) together with the conjunction 'than'. In Hebrew the form of the adjective is not modified in this way, and comparison is expressed by means of the normal form of the adjective in the appropriate gender and number followed by the preposition מִן in the sense of '(distinct) from' (see already to some extent above pp.53f.). For example:

טוֹב הַמֶּלֶךְ מִן־הַנָּבִיא - The king is good-as-distinct-from (i.e. better than) the prophet.

This form of expression is also found with (stative) verbs. For example:

אֶגְדַּל מִמְּךָ - I shall be great-as-distinct-from (i.e. greater than) you.

Exactly the same form of expression in Hebrew may express what we express in English by means of the phrase 'too ... for ...'. For example:

כָּבֵד מִמְּךָ הַדָּבָר - The affair is too difficult (lit. 'heavy') for you.

It is used more commonly in the comparative sense, but only the wider context will make it really clear which sense is intended and in which way it may best be translated.

## III

The *superlative* (English 'greatest'/'most hopeful') is also expressed in Hebrew by the normal form of the adjective, often either simply with the definite article, e.g.

הוּא הַגָּדוֹל   - He is the greatest (lit. 'the great one [among those referred to]')

or in a construct relationship of some kind, e.g.:

קְטֹן בָּנָיו   - the youngest of his sons
*or* his youngest son.

The second of these two senses may also be expressed by

בְּנוֹ הַקָּטֹן   - his youngest son (lit. 'his son, the young[est] one').

A superlative sense may also be expressed by the use of the adverb מְאֹד - 'very, exceedingly':

הוּא עָצוּם מְאֹד   - He is exceedingly powerful.

It may equally be expressed by the use of a singular noun in construct relationship to its own plural:

שִׁיר הַשִּׁירִים - The Song of Songs, i.e. The most beautiful song.

Sometimes, too, the noun אֵל (or even אֱלֹהִים) - 'God' may be used in this way:

הַרְרֵי אֵל - exceedingly high mountains (lit. 'mountains of God').

An example of this may be the phrase רוּחַ אֱלֹהִים in Gen. 1:2, a phrase which is translated as 'spirit of God' in some versions of the Bible, but in others as 'mighty wind' (cf., e.g., REB text and footnote respectively).

## EXERCISE NINETEEN

Translate: **I Samuel 17: 40-43**

We have already met a simplified version of the opening of this passage in sentence No.3 of Exercise 15.

Vocabulary:

Verb:

בָּזָה - to despise

Nouns:

חֲמִשָּׁה - five  כְּלִי - utensil, receptacle

רֹעֶה (pt.) - shepherd  יַלְקוּט - container, wallet

קֶלַע - sling  צִנָּה f - shield

מַרְאֶה - appearance (from רָאָה - to see)

כֶּלֶב - dog

Adjectives:

חָלוּק - smooth  פְּלִשְׁתִּי - Philistine

קָרֵב - approaching  אַדְמֹנִי - red-cheeked, ruddy

Notes:

40: חַלְּקֵי־אֲבָנִים - lit. 'smooth ones of stones', i.e. 'smooth stones'

41: הֹלֵךְ וְקָרֵב - lit. 'going and approaching', i.e. 'coming closer and closer'

42: וַיַּבֵּט - V.C. Imperf. of a verb form which will not be dealt with until Lesson 23 (pp. 142 ff.). The meaning of the verb in question is 'to look'.

וַיִּבְזֵהוּ - V.C. Imperf. of בָּזָה with the direct object appended to the verb form as a suffix. Verbal suffixes will be dealt with in Lesson 24 (pp. 148 f.).

43: הַכֶלֶב - the הַ prefix is a question marker in Hebrew, see Lesson 20 (p. 123 f.). Hence: 'Am I a dog?'

וַיְקַלֵּל - V.C. Imperf. of a verb form which will not be dealt with until Lesson 22 (pp. 136 ff.). The verb in question means 'to curse'.

# LESSON TWENTY

## PARTICLES, ADVERBS AND CONJUNCTIONS

### I

*Particles*

(a) We have already met one particle, the נָא֫- which is appended to Imperative forms to bring out an element of entreaty (see above p. 75). There is another important particle in Hebrew.

Questions in English are indicated partly by word order ('The boy is well' is a statement; 'Is the boy well' is a question), but also by the use of the 'question mark' ('?'; 'Is the boy well?'). Hebrew has no equivalent of the question mark as such, and the interrogative nature of a phrase or sentence would be conveyed by a speaker to a hearer by means of intonation (one's voice rises in pitch at the end of a question). In a written text, therefore, there may be ambiguity. When David is anxious about the fate of his son Absalom after the latter's abortive *coup*, he says to the messenger Ahimaaz

שָׁלוֹם לַנַּ֫עַר - 2 Sam 18:29.

This could be understood as a statement ('It is well with the young man'), but it is clear from the context that it is a question that David is asking ('Is it well with the young man?', 'Is the young man all right?').

Hebrew, however, does have a particle which indicates an interrogative, the particle הֲ immediately prefixed to the first word of the question. It is normally vocalised with ֲ (*hateph patah*), and David's question could have been relieved of ambiguity by being expressed as

הֲשָׁלוֹם לַנַּ֫עַר.

If the first word of the question begins with a *sheva* or with a 'guttural' (unless vocalised with ָ or ֳ ), the ה is vocalised with *patah*:

– 123 –

הַמְעַט הוּא – Is it little? (Num 13:18; see below)

הַאֵלֵךְ – Shall I go?

(note the use of *meteg*; see above p. 25)

If the 'guttural' is vocalised with ֳ or ֱ , the interrogative particle is pointed with *segol*:

הֶחָזָק הוּא – Is it strong? (i.e. the population that lives in the land – Num 13:18)

Disjunctive questions (in English 'whether...or...') are expressed by הֲ before the first part and אִם before the second. Cf. again Num 13:18 where the spies are asked, with reference to the population of the land,

הַמְעַט הוּא אִם־רָב – Is it little (i.e. few in number) or is it numerous?

(b) We have already encountered מִי and מָה as interrogative pronouns (above pp. 38ff.). The following additional question words may be noted:

אַיֵּה – where?

אֵי־מִזֶּה – from where? (whence?)

מֵאַיִן – from where? (whence?)

אָנָה – to where? (whither?)

אֵיכָה/אֵיךְ – how?

(also used in an exclamatory context 'how!')

## II

### Adverbs

(a) Some adverbs which are derived from nouns end in ◌ָם, e.g.:

יוֹמָם (יוֹם – day) – by day

רֵיקָם (רֵיק – empty) – in vain, empty handed

חִנָּם (חֵן – grace) – for nothing, in vain

Sometimes the ā-vowel has become ō:

פִּתְאֹם – suddenly

(b) A number of adverbs we have encountered already. It may be useful to lay them out here and to add to them:

מְאֹד – very (always follows the adjective it qualifies)

שָׁם – there

שָׁמָּה – to there, thither (*He locale*)

כֹּה – thus

(Cf. the very common phrase in prophetic literature, known as 'the messenger formula', which expresses the prophet's relationship to God as his messenger conveying God's message to the people: כֹּה אָמַר יהוה – 'thus has Yahweh spoken/ thus says Yahweh/ this is what Yahweh has said')

כֵּן – thus

עוֹד – still, yet

עַתָּה – now (distinguish carefully from אַתָּה - you)

הִנֵּה – behold (with suffs. הִנְּךָ, הִנְנִי, etc.)

## III

### *Conjunctions*

(a) We are already familiar with ו as the connector both between nouns and between clauses, in the latter instance primarily in its use with verb forms in the Vav Consecutives. In the V.C. Imperfect we noted that the form used is actually the Jussive, as is clear from those instances where there is a distinction between the ordinary Imperfect and the Jussive forms.

When the ו is used with the ordinary Imperfect and vocalised according to its normal rules (see above pp. 27 f.), it expresses purpose: 'in order that...'. In Gen. 24:14, Abraham's servant prays to God that the right wife for Isaac might be the girl who accedes to his request, 'Let down your jar

וְאֶשְׁתֶּה – that I may drink'

i.e. 'Imperfect with simple *vav*' (of שָׁתָה – to drink).

(b) The following also function as conjunctions:

אַף – also, moreover

גַּם – even, also

גַּם ... גַּם – both ... and

נֵם לֹא ... נֵם לֹא – neither...nor

אוֹ – or

אוֹ...אוֹ – either...or

אָז – then

עַל־כֵּן – therefore

(c) We have already observed how אֲשֶׁר functions (above pp. 47 f., 111 f.) and how some prepositions are joined with אֲשֶׁר to form subordinating conjunctions (above p. 112). We have also seen how כ and, less commonly, ב are used with the Infinitive Construct to express subordinate ideas of time (pp. 79 f.). In addition, the following also introduce subordinate clauses:

אִם – if, when

כִּי – (a) for, because;

(b) after verbs of speaking and the like, כִּי introduces *indirect* speech – 'that...'.

פֶּן – lest, so that not

We have already seen that 'but' may be expressed by ו (above pp. 31 f). A very strong contrast, however, may be expressed by אוּלָם:

אוּלָם אֲנִי אֶדְרֹשׁ אֶל־אֵל – But as for me, I will make my request to (דָּרַשׁ אֶל־) God. (Job 5:8)

After a negative, a contrast is expressed by כִּי אִם:

לֹא יִתְנַבֵּא עָלַי טוֹב כִּי אִם־רָע – He does not prophesy concerning me good but (on the contrary) evil. (1 Kgs 22:8)

(יִתְנַבֵּא is the Imperf. of a verb form which will be dealt with in Lesson 22. pp. 136 ff.)

# EXERCISE TWENTY

Translate: **Genesis 20: 1-4**

Vocabulary:

Verbs:

נּוּר - to sojourn, take up temporary residence

בָּעַל - to own, possess

קָרַב - to draw near; euphemism for 'have sexual intercourse with'

Nouns:

חֲלוֹם - dream      בַּעַל - owner, master; husband; Baal

אָדוֹן - lord, master      גּוֹי - people, nation

אָחוֹת *f* - sister (note that this is a singular form)

Proper names:

קָדֵשׁ - Kadesh      שׁוּר - Shur      גְּרָר - Gerar

אֲבִימֶלֶךְ - Abimelech

Notes:

1.    וַיִּסַּע - V.C. Imperf. of נּוּר . For ע״ו verbs see Lesson Sixteen II (p. 104).

2.    אָמַר אֶל - We have already encountered this in the sense of 'say *to*'. Here it means 'say *about*'. 'About' would normally be expressed by עַל in Hebrew, and frequently in the Hebrew Bible there seems to be confusion between the two prepositions אֶל and עַל .

     הוּא - The consonants of this word imply the masculine form of the 3rd sing. of the personal pronoun ( הוּא ), but the sense clearly demands the feminine ( הִיא ). The consonantal text was already too sacred to be changed, so the Masoretes, the Jewish scholars who handed on the text of the Hebrew Bible, retained the consonants as written Kǝtīḇ - ('what is written') but supplied the vowel(s) of the word they wanted us to read and put the consonants in a note in the margin (Qərē - 'read!'). This particular example occurs so frequently in the Pentateuch (Gen. - Deut.) that they simply supply the necessary vowel without the marginal note. This phenomenon, known as Kətīḇ ('what is written') and Qərē ('read!'), is used not only to indicate and correct what were perceived to be errors in the text but also to preserve textual variants which were felt to be too important to ignore when the standard text was being established. There is another example of הִיא/הוּא in verse 3.

3. בְּעֻלַת בַּעַל - the fem. of the passive pt. of the verb בָּעַל in construct relationship to the noun בַּעַל, lit. 'possessed of a husband', i.e. 'she is someone's wife'.

4. אֲדֹנָי - the noun אָדוֹן always has the suffixes appended to its plural form even when the sense of the noun is singular. With the suffix of the 1st person this form - still further differentiated from אֲדֹנַי to אֲדֹנָי - has come to be used as the spoken substitute for the divine name יהוה. Here it occurs in its own right, with Abimelech addressing God, 'Lord!' (with a capital 'L'). In order to differentiate a secular use, the 1st person suffix is appended to the *singular* form of אָדוֹן, and thus אֲדֹנִי means 'my lord' (with a small 'l') or 'sir!'.

# LESSON TWENTY–ONE

## THE SCHEME OF THE VERB – QAL AND NIPHAL

### I

The verb forms which we have looked at so far (Perfect, Imperfect and related forms, Infinitives and Participles) have all belonged to what is known as the 'simple' form of the verb or, to give it its Hebrew designation, the Qal ( קַל is an adjective meaning 'light', i.e. unencumbered with prefixes, infixes, etc. ). Thus שָׁמַר, in all the forms of it which we have seen so far, is usually described as 'the Qal of שׁמר'.

But by means of prefixed and/or infixed letters and/or the doubling of the middle letter of a root, Hebrew is able to provide a wide range of refinements of the basic meaning of a verb. Hebrew Grammars have traditionally used the verb קטל as the verb paradigm when laid out in tabular form (see below pp. 176f. ). We have hitherto used שׁמר as our Qal paradigm, but, as we shall shortly see, there is one aspect of שׁמר which makes it less suitable as a paradigm for all forms of the verb. We shall therefore revert at this point to the more traditional קטל, though we must keep in mind that

(a) קטל is a comparatively rare verb in Hebrew, and it was for this reason that we have used שׁמר until now, and

(b) very few verbs exist in all or even many of the possible forms. For these reasons much of what we have to say about the forms and meanings of קטל in the following paragraphs does not neccessarily apply to קָטַל itself, but there is always some verb to which it does apply. It is, nevertheless, useful at this stage to keep to the same root throughout all the verb forms without introducing the complexity aroused by constantly switching to forms which are actually found in the text of the Hebrew Bible.

The Qal of קֹטֵל, namely קָטַל, means 'to kill'. By prefixing the letter נ to the root, Hebrew can express what it really a reflexive form ( 'kill oneself' ) but is most commonly found expressing the *passive* of the Qal, i.e. 'to be killed': נִקְטַל . Like all the forms cited, this is the 3rd m.s. of the Perfect of this form.

By doubling the *middle* letter of the root, Hebrew expresses what is most commonly thought of as ( though again probably not originally so intended ) an *intensive* sense. If the Qal means 'to kill', the form קִטֵּל would mean 'to kill "intensively"', i.e. possibly 'frequently' or 'thoroughly'. קִטֵּל is the *active* form while קֻטַּל ( still with the doubled middle letter but with a varied vowel-pattern ) is the *passive* ( 'to be killed thoroughly' ). Still with the doubled middle letter but with, in addition, a prefixed hit- ( הִתְ ), we find a *reflexive* form which is probably the reflexive of the basic sense of the verb rather than of the intensive sense strictly speaking: הִתְקַטֵּל - 'to kill oneself'.

By prefixing a ה to the simple form Hebrew produces a *causative* sense. The *active* form has, in addition, a long ī-vowel between the second and third letters of the root. הִקְטִיל - 'to cause ( someone ) to kill ( someone else )' –is the *active* form, while הָקְטַל ( hoqtal ) - 'to be caused ( made ) to kill ( someone )' - is the *passive*.

Thus, on the basis of the simple triliteral root, Hebrew can produce a rich variety of shades of the basic sense of the verb by means of these variants of the root. We have seen already when looking at the so-called 'irregular' verbs ( פ״א, ע״ו, ל״ה etc. ) that the root פעל was used by the *earliest* Hebrew grammarians as their paradigm. So, too, these *derived stems* have technical names formed on the paradigm of פעל : the Niphal ( נִפְעַל ); the Piel ( פִּעֵל ); the Pual ( פֻּעַל ); the Hitpael ( הִתְפַּעֵל ); the Hiphil ( הִפְעִיל ); and the Hophal ( הָפְעַל ).

We may lay this out in tabulated form:

| | |
|---|---|
| Qal | קָטַל |
| Niphal | נִקְטַל |
| Piel | קִטֵּל |
| Pual | קֻטַּל |
| Hitpael | הִתְקַטֵּל |
| Hiphil | הִקְטִיל |
| Hophal | הָקְטַל |

## II

We have already dealt in detail with the Qal of the 'regular' verb and of the different classes of 'weak' verbs. The forms of the Perfect, Imperfect, and Imperative of these derived stems follow the same phonetic rules as those of the Qal. It is important, therefore, that the student should be thoroughly familiar with the latter, in which case no difficulties will be found with the derived stems.

## III

The Niphal ( נִקְטַל ) sometimes has a reflexive meaning, i.e. the subject does the action to him/herself. For example:

נִשְׁמַר - to guard oneself, be on one's guard, beware

נִסְתַּר - to hide oneself.

If one 'hides oneself', one then 'is hidden'. Reflexive connotations lead naturally to 'passive' ones (where the subject is the receiver of the action of the verb), and the most common usage of the Niphal is as the passive of the Qal. For example:

נִשְׁבַּר - to be broken

נִקְבַּר - to be buried.

The characteristic of the Niphal is the prefixed נ - נִקְטַל . In the Imperfect, that נ, occurring, as it there does, at the end of a syllable, is assimilated to the first root letter, and the vowel-pattern is ā – ē:

יִנְקָטֵל ‹ ·יַקָטֵל

The following five parts might be regarded as 'the principal parts' of a Hebrew verb (for a tabulated presentation of these see below, p.174). It is to these that are added the afformatives and preformatives already known from the Perfect, Imperfect and Imperative of the Qal.

| | |
|---|---|
| Perfect | נִקְטַל |
| Infinitive | הִקָּטֵל |
| Imperfect | יִקָּטֵל |
| Imperative | הִקָּטֵל |
| Participle | נִקְטָל |

Note that the final vowel in the Perfect is *patah* (a), while that of the Participle is *qames* (ā). Note, too, that *the characteristic of the Infinitive, Imperfect and Imperative is the doubling of the first root letter* (as the result of the assimilation of the נ ). The ה of the Infinitive and Imperative should not be confused with the ה of the Hiphil (see further below).

### IV

The following points should be noted with regard to those verbs with 'gutturals' or weak letters in their roots.

1. פ-gutturals: The vowel of the נ preformative is usually e:

נֶחְשָׁב – to be accounted

In the case of א or ה (and sometimes ע ), the *sheva* at the end of the first syllable is the composite *sheva* (*hateph*) corresponding to the e: e.g.:

נֶאֱסֹף – to be gathered, taken away

When followed by a *vocal sheva*, that *hateph* becomes a full vowel:

נֶאֶסְפָה (3rd f.s. Perf.)

In the Imperfect Niphal (and related forms), the non-doubling character of the initial 'guttural' causes the lengthening of the preformative vowel: i > ē. For example:

יֵעָמֵד - he will be set

יֵאָמֵר - it will be said

2. ל-gutturals: The long ē of the Imperfect is replaced by a:

יִשָּׁבַע - he will swear (an oath)

In the case of ל''א verbs, however, the ē is retained:

יִמָּצֵא - he will be found

3. פ''ו : Here the original ו (which is not in evidence in the Qal, see above pp. 56 f. ) makes its appearance:

ילד      Niph. Perf. נוֹלַד - to be born

         Imperf.     יִוָּלֵד    (with the ו being treated as an ordinary consonant)

4. ע''ו : From the root כון we have:

         Perf.         נָכוֹן - to be established

         Imperf.      יִכּוֹן  (from *יִנְכּוֹן )

5. פ''ן : Assimilation of the vowelless נ of the root occurs in the Perf. and Pt. From the root נגף we have:

         Perf.            נִגַּף (from *נִנְגַּף ) – to be

                                               smitten

         Pt.               נִגָּף

6. ע''ע : The forms here are (from סבב):

         Perf.          נָסַב - to turn round

         Imperf.      יִסַּב

# V

As was said earlier (above p. 129), very few verbs are found in all seven derived stems. A number of verbs are not found in the Qal, and it is then one of the derived stems which expresses the basic meaning of the verb. The Niphal sometimes fulfils this function, and two fairly common verbs in this category are:

נִמְלַט – to escape (this is basically a reflexive sense 'to save oneself', but מלט is not found in the Qal).

נִלְחַם – to fight (here one could argue a case for this expressing reciprocity, 'fight one another'; the Qal does exist but is extremely rare and is considered by some to be a secondary derivation from the Niphal).

## EXERCISE TWENTY - ONE

Vocabulary:

Verbs:

שָׁקַל – to weigh; Niph. passive

שׁחת – Niph. to be corrupted, be spoiled

מָלֵא – to be full, fill; Niph. passive

גָּרַשׁ – to drive out; Niph. passive

סָתַר – to hide; Niph. reflexive and passive

לחם – Niph. to fight

שׁען – Niph. to lean, rest on

בָּרַח – to flee        מלט – Niph. to escape

שׁבע – Niph. to swear or take an oath

צָעַק – to cry out; Niph. to be called out, be summoned

חָנָה – to encamp

אָסַף – to gather; Niph. be gathered, assemble

Nouns:

חָמָס – violence        גְּבוּרָה f – strength

אֱמֶת f – truth    יָרֵךְ (cstr. יֶרֶךְ) f – thigh

עַמּוֹן – Ammon        גִּלְעָד – Gilead

מִצְפָּה – Mizpah

Other:

עוֹד – still, yet;    עוֹד ... לֹא – no longer

In order to help students in the identification of verb forms we shall now introduce, in addition to translation, another type of exercise, namely 'Parsing'. To *parse* a verb is to describe it in terms of its person, its gender, its number, its form and to indicate the root from which it comes. For example, the verb in the first of the following sentences ( יִכָּתְבוּ ) is the 3rd person masculine plural of the imperfect Niphal of כָּתַב. The first word in sentence 2 is the 3rd person feminine singular of the V.C. Imperf. Niphal of שָׁחַת. It is always best to keep to the same order of information: person, gender, number, form, root; one can then be sure of not omitting essential information.

Parse:

נִכְתְּבוּ, יִשָּׁקֵל, הִשָּׁפֵט, לְהִלָּחֵם, תִּזָּכַרְנָה, נֶאֶסְפוּ, אֶעָמֵד,
יִמָּצְאוּ, נוֹשָׁב, אָקוֹם:

Translate:

1. לֹא יִכָּתְבוּ הָרְשָׁעִים בְּסֵפֶר חַיִּים:

2. וַתִּשָּׁחֵת הָאָרֶץ לִפְנֵי יהוה וַתִּמָּלֵא הָאָרֶץ חָמָס:

3. נִגְרַשְׁתִּי הַיּוֹם מֵעַל־פְּנֵי־הָאֲדָמָה וּמִפָּנֶיךָ אֶסָּתֵר:

4. וְהָאֹיֵב בָּא אֶל־הָעִיר הַזֹּאת וְלֹא יָכֹל לְהִלָּחֵם עָלֶיהָ:

5. בַּיּוֹם הַהוּא לֹא יִשָּׁעֵן עוֹד יִשְׂרָאֵל עַל־גְּבוּרָתוֹ וְעַל־זְהָבוֹ וְנִשְׁעַן עַל־יְהוָה קְדוֹשׁ יִשְׂרָאֵל בֶּאֱמֶת:

6. וַיִּשְׁלַח שָׁאוּל מַלְאָכִים אֶל־בֵּית דָּוִד לְשָׁמְרוֹ וְלַהֲרֹג אֹתוֹ בַּבֹּקֶר וַיֵּלֶךְ דָּוִד וַיִּבְרַח וַיִּמָּלֵט בַּלַּיְלָה הַהוּא:

7. וַיָּשֶׂם הָעֶבֶד אֶת־יָדוֹ תַּחַת יֶרֶךְ אַבְרָהָם אֲדֹנָיו וַיִּשָּׁבַע לוֹ עַל־הַדָּבָר הַזֶּה:

8. וַיִּצָּעֲקוּ בְּנֵי עַמּוֹן וַיַּחֲנוּ בַּגִּלְעָד וַיֵּאָסְפוּ בְּנֵי יִשְׂרָאֵל וַיַּחֲנוּ בַּמִּצְפָּה:

# LESSON TWENTY–TWO
## THE SO-CALLED 'INTENSIVES' PIEL, PUAL AND HITPAEL

### I

The group of forms in which the middle letter of the root is doubled are often regarded as 'intensive' forms. For example:

שָׁבַר - to break

שִׁבֵּר - to shatter, smash to pieces.

This may well not have been their original sense, and these forms have a fairly wide range of meanings in Hebrew, with a 'causative' sense a fairly common one.

The Piel ( קִטֵּל ) is the *active* form, the Pual ( קֻטַּל ) is the *passive*, and the Hitpael ( הִתְקַטֵּל ) is a reflexive form, though not necessarily expressing the reflexive of the intensive sense.

The 'principal parts' of these derived stems are as follows:

| PIEL | Perfect | קִטֵּל |
| | Infinitive | קַטֵּל |
| | Imperfect | יְקַטֵּל |
| | Imperative | קַטֵּל |
| | Participle | מְקַטֵּל |
| | | |
| PUAL | Perfect | קֻטַּל |
| | Infinitive | קֻטַּל |
| | Imperfect | יְקֻטַּל |
| | Imperative | NOT FOUND |
| | Participle | מְקֻטָּל |
| | | |
| HITPAEL | Perfect | הִתְקַטֵּל |
| | Infinitive | הִתְקַטֵּל |
| | Imperfect | יִתְקַטֵּל |
| | Imperative | הִתְקַטֵּל |
| | Participle | מִתְקַטֵּל |

Notes:

1. All participles after the Niphal are characterised by a prefixed מ.

2. The Pual (passive) Participle has a long ā; cf. the Niphal Participle (also passive).

3. Characteristic of the Piel (and Pual) Imperfect is the vocalisation of the preformative with *sheva* - יְקַטֵּל.

4. If the verbal root begins with a sibilant ( ס, שׂ, שׁ ), in the Hitpael the ת of the preformative and the sibilant change places (a phenomenon known as *metathesis*). Thus the Hitpael of שָׁמַר is הִשְׁתַּמֵּר - to take heed to oneself, be on one's guard. It is for this reason that שָׁמַר is not a suitable paradigm for all the derived forms (see above p. 129). In the case of צ, the ת is, in addition, modified to ט (metathesis and partial assimilation). Thus, the Hitpael of צדק is הִצְטַדֵּק - to justify oneself. If the verbal root begins with a dental consonant ( ד, ט, ת ), then the ת of the Hitpael preformative assimilates completely. Thus the Hitpael of טהר ('to be clean, pure') is הִטַּהֵר ( > * הִתְטַהֵר ) - to purify oneself. Note, in this last example, the absence of the characteristic *dagesh* from the middle consonant which, in this instance, is the 'guttural' ה.

## II

The following points should be noted with regard to those verbs with 'gutturals' or weak letters in their roots. These points are applicable, where relevant, also to the Pual and the Hitpael.

1. ע-gutturals: 'Gutturals' tend to have a-vowels associated with them, so the Perfect Piel often (though not invariably) has a instead of ē. Thus the Piel of נחם is נִחַם - to comfort. In the case of נחם the Piel and the Niphal are identical in the Perfect, but the Imperfects

are different: Niphal נֶחַם and Piel יְנַחֵם. If the ע-letter is א or ר, the preceding vowel is normally lengthened in compensation.

בֵּרַךְ - יְבָרֵךְ - to bless

מֵאֵן - יְמָאֵן - to refuse

This does not normally occur with ה, ח or ע. See, e.g., נֶחַם (above) and also הִטַּהֵר in I, note 4 above.

2. ל-gutturals: As was the case with the Niphal (see above p. 133), the long ē-vowel is replaced by a. Thus

שִׁלַּח - יְשַׁלַּח - to set free

Again in the case of ל״א verbs, the ē-vowel is retained. Thus

מִלֵּא - יְמַלֵּא - to fill

3. ע״ו : The so-called 'Intensives' from ע״ו roots are not usually formed by the doubling of the weak middle letter but with the reduplication of either

(i) the final letter: Thus from רום ('to be high, exalted')

רוֹמֵם - יְרוֹמֵם - to exalt

The passive is of the form

רוֹמַם - יְרוֹמַם

or (ii) the first *and* the last letters: Thus from כול ('to contain, include')

כִּלְכֵּל - יְכַלְכֵּל - to include; supply

4. ע״ע : Here the regular form is quite common. Thus from הלל (not found in the Qal) we have

הִלֵּל - יְהַלֵּל - to praise

Note the m. pl. Imperative here ( הַלְלוּ ) with no *dagesh* in the ל (see above p. 106 for those consonants which omit *dagesh* when vocalised with *sheva*). In the expression

הַלְלוּ־יָה

יָה is a form of the divine name יהוה, and the expression as a whole means 'Praise Yahweh/the Lord' (cf. especially

Pss 146-150 ). The phrase has, of course, passed into English as 'Hallelujah'.

But we also find forms identical with those under ע״ו (i) above. Thus from סבב - to go round, we have

יְסֹבֵב - סֹבֵב - to encompass, enclose

## III

1. (a) The *Piel* (of which the *Pual*, when found, is invariably the passive) is, as we have noted, often the *intensive* of the sense expressed by the Qal.

שָׁבַר - to break

שִׁבֵּר - to shatter

שָׁאַל - to ask

שִׁאֵל - to enquire carefully, practise beggary

(b) It may often, however, have a *causative* sense.

לָמַד - to learn

לִמַּד - to teach (i.e. cause to learn ).

Note the a- vowel here, exceptionally

חָיָה - to live

חִיָּה - to preserve alive; bring to life

(c) As a kind of sub-division of this last sense, there is also a *factitive* sense, i.e. making something be something.

אָמַץ - to be strong

אִמֵּץ - to make strong or courageous

2 (a) The Hitpael is, strictly speaking, the reflexive of the Piel. Thus

קָדֵשׁ - to sanctify (make holy )

הִתְקַדֵּשׁ - to sanctify oneself

(b) But it may also express the idea of 'showing oneself' or 'giving oneself out as' doing the action of the simple verb.

נָקַם - to take vengeance

הִתְנַקֵּם - to show oneself vengeful

עָשַׁר - to become rich

הִתְעַשֵּׁר - to pretend to be rich

נִבָּא (Niph.) - to prophesy

הִתְנַבֵּא - to act like a prophet, rave

## IV

Just as there were verbs which did not occur (or occurred but rarely) in the Qal and whose basic sense was expressed by the Niphal, so, too, there are verbs whose basic sense is expressed by the Piel. The most common of these is

דִּבֶּר - יְדַבֵּר - to speak.

Note that this verb always has ē and not ē̆ in the 3rd m.s. of the Perf (דִּבֵּר is the pausal form, see sentence 2 in the Exercise). If דִּבֵּר ever had the sense of 'chatter' (i.e. 'speak intensively'), it has long since lost such a sense and is simply the common verb for 'to speak'.

## EXERCISE TWENTY-TWO

Vocabulary:

Verbs:

סָפַר - to count; Pi. to recount, declare

חוה - Pi. (Imperf. יְחַוֶּה) to make known

גָּדַל - to be great, grow; Pi. to bring up (a child), magnify

פָּשַׁע בְּ - to rebel against

כָּבֵד - to be heavy; Pi. to make heavy, harden

קָדַשׁ - to be set apart, i.e. be holy; Pi. to make holy, sanctify; Hitp. to sanctify oneself

הָלַךְ - to walk; Hitp. to walk to and fro

סָתַר - to hide; Hitp. (הִסְתַּתֵּר; note metathesis - p. 137, note 4) to hide oneself

נבא – Hitp. to act like a prophet, rave

הלל – Pi. to praise

צוה – Pi. ( צִוָּה ) to order, command

בָּרָא – to create (only God is the subject of בָּרָא );
Niph. passive

Nouns:

כָּבוֹד – glory      דַּעַת *f* – knowledge

פַּרְעֹה – Pharaoh      לֵבָב, לֵב – heart

גַּן ( הַגָּן ) – garden

תָּוֶךְ (cstr. תּוֹךְ ) – middle      בְּתוֹךְ – in the middle of

עֵץ – tree (or collectively 'trees')

שֵׁם – name

Parse:

יְדַבְּרוּ, תְּכַבְּדִי, יְכַפֵּר, אֶסְתַּתֵּר, תְּגֻלּוּ, הִתְנַבֵּא, אֲבָרֶךְ, מְשַׁלַּח,
שִׁלְּחוּ, הִתְהַלַּכְנָה:

Translate:

1. הַשָּׁמַיִם מְסַפְּרִים כְּבוֹד־אֵל וְלַיְלָה לְּלַיְלָה יְחַוֶּה־דָּעַת:

2. שִׁמְעוּ שָׁמַיִם כִּי יהוה דִּבֵּר בָּנִים גִּדַּלְתִּי וְהֵם פָּשְׁעוּ בִי:

3. וְלָמָּה תְכַבְּדוּ אֶת־לְבַבְכֶם כַּאֲשֶׁר כִּבְּדוּ מִצְרַיִם וּפַרְעֹה
אֶת־לִבָּם:

4. זִכְרוּ אֶת־יוֹם הַשַּׁבָּת לְקַדְּשׁ אֹתוֹ:

5. וַיִּשְׁמְעוּ אֶת־קוֹל יהוה אֱלֹהִים מִתְהַלֵּךְ בַּגָּן וַיִּסְתַּתֵּר
הָאָדָם וְאִשְׁתּוֹ מִפְּנֵי יהוה אֱלֹהִים בְּתוֹךְ עֵץ הַגָּן:

6. וַיִּתְנַבֵּא גַם־הוּא לִפְנֵי שְׁמוּאֵל כָּל־הַיּוֹם הַהוּא וְכָל־
הַלָּיְלָה עַל־כֵּן יֹאמְרוּ הֲגַם שָׁאוּל בַּנְּבִיאִים:

7. יְהַלְלוּ אֶת־שֵׁם יהוה כִּי הוּא צִוָּה וְנִבְרָאוּ:

# LESSON TWENTY – THREE

## THE CAUSATIVES – HIPHIL AND HOPHAL

### I

The characteristic of these derived stems is the pre-fixed ה in the Perfect. In the active form (Hiphil), the vowel between the second and third letters of the root is ī (written with a י ).

The 'principal parts' of the verb here are as follows:

| HIPHIL | Perfect | הִקְטִיל |
|---|---|---|
| | Infinitive | הַקְטִיל |
| | Imperfect | יַקְטִיל |
| | Imperative | הַקְטֵל |
| | Participle | מַקְטִיל |
| HOPHAL | Perfect | הָקְטַל |
| | Infinitive | הָקְטַל |
| | Imperfect | יָקְטַל |
| | Imperative | NOT FOUND |
| | Participle | מָקְטָל |

Notes:

1. Note the shortening of the ī-vowel to ē in the Imperative of the Hiphil. This occurs also in the Jussive.

    Imperf. יַקְטִיל   Jussive יַקְטֵל   V.C. Imperf. וַיַּקְטֵל

    There is, however, no shortening of the ē to e in the V.C. Imperfect, as we might expect on the pattern of פ״ו and ע״ו/ע״י verbs (above pp. 103f. and see below pp. 143f. on these same classes of verbs).

2. The vowel of the preformative in the Hophal is o (hoqtal).

3. Note that, as in the case of the Niphal and Pual, in this passive form too (Hophal), the vowel of the final syllable of the Participle is ā (moqtāl).

## II

The following points should be noted with regard to those verbs with 'gutturals' or weak letters in their roots.

1. פ-gutturals : The vowel of the preformative in these verbs is usually *e*:

הֶחְבִּיא - to hide, keep hidden

If the guttural in question is א or ה, then the *sheva* which closes that opening syllable is usually the *hateph* corresponding to the preceding short vowel:

הֶאֱמִין - to believe, trust

2. ל-gutturals : In the Hiphil Perfect, a *patah* furtive appears between the long ī -vowel and the final guttural (on *patah* furtive, see above pp. 18f. ):

הִשְׁלִיחַ - יַשְׁלִיחַ - to let loose

In the Jussive (and V.C. Imperf. and Imper. ), the long *ē* is *replaced* by *patah*:

יַשְׁלַח (Jussive ) - וַיִּשְׁלַח ( V.C. Imperf. ) -

הַשְׁלַח ( Imper. )

In the case of ל״א verbs, however, the long ī and the long *ē* both remain:

הִמְצִיא - יַמְצֵא (Jussive ) - to cause to find

3. פ״י : The forms here are:

הֵינִיק - יֵינִיק - to suckle

4. פ״ו : Here the original ו, which is not in evidence in the Qal ( יָלַד ), again, as in the Niphal (above p. 133 ), makes its appearance:

הוֹלִיד - יוֹלִיד - to cause to bring forth
(children )

The Jussive is יוֹלֵד and in the V.C. Imperf. there is the retraction of accent to the penultimate syllable with the consequent shortening of the *ē* to *e*: וַיּוֹלֶד. This is the same phenomenon which we have already observed in the Qal of some פ״ו verbs (see above pp. 103 ff. ). In the Hophal of these verbs we find û instead of o as the preformative vowel: הוּלַד.

**5. ע״ו** : The forms here are (from קוּם):

הֵקִים - יָקִים - to raise

In the Perfect the afformatives have ō as the bearer vowel since the ī is unchangeable; e.g. הֲקִימֹתָ etc. Cf. סָבַב (above, p. 59). The Jussive is יָקֵם and again in the V.C. Imperf. there is the shortening of the final vowel (ē > e) : וַיָּקֶם. Although the vowel of the preformative in the Imperfect is ā, that of the Participle is ē : מֵקִים. In the Hophal the pattern is

הוּקַם (Perf.) - יוּקַם (Imperf.) - מוּקָם (Pt.)

**6.** פ״נ : Again we have the assimilation of the vowel-less נ both in the Hiphil and in the Hophal.

הִגִּיד ( > *הִנְגִּיד ) - יַגִּיד - to report, tell

In the Hophal we find u (in place of o ) before the doubled consonant :

יֻגַּד - הֻגַּד

**7.** ע״ע : Here the characteristic ī of the Hiphil is replaced by ē.

הֵסֵב - יָסֵב (ā in an open syllable) – to turn

The Imper. is הָסֵב and the Pt. מֵסֵב (cf. ע״ו verbs above, where it is also the case that the preformative of the Participle has the vowel of the Perfect as opposed to that of the Imperfect ). If the reduplicating letter is a 'guttural' (as, e.g., in the root רעע ), then the second vowel of the Hiphil is *patah* :

הֵרַע - to do harm, treat in an evil fashion

## III

1. The primary meaning of the Hiphil (of which the Hophal, when found, is invariably the passive ) is as the causative of the Qal. Thus, from פָּקַד - to oversee, we

have הִפְקִיד - to cause someone to oversee (someone else), i.e. to appoint someone as overseer, put someone in charge of (someone else). Similarly, from קָדַשׁ - to be holy, we have הִקְדִּישׁ - to sanctify.

2. Sometimes the sense of the Hiphil is what one might call 'declaratory'. From צָדַק - to be in the right, for example, we find הִצְדִּיק - to *declare* someone to be in the right, i.e. to acquit. Similarly, from רָשַׁע - to be guilty, we find הִרְשִׁיעַ - to *declare* someone to be guilty, i.e. to condemn, to convict.

3. If in the Qal the verb takes a direct object (that is, if it is what is known as a 'transitive' verb), in the Hiphil it may take a *double* direct object. From נָחַל - to inherit, we have הִנְחִיל - to cause (someone) to inherit (something). For example:

הִנְחִיל אֶת־הָאֲנָשִׁים (אֶת־)הָאָרֶץ - He caused the men to inherit the land

where both הָאֲנָשִׁים and הָאָרֶץ are direct objects of the Hiphil הִנְחִיל. The אֶת־ is often dropped from the second or remoter object.

## IV

A number of verbs, again, are found only or mainly in the Hiphil, sometimes with no particular 'causative' sense:

הֶחֱרִישׁ - to be silent
הִגִּיד - to report, tell (from נגד )
הִמְטִיר - to send rain

הִמְטִיר is almost certainly formed on the basis of the noun מָטָר - rain. The usual development in Hebrew is from verb to noun; when the process works in the reverse direction, the verb is known as a 'denominative' ('from the noun [Latin *nomen*]') verb.

הִשְׁקָה - to give drink to someone

הִשְׁקָה acts as the causative of שָׁתָה - to drink which has no Hiphil of its own.

הֶאֱמִין - to trust, believe

- 145 -

הִגִּישׁ - to bring (near) (from נגשׁ)

הֵיטִיב - to do (something) well, deal well
(with someone)

# EXERCISE TWENTY-THREE

Vocabulary:

Verbs:

מָלַךְ - to be king, reign; Hiph. to make king

שָׁכַן - to dwell; Hiph. to place

בדל - Hiph. to divide

יָצָא - to go out; Hiph. to send out, bring out

נבט - Hiph. (הִבִּיט) to look

שׁלךְ - Hiph. to cast, throw

נצל - Hiph. (הִצִּיל) to save, deliver

שׁוּב - to return; Hiph. (הֵשִׁיב) to restore

Nouns:

קֶדֶם - East;   מִקֶּדֶם לְ - to the East of ...

עֵדֶן - Eden

זֶרַע - seed; descendants

בּוֹר - pit     כְּרוּב - cherub

רְאוּבֵן - Reuben    חוּץ - out-of-doors,
outside

Other:

לְמַעַן - so that, in order that

Parse:

הִשְׁמַדְתִּי, יַזְכִּיר, וַיִּשְׁכֵּן, הִמְטַרְתָּ, הַבְדִּיל, תַּסְתֵּר, הָעֱמַדְתִּי,
יוּשַׁב, הֻבְדַּל, מָשְׁלָךְ:

- 146 -

Translate :

1. אַתָּה הַמְלַכְתָּ אֹתִי תַּחַת דָּוִד אָבִי :

2. וַיַּשְׁכֵּן יהוה מִקֶּדֶם לְגַן־עֵדֶן אֶת־הַכְּרוּבִים לִשְׁמֹר אֶת־
דֶּרֶךְ עֵץ הַחַיִּים :

3. וַיַּרְא אֱלֹהִים אֶת־הָאוֹר כִּי־טוֹב וַיַּבְדֵּל אֱלֹהִים בֵּין
הָאוֹר וּבֵין הַחֹשֶׁךְ :

4. וַיּוֹצֵא אֹתוֹ הַחוּצָה וַיֹּאמֶר הַבֶּט־נָא הַשָּׁמַיְמָה וּסְפֹר
הַכּוֹכָבִים אִם־תּוּכַל לִסְפֹּר אֹתָם וַיֹּאמֶר לוֹ כֹּה יִהְיֶה
זַרְעֶךָ :

5. וַיֹּאמֶר אֲלֵיהֶם רְאוּבֵן אַל־תִּשְׁפְּכוּ־דָם הַשְׁלִיכוּ אֹתוֹ
אֶל־הַבּוֹר הַזֶּה אֲשֶׁר בַּמִּדְבָּר לְמַעַן הַצִּיל אֹתוֹ מִיָּדָם
לַהֲשִׁיבוֹ אֶל־אָבִיו :

# LESSON TWENTY—FOUR

## THE VERB WITH SUFFIXES

We are already familiar with one way in which Hebrew expresses the direct object of a verb when that object is a pronoun, namely by the use of the pronominal suffixes appended to the object marker אֵת ( אֹתִי, אֹתְךָ, etc., see above p. 70 ). But commonly such a pronominal object is expressed by means of a pronominal suffix appended directly to the verb-form itself.

It will be clear from the Table on pp. 196f. that these suffixes are very similar to those which are added to nouns (see above pp. 67ff.). The following are the main differences:

1. The suffix which expresses the 1st s. ('me'), is not, as in the noun, ִי , but נִי_ (see already the forms of הִנֵּה with suffixes above, p. 125 ).

2. The suffixes which express the 3rd s., m. and f., ('him'/'her') are, with the Imperfect and Imperative, הוּ_ and הָ_ respectively.

3. Where the verb-form ends in a consonant, a 'helping vowel' is sometimes needed between verb and suffix. In the Perfect that vowel is a:

שְׁמָרַנִי   =   נִי   +   שָׁמַר - he has guarded me

while in the Imperfect and Imperative it is ê:

יִשְׁמְרֵנִי   =   נִי   +   יִשְׁמֹר - he will guard me

It will also be clear from the Table that in most cases the addition of the suffixes causes a shift in the position of the accent in the word, thereby occasioning modification of the vowels. In few cases, however, will this cause any difficulty in the identification of forms.

Singular suffixes added to Imperfect and Imperative forms are sometimes strengthened by the addition of a נ. This נ is known as 'energic nun' (*nun energicum* in older,

Latin terminology), since it was thought that it added strength or force to the expression. If that idea was originally an element of the form in question, it is no longer obviously so. The נ is usually assimilated to the following consonant:

יְקְטֵל + נ + נִי > יְקְטְלֵנִי

יְקְטֵל + נ + הָ > יְקְטְלֶךָ

If the following consonant is a ה, the ה seems to be regressively assimilated to the נ:

יְקְטֵל + נ + הוּ > יְקְטְלֶנּוּ

The Participle is primarily a noun - and, as we have seen (above p. 98), is a prominent constituent of the third declension - and the suffixes appended to it are almost always those of the noun.

The same is the case with the Infinitive Construct, with one important distinction. In the case of the suffix of the 1st s., the noun suffix ( ִי ) is used to denote the *subject* of the Infinitive:

יוֹם פָּקְדִי - the day of my visiting, i.e. when I visit, while the verb suffix ( נִי ) is used to denote the *object* of the Infinitive:

לְפָקְדֵנִי - to visit me

In the other persons (3rd and 2nd) the suffix may express either the subject or the object. We are already familiar with the use of the Infinitive Construct with suffixes and prefixed by the preposition כ or ב to express a subordinate idea of time (see above pp. 79f.).

# EXERCISE TWENTY-FOUR

Translate: **Isaiah 41: 8–10**

Vocabulary:

Verbs:

חָזַק – to be strong; Hiph. to seize, grasp

מָאַס – to reject

שָׁעָה – to gaze; Hitp. to gaze about (in anxiety)

אָמֵץ – to be strong; Pi. to strengthen

עָזַר – to help      תָּמַךְ – to grasp, lay hold of

Nouns:

אֹהֵב (pt.) – friend, lover    קָצָה f – end, extremity

אָצִיל – extremity, remote corner

יָמִין – right hand      צֶדֶק – righteousness

Notes:

10: אַל־תִּירָא – the negative particle אַל with the Jussive (2nd m. sing.) of יָרֵא.

תִּשְׁתָּע – 2nd m. sing. Jussive (apocopated as is usual in ל״ה verbs – see p. 105) of the Hitp. (with metathesis – see p. 137 note 4) of שָׁעָה: יִשְׁתָּעֶה – הִשְׁתָּעָה.

בִּימִין צִדְקִי – prep. בְּ and cstr. form of יָמִין in construct relationship to צֶדֶק with suffix of 1st sing. Lit. 'with the right hand of my righteousness'. This may be an instance of the cstr. being used in a way which we would express adjectivally (see above p. 64), i.e. 'with my righteous right hand'.

# LESSON TWENTY–FIVE

## NUMBERS

There are two kinds of numbers, *cardinal* numbers which answer the question 'How many?' (i.e. one, two, three, etc.) and *ordinal* numbers which answer the question 'In what order?' (i.e., first, second, third, etc.).

The numbers in Hebrew are often thought to be difficult and complicated and are often not properly tackled by students. What, admittedly, *is* difficult is to know the *precise form* of the number that is used in any given situation, whether it stands before or after the noun it regulates and whether the noun should be singular or plural. In other words, the difficulties arise out of the relationship between the number and what is being enumerated, that is out of the *syntax* of the numbers. However, for the purposes of reading Hebrew (as opposed to being able to write it correctly) only three aspects of the numbers need be known.

**1.** The *consonantal shape* of the number (mainly the units) remains constant whatever the precise form that the number takes.

**2.** Numbers which have the plural ending ( ים_ ) are the *tens* (twenty, thirty, etc.).

**3.** Numbers which end in ◌ִי (feminine ית_ ) are *ordinal* numbers, and these have a special form only from 2 to 10.

A complete list of the cardinal numbers in their varied forms will be found below on pp. 198 f.

### I

The following are the *consonantal shapes* of the numbers 1 to 10:

| | |
|---|---|
| 1 | אֶחָד (m.) / אַחַת (f.) |
| 2 | שְׁנַיִם (m.) / שְׁתַּיִם (f.) |

| | |
|---|---|
| 3 | שָׁלֹשׁ |
| 4 | ארבע |
| 5 | חמשׁ |
| 6 | שֵׁשׁ |
| 7 | שֶׁבַע |
| 8 | שמנה |
| 9 | חֵשַׁע |
| 10 | עשׂר |

Notes:

1.  '1' is an adjective and follows its noun.

2.  '2-10' are nouns and occur either in construct form *before* the noun which they enumerate or in the absolute form, again, normally *before* the noun.

3.  In the case of '3-10', what appears to be a feminine form occurs with masculine nouns, and a shorter form occurs with feminine nouns. This odd phenomenon may be due to the fact that the number was originally a feminine noun meaning 'a triad' etc. This feminine noun occurs in a construct relationship with the main (masculine) class of nouns. Feminine nouns (a smaller class) subsequently acquired a differentiated (non-feminine) form of the numbers.

## II

The 'teens' are compounds of the units and עשׂר (10), with no connective between the two elements.
For example:

אַחַד עָשָׂר, שְׁנִים עָשָׂר, etc.

These numbers usually stand *before* the noun which is enumerated. The noun is usually plural, though some common words (e.g. יוֹם - day; שָׁנָה - year; אִישׁ - man) occur in the singular.

## III

עֶשְׂרִים, the plural form of עֶשֶׂר (10), is used for '20', but the other 'tens' are the plural forms of the corresponding units:

שְׁלֹשִׁים – 30

אַרְבָּעִים – 40

etc. Tens and units are usually connected by וּ and may occur in either order:

שִׁבְעִים וְשִׁבְעָה or שִׁבְעָה וְשִׁבְעִים – seven and seventy
*or* seventy and seven

These numbers usually precede the noun, which is then often in the singular.

## IV

מֵאָה is '100'. The dual, מָאתַיִם, is '200'. The other 'hundreds' are combinations of the units with the plural מֵאוֹת , e.g.:

שְׁלֹשׁ מֵאוֹת – 300

אֶלֶף is '1,000', with a similar usage as in the case of מֵאָה:

אַלְפַּיִם – 2,000

שְׁלֹשָׁה אֲלָפִים – 3,000

רְבָבָה and רִבּוֹ ( רִבּוֹא), both from the verb רָבַב –'to be many', occur in the general sense of 'myriads, large number' and in the specific numerical sense of '10,000'.

## V

There are special forms for the *ordinal* numbers only from 1 to 10.

רִאשׁוֹן – first, is an adjectival form derived from רֹאשׁ – 'head'. From שֵׁנִי ('second') onwards the characteristic ending is ִי_ in the masculine forms and ִית_ in the feminine ( שֵׁנִית; שְׁלִישִׁי and שְׁלִישִׁית; etc. ). For the form cf. that of the 'gentilic' adjective (above p. 119). From '11' onwards the cardinal numbers serve also as the ordinals, and only the context will make it clear which is intended. אַחֲרוֹן is 'last' (cf. the preposition אַחֲרֵי – 'after').

## VI

The use of the letters of the Hebrew alphabet as numbers, although of Mediaeval origin, should be noted, since they are used for chapter and verse numbers in some editions of the Hebrew Bible, especially those printed in Israel. The numerical values of the letters are indicated in the alphabet list on p. 3. Additional numbers are indicated by combinations of letters, e.g. יא '11' (i.e. 10 [ י] + 1 [ א] and written in the Hebrew order, from right to left).

Particular note should be made of the Hebrew equiv-alents of 15 and 16. By analogy one would expect these to be יה and יו respectively. But these particular combin-ations of letters are forms of the divine name יהוה, so 15 is represented by טו (9+6) and 16 by טז (9+7).

Numbers beyond 400 ( ת, the last letter of the alphabet) are also indicated by combinations:

| | | |
|---|---|---|
| תק | – | 500 (400 + 100) |
| תת | – | 800 (400 + 400) |
| תתר | – | 1,000 (400 + 400 + 200) |

## EXERCISE TWENTY-FIVE

Translate: **Jeremiah 52 : 28-30**

Vocabulary:

Verb:

        גָּלָה – to uncover; depart, go into exile
                Hiph. to carry into exile, deport

Nouns:

        שָׁנָה – year         רַב – chief
        טַבָּח – cook; (pl.) guardsmen, bodyguard

Proper names:

נְבוּכַדְרֶאצַּר - Nebuchadrezzar; the spelling with `n´ (Nebuchadnezzar), though equally commonly found in the Hebrew Bible, is etymologically incorrect

נְבוּזַרְאֲדָן - Nebuzaradan, one of Nebuchadrezzar's generals

Notes:

40 : טַבָּחִים - the noun טַבָּח is derived from the verb טָבַח - to slaughter (for food as opposed to sacrifice; the latter is expressed by the verb זָבַה ). The noun form with the doubled middle consonant is the so-called occupational form (cf. גַּנָּב - thief, from גָּנַב - to steal). A טַבָּח, therefore, was a butcher who also cooked the meat. In the context of a royal court the butcher/cook was also the royal bodyguard. In the formality of the court of Babylon and, no doubt, also that of Judah, this no longer corresponded to reality, but the antique title remained.

# THE NEXT STEP

## READING THE HEBREW BIBLE

You have already begun, in some of the previous chapters, to read short portions from the Hebrew Bible itself, but now that we have completed our coverage of the basic grammar, you are in a position to venture on this for yourself. If you are learning Hebrew as part of a University or College course, you will have a prescription of set texts on which to work, and your teacher will provide you with the right kind of guidance. If, however, you are working on your own, a few initial words of caution might prove useful.

Do not expect to run before you can walk. Some parts of the Hebrew Bible are more difficult than others, and, on the whole, the prophetic books and the poetry (the Psalms and Job, for example) are not the best places to begin. Choose, rather, a little narrative section - perhaps even only a single chapter to begin with (the story of Abraham's sacrifice of Isaac in Gen. 22:1-18, for example) - from Genesis or the books of Samuel or Kings, a story with which you are already familiar and which you enjoy. You can then progress to one of the two fairly short narrative books, Jonah and Ruth. It is better at first to choose something fairly simple and uncomplicated, and then, when you succeed in that, you will have a sense of accomplishment. Resist the temptation to want to start with Isaiah or Jeremiah. The Hebrew of these books - and of the prophets generally - is difficult, and the sense of frustration you would experience could bring only disappointment.

Try to work with the Hebrew text first before looking at one or other of the English versions. It is too easy - and self-deluding - to think that you are reading Hebrew while you have the English version open beside you. There is perhaps a place for that activity, and it is no doubt useful when you want to read something through fairly quickly and have the overall feel of a section, but it is not the way in which to learn the language. And remember that, having worked to the end of this volume, you are only now just beginning to learn Hebrew!

This Grammar has been an *introductory* one and has made no attempt to cope with every aspect of Hebrew grammar or explain all the forms you will encounter in the course of your future reading. For that you will need to be pointed in other directions, and such is the principal function of this final chapter.

I

*Editions of the Hebrew Bible*

a) The most readily available edition of the Hebrew Bible is that published by the British and Foreign Bible Society (BFBS) and edited by N. H. Snaith. It is designated on its title page and on the cover by the names of the Hebrew Bible's three component parts: תּוֹרָה ('Law') – נְבִיאִים ('Prophets') – כְּתוּבִים ('Writings'). The initial letters of these three terms are used as an acronym by Jews to refer to their Bible – תָּנָךְ . For details as to the precise contents of these three parts of the Bible see any of the standard Introductions to the Old Testament (e.g. O. Eissfeldt, *The Old Testament. An Introduction*, Blackwell, 1965) or, indeed, the contents pages provided in the edition at the beginning of each of the three sections. The currently available printing of the BFBS text has been photomechanically reduced from its original format. Some people may find the print too small for comfort – though it is admirably clear – and it is no doubt possible to obtain the larger format – or indeed a copy of the pre-Snaith BFBS edition – second-hand.

b) The above edition of the Hebrew Bible is 'un-critical', in the sense that it contains no editorial matter intervening between the text and the reader. While it is perfectly suitable for the beginner - and, indeed, for many other types of user - anyone who intends to pursue serious scholarly work on the Hebrew Bible will need eventually to acquire a 'critical' edition, one which contains some kind of information about variant readings in the manuscript traditions and observations on text-critical matters derived from an examination of the early translations of the Hebrew Bible into other languages (primarily Greek and Aramaic). The standard critical edition currently available is *Biblia Hebraica Stuttgartensia* (ed. Elliger and Rudolph) published by the German Bible Society (the Deutsche Bibelgesellschaft) in Stuttgart. This is most readily available through the Bible Societies (in England and Wales the Bible Society; in Scotland the National Bible Society of Scotland) who operate a discount scheme for the purchase of Bibles by *bona fide* theological students. A 'guide' to BHS (as it is known) is available: E. Würthwein, *The Text of the Old Testament (An Introduction to the Biblia Hebraica)*, SCM Press, 1980. The earlier edition of *Biblia Hebraica* (ed. R. Kittel, 1937 with subsequent reprintings; 'BHK') may also be found second-hand.

## II

*Grammars*

More detailed grammatical treatment of Hebrew than is provided here may be found in other 'introductory' grammars.

a) Previous editions of Davidson may be found second-hand; editions prior to the 25th are probably not so useful.

b) J. Weingreen, *A Practical Grammar for Classical Hebrew* (Oxford, 1959).

c) T. O. Lambdin, *Introduction to Biblical Hebrew* (Darton, Longman and Todd, 1973).

d) A more advanced treatment may be found in *Davidson's Introductory Hebrew Grammar - Syntax*, 4th edition,

J. C. L. Gibson (T & T Clark, 1994).

e) The standard reference Grammar in English, though heavily Latinate in its terminology, is *Gesenius' Hebrew Grammar*, ed. and enlarged by E. Kautzsch, translated by A. E. Cowley (Oxford, 1910). This is known as 'Gesenius-Kautzsch' and is abbreviated as GK. References to it are always by chapter number (§) and paragraph letter (e.g. GK § 31c). It has an Index of Hebrew Words and an Index of Passages, so that a particular form or a particular passage where problems or difficulties are experienced can be easily found in the body of the Grammar.

## III

*Dictionaries*

a) The most convenient small dictionary, though now somewhat dated, is *Langenscheidt's Hebrew-English Pocket Dictionary to the Old Testament*, part of a well-known and long-established series of dictionaries in many languages and in all sizes (published in the UK by Hodder).

b) Also small is the English version by W. Johnstone of G. Fohrer, *Hebrew and Aramaic Dictionary of the Old Testament*. This was originally published in 1973 by SCM Press. It is now no longer available in the UK but has, in the USA, reverted, still in English translation, to the publishers of the German original, de Gruyter (USA).

c) A larger, but for the beginner not overwhelming, dictionary is W. L. Holladay, *A Concise Hebrew and Aramaic Lexicon of the Old Testament* (E. J. Brill, Leiden, 1971; available in North America through Eerdmans). This is a 'concise' version of the *Lexicon in Veteris Testamenti Libros* by Koehler and Baumgartner (KB), now in its 3rd but still incomplete edition with meanings now given only in German (the 1st and 2nd editions had meanings in both German and English). An English translation of the 3rd edition is now promised.

d) The standard dictionary for the English-speaking world is Brown, Driver and Briggs, *Hebrew and English Lexicon of the Old Testament* (Oxford, 1907 with reprints and, from 1953 onwards, with corrections). This, on the basis of the initials of its compilers, is referred to as BDB. The difficulty for beginners in using BDB is that every word has to be looked for under the triliteral root from which it is ultimately derived. The other dictionaries mentioned here are arranged, for the most part, alphabetically. An Index to BDB compiled by Bruce Einspahr is available. It was published in 1976 in the UK by Samuel Bagster and is available in the USA from Moody.

e) A new 8-volume *Dictionary of Classical Hebrew* edited by Professor David Clines and covering the language not only of the Bible but also of later Hebrew texts such as the Dead Sea Scrolls, is in process of publication by Sheffield Academic Press.

## IV

*Vocabulary*

Some students may wish to build up a knowledge of Hebrew words in a systematic way, and three books are available which, in their different ways, list the words occurring in the Hebrew Bible in the order of their frequency of occurrence. In this way students can learn the most common words first (those occurring more than 500 times) and gradually work their way - stopping where they feel it desirable - down to the less common words (those occurring 10 times).

a) G. M. Landes, *A Student's Vocabulary of Biblical Hebrew* (Charles Scribner's Sons, New York, 1961).

b) J. D. W. Watts, *Lists of Words occurring frequently in the Hebrew Bible* (originally published by Brill of Leiden, 2nd edn. 1967, but now available from Eerdmans Publishing Co., USA).

c) L. A. Mitchel, *A Student's Vocabulary for Biblical Hebrew and Aramaic* (Academie Books, Zondervan Publishing House, Grand Rapids, Michigan, USA, 1984).

## V

*Additional Lexicographical Tools*

a) T. A. Armstrong *et al.*, *A Reader's Hebrew-English Lexicon of the Old Testament* (4 vols., Regency Reference Library, Zondervan, Grand Rapids, Michigan, USA, 1980-88). Here the lexicographical listing is chapter by chapter and book by book in the order in which these occur in the Hebrew Bible. Words occurring 50 times or more in the Old Testament are listed separately in an Appendix and not in the ongoing context. Users of the Lexicon are, therefore, 'encouraged to master this list'.

b) A more long-standing tool which lists alphabetically every form which occurs in the Hebrew Bible and indicates the root under which the word should then be looked up for its meaning is B. Davidson, *Analytical Hebrew and Chaldee Lexicon* (S. Bagster and Sons Ltd., London; in the USA it too is published by Zondervan).

Further help of an elementary nature on the reading of selected books can be found in the now out-of-print volumes by N. H. Snaith entitled *Notes on the Hebrew Text of...* and published by Epworth Press. These could be found second-hand or in libraries. Some commentaries on individual books do refer to the Hebrew text and to specific points in it, but these will tend to be not of an elementary nature but on points of textual criticism, of linguistic interest and of exegesis and may not be particularly helpful to those just beginning to read the Hebrew Bible.

It is not to be imagined that students must acquire a whole battery of books before they can begin to read. Much can be done with very little. What is required as a minimum is a copy of the text, a good Grammar and a dictionary. In the light of the information supplied in this chapter, make your decisions as to what, in these categories, will best suit *your* needs. If you have access to a good library - for the most part this will have to be a College or University one - have a look at some of these tools before you make that decision, or take the advice of a good teacher or other reliable informant. Arm yourself with the tools and along with patience and determination venture forth on a journey that will provide you with a lifetime's fascination and reward!

# PARADIGMS

# THE VOCALISATION OF THE DEFINITE ARTICLE

1. Before ordinary consonants:

הַמֶּ֫לֶךְ – הַ-

2. Before 'gutturals':

(i)  ע, ר, א

הָעָבַד, הָרֹאשׁ, הָאִישׁ – הָ-

(ii)  ה, ח

הַהֵיכָל, הַחֶ֫רֶב – הַ-

3. But before:

(i)  הָ

הָהָר – הָ-

(ii)  עָ, הָ

הֶעָמָל, הֶהָרִים – הֶ-

(iii)  חֶ, חָ

הֶחָלִי, הֶחָכָם – הֶ-

*Notes:*

1. Before *accented* הָ, the article, falling in the pretonic syllable, takes qāmeṣ, as in 3 (i).
2. Before *unaccented* עָ and הָ, the article, falling *before* the pretonic syllable, takes segōl, as in 3(ii).
3. Before חָ, accented or unaccented, and חֶ, the article takes segōl, as in 3(iii).

# NOUNS: FIRST DECLENSION

| | word | old man | star | desert | hand |
|---|---|---|---|---|---|
| Sing. abs. | דָּבָר | זָקֵן | כּוֹכָב | מִדְבָּר | יָד |
| cstr. | דְּבַר | זְקַן | כּוֹכַב | מִדְבַּר | יַד |
| w.1 s.suf. | דְּבָרִי | זְקֵנִי | כּוֹכָבִי | מִדְבָּרִי | יָדִי |
| 2 s.m. | דְּבָרְךָ | זְקֵנְךָ | כּוֹכָבְךָ | מִדְבָּרְךָ | יֶדְךָ |
| 2 pl.m. | דְּבַרְכֶם | זְקֶנְכֶם | כּוֹכַבְכֶם | מִדְבַּרְכֶם | יֶדְכֶם |
| Plur.abs. | דְּבָרִים | זְקֵנִים | כּוֹכָבִים | מִדְבָּרִים | יָדוֹת |
| cstr. | דִּבְרֵי | זִקְנֵי | כּוֹכְבֵי | מִדְבְּרֵי | יְדוֹת |
| w.1 s.suf. | דְּבָרַי | זְקֵנַי | כּוֹכָבַי | מִדְבָּרַי | יָדֹתַי |
| 2 s.m. | דְּבָרֶיךָ | זְקֵנֶיךָ | כּוֹכָבֶיךָ | מִדְבָּרֶיךָ | יָדֹתֶיךָ |
| 2 pl.m. | דִּבְרֵיכֶם | זִקְנֵיכֶם | כּוֹכְבֵיכֶם | מִדְבְּרֵיכֶם | יְדֹתֵיכֶם |

| | blood | river | wicked | joyful | army |
|---|---|---|---|---|---|
| Sing.abs. | דָּם | נָהָר | רָשָׁע | שָׂמֵחַ | צָבָא |
| cstr. | דַּם | נְהַר | רְשַׁע | שְׂמֵחַ | צְבָא |
| w.1.s.suf | דָּמִי | נַהֲרִי | רְשָׁעִי | שְׂמֵחִי | צְבָאִי |
| 2.s.m. | דָּמְךָ | נַהֲרְךָ | רְשָׁעֲךָ | שְׂמֵחֲךָ | צְבָאֲךָ |
| 2.pl.m. | דִּמְכֶם | נַהַרְכֶם | רִשְׁעֲכֶם | שְׂמֵחֲכֶם | צְבָאֲכֶם |
| Plur.abs. | דָּמִים | נְהָרִים | רְשָׁעִים | שְׂמֵחִים | צְבָאוֹת |
| cstr. | דְּמֵי | נַהֲרֵי | רִשְׁעֵי | שִׂמְחֵי / שְׂמֵחֵי | צִבְאוֹת |
| w.1.s.suf. | דָּמַי | נְהָרַי | רְשָׁעַי | שְׂמֵחַי | צִבְאֹתַי |
| 2.s.m. | דָּמֶיךָ | נְהָרֶיךָ | רְשָׁעֶיךָ | שְׂמֵחֶיךָ | צִבְאֹתֶיךָ |
| 2.pl.m. | דְּמֵיכֶם | נַהֲרֵיכֶם | רִשְׁעֵיכֶם | שְׂמֵחֵיכֶם | צִבְאֹתֵיכֶם |

| | rising | dead | leaf | field | beautiful |
|---|---|---|---|---|---|
| Sing.abs. | קָם | מֵת | עָלֶה | שָׂדֶה | יָפֶה |
| cstr. | קָם | מֵת | עֲלֵה | שְׂדֵה | יְפֵה |
| w.1.s.suf | קָמִי | מֵתִי | עָלִי | שָׂדִי | (יָפִי) |
| 2.s.m. | קָמְךָ | מֵתְךָ | עָלְךָ | שָׂדְךָ | (יָפְךָ) |
| 2.pl.m. | קָמְכֶם | מֵתְכֶם | עֲלְכֶם | שָׂדְכֶם | (יָפְכֶם) |
| Plur.abs. | קָמִים | מֵתִים | עָלִים | שָׂדוֹת | יָפִים |
| cstr. | קָמֵי | מֵתֵי | עֲלֵי | שְׂדוֹת | יְפֵי |
| w.1.s.suf. | קָמַי | מֵתַי | עָלַי | שְׂדֹתַי | (יָפַי) |
| 2.s.m. | קָמֶיךָ | מֵתֶיךָ | עָלֶיךָ | שְׂדֹתֶיךָ | (יָפֶיךָ) |
| 2.pl.m. | קָמֵיכֶם | מֵתֵיכֶם | עֲלֵיכֶם | שְׂדֹתֵיכֶם | (יְפֵיכֶם) |

# FIRST DECLENSION

| FEM. | righteousness | corpse | fish | rising |
|---|---|---|---|---|
| Sing. abs. | צְדָקָה | נְבֵלָה | דָּגָה | קָמָה |
| cstr. | צִדְקַת | נִבְלַת | דְּגַת | קָמַת |
| w.1.s.suf. | צִדְקָתִי | נִבְלָתִי | דְּגָתִי | קָמָתִי |
| 2.s.m. | צִדְקָתְךָ | נִבְלָתְךָ | דְּגֵתְךָ | קָמָתְךָ |
| 2.pl.m. | צִדְקַתְכֶם | נִבְלַתְכֶם | דְּגַתְכֶם | קָמַתְכֶם |
| Plur. abs. | צְדָקוֹת | נְבֵלוֹת | דָּגוֹת | קָמוֹת |
| cstr. | צִדְקוֹת | נִבְלוֹת | דְּגוֹת | קָמוֹת |
| w.1.s.suf. | צִדְקֹתַי | נִבְלֹתַי | דְּגֹתַי | קָמֹתַי |
| 2.s.m. | צִדְקֹתֶיךָ | נִבְלֹתֶיךָ | דְּגֹתֶיךָ | קָמֹתֶיךָ |
| 2.pl.m. | צִדְקֹתֵיכֶם | נִבְלֹתֵיכֶם | דְּגֹתֵיכֶם | קָמֹתֵיכֶם |

| | dead | beautiful |
|---|---|---|
| Sing. abs. | מֵתָה | יָפָה |
| cstr. | מֵתַת | יְפַת |
| w.1.s.suf. | מֵתָתִי | (יְפָתִי) |
| 2.s.m. | מֵתָתְךָ | (יְפָתְךָ) |
| 2.pl.m. | מֵתַתְכֶם | (יְפַתְכֶם) |
| Plur. abs. | מֵתוֹת | יָפוֹת |
| cstr. | מֵתוֹת | יְפוֹת |
| w.1.s.suf. | מֵתֹתַי | (יְפֹתַי) |
| 2.s.m. | מֵתֹתֶיךָ | (יְפֹתֶיךָ) |
| 2.pl.m. | מֵתֹתֵיכֶם | (יְפֹתֵיכֶם) |

---

| DUAL | hands | lips |
|---|---|---|
| Abs. | יָדַיִם | שְׂפָתַיִם |
| cstr. | יְדֵי | שְׂפָתֵי |
| w.1.s.suf. | יָדַי | שְׂפָתַי |
| 2.s.m. | יָדֶיךָ | שְׂפָתֶיךָ |
| 2.pl.m. | יְדֵיכֶם | שִׂפְתֵיכֶם |

# SECOND DECLENSION

| MASC. | king | book | morning | young man | terror |
|---|---|---|---|---|---|
| Sing. abs. | מֶלֶךְ | סֵפֶר | בֹּקֶר | נַעַר | פַּחַד |
| cstr. | מֶלֶךְ | סֵפֶר | בֹּקֶר | נַעַר | פַּחַד |
| w.1.s.suf. | מַלְכִּי | סִפְרִי | בְּקְרִי | נַעֲרִי | פַּחְדִּי |
| 2.s.m. | מַלְכְּךָ | סִפְרְךָ | בְּקְרְךָ | נַעַרְךָ | פַּחְדְּךָ |
| 2.pl.m. | מַלְכְּכֶם | סִפְרְכֶם | בְּקְרְכֶם | נַעַרְכֶם | פַּחְדְּכֶם |
| Plur. abs. | מְלָכִים | סְפָרִים | בְּקָרִים | נְעָרִים | פְּחָדִים |
| cstr. | מַלְכֵי | סִפְרֵי | בְּקְרֵי | נַעֲרֵי | פַּחֲדֵי |
| w.1.s.suf. | מְלָכַי | סְפָרַי | בְּקָרַי | נְעָרַי | פְּחָדַי |
| 2.s.m. | מְלָכֶיךָ | סְפָרֶיךָ | בְּקָרֶיךָ | נְעָרֶיךָ | פְּחָדֶיךָ |
| 2.pl.m. | מַלְכֵיכֶם | סִפְרֵיכֶם | בְּקְרֵיכֶם | נַעֲרֵיכֶם | פַּחֲדֵיכֶם |

| | breadth | seed | spear | sin | death | olive-tree |
|---|---|---|---|---|---|---|
| Sing. abs. | רֹחַב | זֶרַע | רֹמַח | חֵטְא | מָוֶת | זַיִת |
| cstr. | רֹחַב | זֶרַע | רֹמַח | חֵטְא | מוֹת | זֵית |
| w.1.s.suf. | רָחְבִּי | זַרְעִי | רָמְחִי | חֶטְאִי | מוֹתִי | זֵיתִי |
| 2.s.m. | רָחְבְּךָ | זַרְעֲךָ | רָמְחֲךָ | חֶטְאֲךָ | מוֹתְךָ | זֵיתְךָ |
| 2.pl.m. | רָחְבְּכֶם | זַרְעֲכֶם | רָמְחֲכֶם | חֶטְאֲכֶם | מוֹתְכֶם | זֵיתְכֶם |
| Plur. abs. | (רְחָבִים) | זְרָעִים | רְמָחִים | חֲטָאִים | מוֹתִים | זֵיתִים |
| cstr. | (רְחָבֵי) | זְרָעֵי | רָמְחֵי | חֲטָאֵי | מוֹתֵי | זֵיתֵי |
| w.1.s.suf. | (רְחָבַי) | זְרָעַי | רָמְחַי | חֲטָאַי | מוֹתֵי | זֵיתֵי |
| 2.s.m. | (רְחָבֶיךָ) | זְרָעֶיךָ | רְמָחֶיךָ | חֲטָאֶיךָ | מוֹתֶיךָ | זֵיתֶיךָ |
| 2.pl.m. | (רְחָבֵיכֶם) | זְרָעֵיכֶם | רָמְחֵיכֶם | חֲטָאֵיכֶם | מוֹתֵיכֶם | זֵיתֵיכֶם |

| | army, power | honey | stench | fruit | half | sickness |
|---|---|---|---|---|---|---|
| Sing. abs. | חַיִל | דְּבַשׁ | בְּאֹשׁ | פְּרִי | חֵצִי | חֳלִי |
| cstr. | חֵיל | דְּבַשׁ | בְּאֹשׁ | פְּרִי | חֵצִי | חֳלִי |
| w.1.s.suf. | חֵילִי | דֻּבְשִׁי | בָּאְשִׁי | פִּרְיִי | חֶצְיִי | חָלְיִי |
| 2.s.m. | חֵילְךָ | דֻּבְשְׁךָ | בָּאְשְׁךָ | פִּרְיְךָ | חֶצְיְךָ | חָלְיְךָ |
| 2.pl.m. | חֵילְכֶם | דֻּבְשְׁכֶם | בָּאְשְׁכֶם | פִּרְיְכֶם | חֶצְיְכֶם | חָלְיְכֶם |
| Plur. abs. | חֲיָלִים | | | | | חֳלָיִים |
| cstr. | חֵילֵי | | | | | חֳלָיֵי |
| w.1.s.suf. | (חֲיָלִי) | | | | | (חֳלָיַי) |
| 2.s.m. | (חֲיָלֶיךָ) | | | | | (חֳלָיֶךָ) |
| 2.pl.m. | חֵילֵיכֶם | | | | | (חֳלָיֶכֶם) |

# SECOND DECLENSION

| FEM. | queen | ewe-lamb | desert | kingdom |
|---|---|---|---|---|
| Sing. abs. | מַלְכָּה | כִּבְשָׂה | חָרְבָּה | מַמְלָכָה |
| cstr. | מַלְכַּת | כִּבְשַׂת | חָרְבַּת | מַמְלֶכֶת |
| w.1.s.suf. | מַלְכָּתִי | כִּבְשָׂתִי | חָרְבָּתִי | מַמְלַכְתִּי |
| 2.s.m. | מַלְכָּתְךָ | כִּבְשָׂתְךָ | חָרְבָּתְךָ | מַמְלַכְתְּךָ |
| 2.pl.m. | מַלְכַּתְכֶם | כִּבְשַׂתְכֶם | חָרְבַּתְכֶם | מַמְלַכְתְּכֶם |
| Plur. abs. | מְלָכוֹת | כְּבָשׂוֹת | חֲרָבוֹת | מַמְלָכוֹת |
| cstr. | מַלְכוֹת | כִּבְשׂוֹת | חָרְבוֹת | מַמְלְכוֹת |
| w.1.s.suf. | מַלְכוֹתַי | כִּבְשׂוֹתַי | חָרְבוֹתַי | מַמְלְכוֹתַי |
| 2.s.m. | מַלְכֹתֶיךָ | כִּבְשֹׂתֶיךָ | חָרְבֹתֶיךָ | מַמְלְכֹתֶיךָ |
| 2.pl.m. | מַלְכֹתֵיכֶם | כִּבְשֹׂתֵיכֶם | חָרְבֹתֵיכֶם | מַמְלְכֹתֵיכֶם |

| | nurse | tunic |
|---|---|---|
| Sing. abs. | מֵינֶקֶת | כֻּתֹּנֶת , / כְּתֹנֶת |
| cstr. | מֵינֶקֶת | כְּתֹנֶת |
| w.1.s.suf. | מֵינַקְתִּי | כֻּתָּנְתִּי |
| 2.s.m. | מֵינַקְתְּךָ | כֻּתָּנְתְּךָ |
| 2.pl.m. | מֵינַקְתְּכֶם | כֻּתָּנְתְּכֶם |
| Plur. abs. | מֵינִיקוֹת | כֻּתֳּנוֹת |
| cstr. | מֵינִיקוֹת | כָּתֳנוֹת |
| w.1.s.suf. | מֵינִיקוֹתַי | כֻּתֳּנוֹתַי |
| 2.s.m. | מֵינִיקֹתֶיךָ | כֻּתֳּנֹתֶיךָ |
| 2.pl.m. | מֵינִיקֹתֵיכֶם | כֻּתֳּנֹתֵיכֶם |

---

| DUAL | feet | knees | ears | sides |
|---|---|---|---|---|
| bs. | רַגְלַיִם | בִּרְכַּיִם | אָזְנַיִם | יַרְכָתַיִם |
| Cstr. | רַגְלֵי | בִּרְכֵּי | אָזְנֵי | יַרְכְתֵי |
| w.1.s.suf. | רַגְלַי | בִּרְכַּי | אָזְנַי | (יַרְכָתַי) |
| 2.s.m. | רַגְלֶיךָ | בִּרְכֶּיךָ | אָזְנֶיךָ | (יַרְכָתֶיךָ) |
| 2.pl.m. | רַגְלֵיכֶם | בִּרְכֵּיכֶם | אָזְנֵיכֶם | (יַרְכְתֵיכֶם) |

# THIRD DECLENSION

|  | killing | staff | name | priest |
|---|---|---|---|---|
| *Sing. abs.* | קֹטֶל | מַקֵּל | שֵׁם | כֹּהֵן |
| *cstr.* | קֹטֶל | מַקֵּל | שֵׁם | כֹּהֵן |
| *w.1.s.suf.* | קָטְלִי | מַקְלִי | שְׁמִי | כֹּהֲנִי |
| *2.s.m.* | קָטְלְךָ | מַקֶּלְךָ | שִׁמְךָ | כֹּהֶנְךָ |
| *2.pl.m.* | קָטְלְכֶם | מַקֶּלְכֶם | שִׁמְכֶם | כֹּהֶנְכֶם |
| *Plur. abs.* | קְטָלִים | מַקְלוֹת | שֵׁמוֹת | כֹּהֲנִים |
| *cstr.* | קָטְלֵי | מַקְלוֹת | שְׁמוֹת | כֹּהֲנֵי |
| *w.1.s.suf.* | קְטָלַי | מַקְלוֹתַי | שְׁמוֹתַי | כֹּהֲנַי |
| *2.s.m.* | קְטָלֶיךָ | מַקְלֹתֶיךָ | שְׁמֹתֶיךָ | כֹּהֲנֶיךָ |
| *2.pl.m.* | קְטָלֵיכֶם | מַקְלֹתֵיכֶם | שְׁמֹתֵיכֶם | כֹּהֲנֵיכֶם |

|  | altar | possessor | cattle |
|---|---|---|---|
| *Sing. abs.* | מִזְבֵּחַ | קֹנֶה | מִקְנֶה |
| *cstr.* | מִזְבַּח | קֹנֵה | מִקְנֵה |
| *w.1.s.suf.* | מִזְבְּחִי | קֹנִי | מִקְנִי |
| *2.s.m.* | מִזְבַּחֲךָ | קֹנְךָ | מִקְנְךָ |
| *2.pl.m.* | מִזְבַּחֲכֶם | קֹנְכֶם | מִקְנְכֶם |
| *Plur. abs.* | מִזְבְּחוֹת | קֹנִים | מִקְנִים |
| *cstr.* | מִזְבְּחוֹת | קֹנֵי | מִקְנֵי |
| *w.1.s.suf.* | מִזְבְּחוֹתַי | קֹנַי | מִקְנַי |
| *2.s.m.* | מִזְבְּחֹתֶיךָ | קֹנֶיךָ | מִקְנֶיךָ |
| *2.pl.m.* | מִזְבְּחֹתֵיכֶם | קֹנֵיכֶם | מִקְנֵיכֶם |

# FOURTH DECLENSION

| MASC. | people | mountain | arrow | statute |
|---|---|---|---|---|
| *Sing. abs.* | עַם | הַר | חֵץ | חֹק |
| *cstr.* | עַם | הַר | חֵץ | חָק־ |
| *w.1.s.suf.* | עַמִּי | הָרִי | חִצִּי | חֻקִּי |
| *2.s.m.* | עַמְּךָ | הָרְךָ | חִצְּךָ | חֻקְּךָ |
| *2.pl.m.* | עַמְּכֶם | הַרְכֶם | חִצְּכֶם | חֻקְּכֶם |
| *Plur. abs.* | עַמִּים | הָרִים | חִצִּים | חֻקִּים |
| *cstr.* | עַמֵּי | הָרֵי | חִצֵּי | חֻקֵּי |
| *w.1.s.suf.* | עַמַּי | הָרַי | חִצַּי | חֻקַּי |
| *2.s.m.* | עַמֶּיךָ | הָרֶיךָ | חִצֶּיךָ | חֻקֶּיךָ |
| *2.pl.m.* | עַמֵּיכֶם | הָרֵיכֶם | חִצֵּיכֶם | חֻקֵּיכֶם |

| MASC. | small | nose, nostrils |
|---|---|---|
| *Sing. abs.* | קָטֹן | אַף |
| *cstr.* | קְטֹן | אַף |
| *w.1.s.suf.* | קְטַנִּי | אַפִּי |
| *2.s.m.* | קְטָנְךָ | אַפְּךָ |
| *2.pl.m.* | קְטָנְכֶם | אַפְּכֶם |
| | | **DUAL** |
| *Plur. abs.* | קְטַנִּים | אַפַּיִם |
| *cstr.* | קְטַנֵּי | אַפֵּי |
| *w.1.s.suf.* | קְטַנַּי | אַפַּי |
| *2.s.m.* | קְטַנֶּיךָ | אַפֶּיךָ |
| *2.pl.m.* | קְטַנֵּיכֶם | אַפֵּיכֶם |

# FOURTH DECLENSION

| FEM. | mother | desolation | measure | statute |
|------|--------|------------|---------|---------|
| Sing. abs. | אֵם | שַׁמָּה | מִדָּה | חֻקָּה |
| cstr. | אֵם | שַׁמַּת | מִדַּת | חֻקַּת |
| w. 1. s. suf. | אִמִּי | שַׁמָּתִי | מִדָּתִי | חֻקָּתִי |
| 2. s. m. | אִמְּךָ | שַׁמָּתְךָ | מִדָּתְךָ | חֻקָּתְךָ |
| 2. pl. m. | אִמְּכֶם | שַׁמַּתְכֶם | מִדַּתְכֶם | חֻקַּתְכֶם |
| Plur. abs. | אִמּוֹת | שַׁמּוֹת | מִדּוֹת | חֻקּוֹת |
| cstr. | אִמּוֹת | שַׁמּוֹת | מִדּוֹת | חֻקּוֹת |
| w. 1. s. suf. | אִמּוֹתַי | שַׁמּוֹתַי | מִדּוֹתַי | חֻקּוֹתַי |
| 2. s. m. | אִמֹּתֶיךָ | שַׁמֹּתֶיךָ | מִדֹּתֶיךָ | חֻקֹּתֶיךָ |
| 2. pl. m. | אִמֹּתֵיכֶם | שַׁמֹּתֵיכֶם | מִדֹּתֵיכֶם | חֻקֹּתֵיכֶם |

| | evil | small |
|------|------|-------|
| Sing. abs. | רָעָה | קְטַנָּה |
| cstr. | רָעַת | קְטַנַּת |
| w. 1. s. suf. | רָעָתִי | קְטַנָּתִי |
| 2. s. m. | רָעָתְךָ | קְטַנָּתְךָ |
| 2. pl. m. | רָעַתְכֶם | קְטַנַּתְכֶם |
| Plur. abs. | רָעוֹת | קְטַנּוֹת |
| cstr. | רָעוֹת | קְטַנּוֹת |
| w. 1. s. suf. | רָעוֹתַי | קְטַנּוֹתַי |
| 2. s. m. | רָעֹתֶיךָ | קְטַנֹּתֶיךָ |
| 2. pl. m. | רָעֹתֵיכֶם | קְטַנֹּתֵיכֶם |

# PREPOSITIONS

| | in, by, with | to, at, for | like | after | into | upon, beside |
|---|---|---|---|---|---|---|
| | בְּ | לְ | כְּ | אַחֲרֵי | אֶל- | עַל |
| **With** | | | | | | |
| 3.s.m. | בּוֹ | לוֹ | כָּמוֹהוּ | אַחֲרָיו | אֵלָיו | עָלָיו |
| 3.s.f. | בָּהּ | לָהּ | כָּמוֹהָ | אַחֲרֶיהָ | אֵלֶיהָ | עָלֶיהָ |
| 2.s.m. | בְּךָ | לְךָ | כָּמוֹךָ | אַחֲרֶיךָ | אֵלֶיךָ | עָלֶיךָ |
| 2.s.f. | בָּךְ | לָךְ | כָּמוֹךְ | אַחֲרַיִךְ | אֵלַיִךְ | עָלַיִךְ |
| 1.s.suf. | בִּי | לִי | כָּמוֹנִי | אַחֲרַי | אֵלַי | עָלַי |
| 3.pl.m. | בָּהֶם, בָּם | לָהֶם | כָּהֶם' | אַחֲרֵיהֶם | אֲלֵיהֶם | עֲלֵיהֶם |
| 3.pl.f. | בָּהֶן | לָהֶן | כָּהֶן' | אַחֲרֵיהֶן | אֲלֵיהֶן | עֲלֵיהֶן |
| 2.pl.m. | בָּכֶם | לָכֶם | כָּכֶם | אַחֲרֵיכֶם | אֲלֵיכֶם | עֲלֵיכֶם |
| 2.pl.f. | בָּכֶן | לָכֶן | כָּכֶן | אַחֲרֵיכֶן | אֲלֵיכֶן | עֲלֵיכֶן |
| 1.pl.c. | בָּנוּ | לָנוּ | כָּמוֹנוּ | אַחֲרֵינוּ | אֵלֵינוּ | עָלֵינוּ |

| | as far as | under | from | with | | between |
|---|---|---|---|---|---|---|
| | עַד | תַּחַת | מִן | אֵת | עִם | בֵּין |
| **With** | | | | | | |
| 3.s.m. | עָדָיו | תַּחְתָּיו | מִמֶּנּוּ | אִתוֹ | עִמּוֹ | בֵּינוֹ |
| 3.s.f. | עָדֶיהָ | תַּחְתֶּיהָ | מִמֶּנָּה | אִתָּהּ | עִמָּהּ | בֵּינָהּ |
| 2.s.m. | עָדֶיךָ | תַּחְתֶּיךָ | מִמְּךָ | אִתְּךָ | עִמְּךָ | בֵּינְךָ |
| 2.s.f. | עָדַיִךְ | תַּחְתַּיִךְ | מִמֵּךְ | אִתָּךְ | עִמָּךְ | בֵּינֵךְ |
| 1.s.suf. | עָדַי | תַּחְתַּי | מִמֶּנִּי | אִתִּי | עִמִּי (עִמָּדִי) | בֵּינִי |
| 3.pl.m. | עֲדֵיהֶם | תַּחְתֵּיהֶם | מֵהֶם | אִתָּם | עִמָּם | בֵּינֵיהֶם |
| 3.pl.f. | עֲדֵיהֶן | תַּחְתֵּיהֶן | מֵהֶן | אִתָּן | עִמָּן | בֵּינֵיהֶן |
| 2.pl.m. | עֲדֵיכֶם | תַּחְתֵּיכֶם | מִכֶּם | אִתְּכֶם | עִמָּכֶם | בֵּינֵיכֶם |
| 2.pl.f. | עֲדֵיכֶן | תַּחְתֵּיכֶן | מִכֶּן | אִתְּכֶן | עִמָּכֶן | בֵּינֵיכֶן |
| 1.pl.c. | עָדֵינוּ | תַּחְתֵּינוּ | מִמֶּנּוּ | אִתָּנוּ | עִמָּנוּ | בֵּינֵינוּ |

---

' Alternatively כָּהֶם or כָּהֵמָה and כָּהֵנָּה

# THE PRINCIPAL PARTS OF THE HEBREW VERB

|  | Qal | Niphal | Piel | Pual | Hitpael | Hiphil | Hophal |
|---|---|---|---|---|---|---|---|
| Perfect | קָטַל כָּבֵד קָטֹן | נִקְטַל | קִטֵּל | קֻטַּל | הִתְקַטֵּל | הִקְטִיל | הָקְטַל |
| Infinitive | קְטֹל | הִקָּטֵל | קַטֵּל | קֻטַּל | הִתְקַטֵּל | הִקְטִיל | הָקְטַל |
| Imperfect | יִקְטֹל יִכְבַּד | יִקָּטֵל | יְקַטֵּל | יְקֻטַּל | יִתְקַטֵּל | יַקְטִיל Jussive יַקְטֵל | יָקְטַל |
| Imperative | קְטֹל כְּבַד | הִקָּטֵל | קַטֵּל | —— | הִתְקַטֵּל | הַקְטֵל | —— |
| Participle | קֹטֵל Passive קָטוּל | נִקְטָל | מְקַטֵּל | מְקֻטָּל | מִתְקַטֵּל | מַקְטִיל | מָקְטָל |

# VERB PARADIGMS

| | Qal | | | Niphal |
|---|---|---|---|---|
| | act. | stat. | | |
| *Perf. Sing.* 3.*m.* | קָטַל | כָּבֵד | קָטֹן | נִקְטַל |
| 3.*f.* | קָטְלָה | כָּבְדָה | קָטְנָה | נִקְטְלָה |
| 2.*m.* | קָטַ֫לְתָּ | כָּבַ֫דְתָּ | קָטֹ֫נְתָּ | נִקְטַ֫לְתָּ |
| 2.*f.* | קָטַלְתְּ | כָּבַדְתְּ | קָטֹנְתְּ | נִקְטַלְתְּ |
| 1.*c.* | קָטַ֫לְתִּי | כָּבַ֫דְתִּי | קָטֹ֫נְתִּי | נִקְטַ֫לְתִּי |
| *Plur.* 3.*c.* | קָטְלוּ | כָּבְדוּ | קָטְנוּ | נִקְטְלוּ |
| 2.*m.* | קְטַלְתֶּם | כְּבַדְתֶּם | קְטָנְתֶּם | נִקְטַלְתֶּם |
| 2.*f.* | קְטַלְתֶּן | כְּבַדְתֶּן | קְטָנְתֶּן | נִקְטַלְתֶּן |
| 1.*c.* | קָטַ֫לְנוּ | כָּבַ֫דְנוּ | קָטֹ֫נּוּ | נִקְטַ֫לְנוּ |
| *Impf. Sing.* 3.*m.* | יִקְטֹל | יִכְבַּד | יִקְטַן | יִקָּטֵל |
| 3.*f.* | תִּקְטֹל | תִּכְבַּד | &c. as | תִּקָּטֵל |
| 2.*m.* | תִּקְטֹל | תִּכְבַּד | with | תִּקָּטֵל |
| 2.*f.* | תִּקְטְלִי (ין) | תִּכְבְּדִי | יִכְבַּד | תִּקָּטְלִי |
| 1.*c.* | אֶקְטֹל | אֶכְבַּד | | אֶקָּטֵל (אִקָּטֵל) |
| *Plur.* 3.*m.* | יִקְטְלוּ (וּן) | יִכְבְּדוּ | | יִקָּטְלוּ |
| 3.*f.* | תִּקְטֹ֫לְנָה | תִּכְבַּ֫דְנָה | | תִּקָּטַ֫לְנָה |
| 2.*m.* | תִּקְטְלוּ (וּן) | תִּכְבְּדוּ | | תִּקָּטְלוּ |
| 2.*f.* | תִּקְטֹ֫לְנָה | תִּכְבַּ֫דְנָה | | תִּקָּטַ֫לְנָה |
| 1.*c.* | נִקְטֹל | נִכְבַּד | | נִקָּטֵל |
| *Imp. Sing.* 2.*m.* | קְטֹל (קָטְלָה) | כְּבַד (כִּבְדָה) | | הִקָּטֵל (הִקָּטֵל) |
| 2.*f.* | קִטְלִי (קָטְלִי) | כִּבְדִי | | הִקָּטְלִי |
| *Plur.* 2.*m.* | קִטְלוּ | כִּבְדוּ | | הִקָּטְלוּ |
| 2.*f.* | קְטֹ֫לְנָה | כְּבַ֫דְנָה | | הִקָּטַ֫לְנָה |
| *Jussive* 3 *sing.* | יִקְטֹל | יִכְבַּד | | יִקָּטֵל (יִקָּטֵל) |
| *vāv cons. impf.* | וַיִּקְטֹל | וַיִּכְבַּד | | וַיִּקָּטֵל (וַיִּקָּטֵל) |
| *Cohort.* 1 *sing.* | אֶקְטְלָה | אֶכְבְּדָה | | אֶקָּטְלָה |
| *vāv cons. perf.* | וְקָטַלְתָּ֫ | &c. | | |
| *Inf. cstr.* | קְטֹל | כְּבַד (כְּבֹד) | | הִקָּטֵל |
| *absol.* | קָטוֹל | כָּבוֹד | | הִקָּטֹל, נִקְטֹל |
| *Part. act.* | קֹטֵל | כָּבֵד | קָטֹן | |
| *pass.* | קָטוּל | | | נִקְטָל |

# VERB

| Piel | Pual | Hitpael | Hiphil | Hophal |
|---|---|---|---|---|
| קִטֵּל (קֻטַּל) | קֻטַּל | הִתְקַטֵּל (־קַטֵּל) | הִקְטִיל | הָקְטַל |
| קִטְּלָה | קֻטְּלָה | הִתְקַטְּלָה | הִקְטִילָה | הָקְטְלָה |
| קִטַּלְתָּ | קֻטַּלְתָּ | הִתְקַטַּלְתָּ | הִקְטַלְתָּ | הָקְטַלְתָּ |
| קִטַּלְתְּ | קֻטַּלְתְּ | הִתְקַטַּלְתְּ | הִקְטַלְתְּ | הָקְטַלְתְּ |
| קִטַּלְתִּי | קֻטַּלְתִּי | הִתְקַטַּלְתִּי | הִקְטַלְתִּי | הָקְטַלְתִּי |
| קִטְּלוּ | קֻטְּלוּ | הִתְקַטְּלוּ | הִקְטִילוּ | הָקְטְלוּ |
| קִטַּלְתֶּם | קֻטַּלְתֶּם | הִתְקַטַּלְתֶּם | הִקְטַלְתֶּם | הָקְטַלְתֶּם |
| קִטַּלְתֶּן | קֻטַּלְתֶּן | הִתְקַטַּלְתֶּן | הִקְטַלְתֶּן | הָקְטַלְתֶּן |
| קִטַּלְנוּ | קֻטַּלְנוּ | הִתְקַטַּלְנוּ | הִקְטַלְנוּ | הָקְטַלְנוּ |

| Piel | Pual | Hitpael | Hiphil | Hophal |
|---|---|---|---|---|
| יְקַטֵּל | יְקֻטַּל | יִתְקַטֵּל | יַקְטִיל | יָקְטַל |
| תְּקַטֵּל | תְּקֻטַּל | תִּתְקַטֵּל | תַּקְטִיל | תָּקְטַל |
| תְּקַטֵּל | תְּקֻטַּל | תִּתְקַטֵּל | תַּקְטִיל | תָּקְטַל |
| תְּקַטְּלִי | תְּקֻטְּלִי | תִּתְקַטְּלִי | תַּקְטִילִי | תָּקְטְלִי |
| אֲקַטֵּל | אֲקֻטַּל | אֶתְקַטֵּל | אַקְטִיל | אָקְטַל |
| יְקַטְּלוּ | יְקֻטְּלוּ | יִתְקַטְּלוּ | יַקְטִילוּ | יָקְטְלוּ |
| תְּקַטֵּלְנָה | תְּקֻטַּלְנָה | תִּתְקַטֵּלְנָה | תַּקְטֵלְנָה | תָּקְטַלְנָה |
| תְּקַטְּלוּ | תְּקֻטְּלוּ | תִּתְקַטְּלוּ | תַּקְטִילוּ | תָּקְטְלוּ |
| תְּקַטֵּלְנָה | תְּקֻטַּלְנָה | תִּתְקַטֵּלְנָה | תַּקְטֵלְנָה | תָּקְטַלְנָה |
| נְקַטֵּל | נְקֻטַּל | נִתְקַטֵּל | נַקְטִיל | נָקְטַל |

| Piel | Pual | Hitpael | Hiphil | Hophal |
|---|---|---|---|---|
| קַטֵּל | — | הִתְקַטֵּל | הַקְטֵל | — |
| קַטְּלִי | — | הִתְקַטְּלִי | הַקְטִילִי | — |
| קַטְּלוּ | — | הִתְקַטְּלוּ | הַקְטִילוּ | — |
| קַטֵּלְנָה | — | הִתְקַטֵּלְנָה | הַקְטֵלְנָה | — |
| יְקַטֵּל | יְקֻטַּל | יִתְקַטֵּל | יַקְטֵל | — |
| וַיְקַטֵּל | וַיְקֻטַּל | וַיִּתְקַטֵּל | וַיַּקְטֵל | וַיָּקְטַל |
| אֲקַטְּלָה | — | אֶתְקַטְּלָה | אַקְטִילָה | — |

| Piel | Pual | Hitpael | Hiphil | Hophal |
|---|---|---|---|---|
| קַטֵּל | (קֻטַּל) | הִתְקַטֵּל | הַקְטִיל | (הָקְטַל) |
| קַטֵּל ,קַטֹּל | קֻטַּל | (הִתְקַטֵּל) | הַקְטֵל | (הָקְטֵל) |
| מְקַטֵּל | | מִתְקַטֵּל | מַקְטִיל | |
| | מְקֻטָּל | | | מָקְטָל |

| | Qal act. | Qal stat. | Niph. |
|---|---|---|---|
| Perf. Sing. 3.*m.* | עָמַד חָתַם | חָכַם הָזַק | נֶעֱמַד נֶחְתַּם |
| 3.*f.* | עָמְדָה &c. | &c. or הָזַק &c. | נֶעֶמְדָה |
| 2.*m.* | עָמַדְתָּ | | נֶעֱמַדְתָּ |
| 2.*f.* | עָמַדְתְּ | | נֶעֱמַדְתְּ |
| 1.*c.* | עָמַדְתִּי | | נֶעֱמַדְתִּי |
| Plur. 3.*c.* | עָמְדוּ | | נֶעֶמְדוּ |
| 2.*m.* | עֲמַדְתֶּם | | נֶעֱמַדְתֶּם |
| 2.*f.* | עֲמַדְתֶּן | | נֶעֱמַדְתֶּן |
| 1.*c.* | עָמַדְנוּ | | נֶעֱמַדְנוּ |
| Impf. Sing. 3.*m.* | יַעֲמֹד יַחְתֹּם | יֶחְכַּם יֶחֱזַק | יֵעָמֵד |
| 3.*f.* | תַּעֲמֹד &c. | תֶּחֱזַק &c. | תֵּעָמֵד |
| 2.*m.* | תַּעֲמֹד | תֶּחֱזַק | תֵּעָמֵד |
| 2.*f.* | תַּעַמְדִי | תֶּחֶזְקִי | תֵּעָמְדִי |
| 1.*c.* | אֶעֱמֹד | אֶחֱזַק | אֵעָמֵד |
| Plur. 3.*m.* | יַעַמְדוּ | יֶחֶזְקוּ | יֵעָמְדוּ |
| 3.*f.* | תַּעֲמֹדְנָה | תֶּחֱזַקְנָה | תֵּעָמַדְנָה |
| 2.*m.* | תַּעַמְדוּ | תֶּחֶזְקוּ | תֵּעָמְדוּ |
| 2.*f.* | תַּעֲמֹדְנָה | תֶּחֱזַקְנָה | תֵּעָמַדְנָה |
| 1.*c.* | נַעֲמֹד | נֶחֱזַק | נֵעָמֵד |
| Imp. Sing. 2.*m.* | עֲמֹד חֲתֹם | חֲכַם חֲזַק | הֵעָמֵד |
| 2.*f.* | עִמְדִי &c. | חִזְקִי &c. | הֵעָמְדִי |
| Plur. 2.*m.* | עִמְדוּ | חִזְקוּ | הֵעָמְדוּ |
| 2.*f.* | עֲמֹדְנָה | חֲזַקְנָה | הֵעָמַדְנָה |
| *Jussive* 3 sing. | יַעֲמֹד יַחְתֹּם | יֶחְכַּם יֶחֱזַק | |
| *vāv cons. impf.* | וַיַּעֲמֹד וַיַּחְתֹּם | וַיִּחְכַּם וַיֶּחֱזַק | |
| *Cohort.* 1 sing. | אֶעֶמְדָה | | |
| *vāv cons. perf.* | וְעָמַדְתָּ | | |
| Inf. cstr. | עֲמֹד חֲתֹם | | הֵעָמֵד |
| absol. | עָמוֹד חָתוֹם | | נַעֲמוֹד נַחְתוֹם |
| Part. act. | עֹמֵד חֹתֵם | חָזֵק | |
| pass. | עָמוּד חָתוּם | | נֶעֱמָד נֶחְתָּם |

| Hiph. | | Hoph. | | Qal |
|---|---|---|---|---|
| הֶחֱתִים | הֶעֱמִיד | הָחֳתַם | הָעֳמַד | אָכַל |
| | הֶעֱמִידָה | | הָעֳמְדָה | &c. |
| | הֶעֱמַדְתָּ | | הָעֳמַדְתָּ | |
| | הֶעֱמַדְתְּ | | הָעֳמַדְתְּ | |
| | הֶעֱמַדְתִּי | | הָעֳמַדְתִּי | |
| | הֶעֱמִידוּ | | הָעֳמְדוּ | |
| | הֶעֱמַדְתֶּם | | הָעֳמַדְתֶּם | |
| | הֶעֱמַדְתֶּן | | הָעֳמַדְתֶּן | |
| | הֶעֱמַדְנוּ | | הָעֳמַדְנוּ | |
| | | | | |
| | יַעֲמִיד | | יָעֳמַד | יֹאכַל |
| | תַּעֲמִיד | | תָּעֳמַד | תֹּאכַל |
| | תַּעֲמִיד | | תָּעֳמַד | תֹּאכַל |
| | תַּעֲמִידִי | | תָּעֳמְדִי | תֹּאכְלִי |
| | אַעֲמִיד | | אָעֳמַד | אֹכַל |
| | יַעֲמִידוּ | | יָעֳמְדוּ | יֹאכְלוּ |
| | תַּעֲמֵדְנָה | | תָּעֳמַדְנָה | תֹּאכַלְנָה |
| | תַּעֲמִידוּ | | תָּעֳמְדוּ | תֹּאכְלוּ |
| | תַּעֲמֵדְנָה | | תָּעֳמַדְנָה | תֹּאכַלְנָה |
| | נַעֲמִיד | | נָעֳמַד | נֹאכַל |
| | | | | |
| | הַעֲמֵד | | — | אֱכֹל |
| | הַעֲמִידִי | | — | אִכְלִי |
| | הַעֲמִידוּ | | — | אִכְלוּ |
| | הַעֲמֵדְנָה | | — | אֲכֹלְנָה |
| | יַעֲמֵד | | | |
| | וַיַּעֲמֵד | | | וַיֹּאכַל (וַיֹּאמֶר) |
| | אַעֲמִידָה | | | אָכְלָה |
| | וְהַעֲמַדְתָּ | | | |
| | | | | |
| | הַעֲמִיד | | | אָכֹל |
| | הַעֲמֵד | | הָעֳמֵד | אָכוֹל |
| | מַעֲמִיד | | | אֹכֵל |
| | | | מָעֳמָד | אָכוּל |

| | Qal | Niphal | |
|---|---|---|---|
| Perf. Sing. 3.m. | (נָחַם) שָׁחַט | נִשְׁחַט | נָחַם |
| 3.f. | שָׁחֲטָה | נִשְׁחֲטָה | |
| 2.m. | שָׁחַטְתָּ | נִשְׁחַטְתָּ | |
| 2.f. | שָׁחַטְתְּ | נִשְׁחַטְתְּ | |
| 1.c. | שָׁחַטְתִּי | נִשְׁחַטְתִּי | |
| Plur. 3.c. | שָׁחֲטוּ | נִשְׁחֲטוּ | |
| 2.m. | שְׁחַטְתֶּם | נִשְׁחַטְתֶּם | |
| 2.f. | שְׁחַטְתֶּן | נִשְׁחַטְתֶּן | |
| 1.c. | שָׁחַטְנוּ | נִשְׁחַטְנוּ | |
| Impf. Sing. 3.m. | יִשְׁחַט | יִשָּׁחֵט | יִנָּחֵם |
| 3.f. | תִּשְׁחַט | תִּשָּׁחֵט | |
| 2.m. | תִּשְׁחַט | תִּשָּׁחֵט | |
| 2.f. | תִּשְׁחֲטִי | תִּשָּׁחֲטִי | |
| 1.c. | אֶשְׁחַט | אֶשָּׁחֵט | |
| Plur. 3.m. | יִשְׁחֲטוּ | יִשָּׁחֲטוּ | |
| 3.f. | תִּשְׁחַטְנָה | תִּשָּׁחַטְנָה | |
| 2.m. | תִּשְׁחֲטוּ | תִּשָּׁחֲטוּ | |
| 2.f. | תִּשְׁחַטְנָה | תִּשָּׁחַטְנָה | |
| 1.c. | נִשְׁחַט | נִשָּׁחֵט | |
| Imp. Sing. 2.m. | שְׁחַט | הִשָּׁחֵט | הִנָּחֵם |
| 2.f. | שַׁחֲטִי | הִשָּׁחֲטִי | |
| Plur. 2.m. | שַׁחֲטוּ | הִשָּׁחֲטוּ | |
| 2.f. | שְׁחַטְנָה | הִשָּׁחַטְנָה | |
| Jussive 3 sing. | יִשְׁחַט | יִשָּׁחֵט | |
| vāv cons. impf. | וַיִּשְׁחַט | וַיִּשָּׁחֵט | |
| Impf. with suff. | יִשְׁחָטֵנִי | | |
| Inf. cstr. | שְׁחֹט | הִשָּׁחֵט | הִנָּחֵם |
| absol. | שָׁחוֹט | נִשְׁחוֹט | |
| Part. act. | שֹׁחֵט | | |
| pass. | שָׁחוּט | נִשְׁחָט | נָחָם |

| Piēl | Pual | Hitp. |
|---|---|---|
| נִחַם בֵּרֵךְ | נֻחַם בֹּרַךְ | הִתְנַחֵם הִתְבָּרֵךְ |
| בֵּרְכָה בֵּרְכָה | בֹּרְכָה | הִתְבָּרְכָה |
| בֵּרַכְתָּ | בֹּרַכְתָּ | הִתְבָּרַכְתָּ |
| בֵּרַכְתְּ | בֹּרַכְתְּ | הִתְבָּרַכְתְּ |
| בֵּרַכְתִּי | בֹּרַכְתִּי | הִתְבָּרַכְתִּי |
| בֵּרְכוּ בֵּרְכוּ | בֹּרְכוּ | הִתְבָּרְכוּ |
| בֵּרַכְתֶּם | בֹּרַכְתֶּם | הִתְבָּרַכְתֶּם |
| בֵּרַכְתֶּן | בֹּרַכְתֶּן | הִתְבָּרַכְתֶּן |
| בֵּרַכְנוּ | בֹּרַכְנוּ | הִתְבָּרַכְנוּ |
| | | |
| יְנַחֵם יְבָרֵךְ | יְנֻחַם יְבֹרַךְ | יִתְנַחֵם יִתְבָּרֵךְ |
| תְּבָרֵךְ | תְּבֹרַךְ | תִּתְבָּרֵךְ |
| תְּבָרֵךְ | תְּבֹרַךְ | תִּתְבָּרֵךְ |
| תְּבָרְכִי תְּבָרְכִי | תְּבֹרְכִי | תִּתְבָּרְכִי |
| אֲבָרֵךְ | אֲבֹרַךְ | אֶתְבָּרֵךְ |
| יְבָרְכוּ יְבָרְכוּ | יְבֹרְכוּ | יִתְבָּרְכוּ |
| תְּבָרַכְנָה | תְּבֹרַכְנָה | תִּתְבָּרַכְנָה |
| תְּבָרְכוּ תְּבָרְכוּ | תְּבֹרְכוּ | תִּתְבָּרְכוּ |
| תְּבָרַכְנָה | תְּבֹרַכְנָה | תִּתְבָּרַכְנָה |
| נְבָרֵךְ | נְבֹרַךְ | נִתְבָּרֵךְ |
| | | |
| נַחֵם בָּרֵךְ | — | הִתְנַחֵם הִתְבָּרֵךְ |
| בָּרְכִי בָּרְכִי | — | הִתְבָּרְכִי |
| בָּרְכוּ בָּרְכוּ | — | הִתְבָּרְכוּ |
| בָּרֵכְנָה | — | הִתְבָּרֵכְנָה |
| | | |
| נַחֵם בָּרֵךְ | נֻחַם בֹּרַךְ | הִתְנַחֵם הִתְבָּרֵךְ |
| בָּרֵךְ | | |
| מְנַחֵם מְבָרֵךְ | | מִתְנַחֵם מִתְבָּרֵךְ |
| | מְנֻחָם מְבֹרָךְ | |

|  | Qal | Niph. | Piël |
|---|---|---|---|
| *Perf. Sing.* 3.*m.* | שָׁלַח | נִשְׁלַח | שִׁלַּח |
| 3.*f.* | שָׁלְחָה | נִשְׁלְחָה | שִׁלְּחָה |
| 2.*m.* | שָׁלַחְתָּ | נִשְׁלַחְתָּ | שִׁלַּחְתָּ |
| 2.*f.* | שָׁלַחַתְּ | נִשְׁלַחַתְּ | שִׁלַּחַתְּ |
| 1.*c.* | שָׁלַחְתִּי | נִשְׁלַחְתִּי | שִׁלַּחְתִּי |
| *Plur.* 3.*c.* | שָׁלְחוּ | נִשְׁלְחוּ | שִׁלְּחוּ |
| 2.*m.* | שְׁלַחְתֶּם | נִשְׁלַחְתֶּם | שִׁלַּחְתֶּם |
| 2.*f.* | שְׁלַחְתֶּן | נִשְׁלַחְתֶּן | שִׁלַּחְתֶּן |
| 1.*c.* | שָׁלַחְנוּ | נִשְׁלַחְנוּ | שִׁלַּחְנוּ |
|  |  |  |  |
| *Impf. Sing.* 3.*m.* | יִשְׁלַח | יִשָּׁלַח | יְשַׁלַּח |
| 3.*f.* | תִּשְׁלַח | תִּשָּׁלַח | תְּשַׁלַּח |
| 2.*m.* | תִּשְׁלַח | תִּשָּׁלַח | תְּשַׁלַּח |
| 2.*f.* | תִּשְׁלְחִי | תִּשָּׁלְחִי | תְּשַׁלְּחִי |
| 1.*c.* | אֶשְׁלַח | אֶשָּׁלַח | אֲשַׁלַּח |
| *Plur.* 3.*m.* | יִשְׁלְחוּ | יִשָּׁלְחוּ | יְשַׁלְּחוּ |
| 3.*f.* | תִּשְׁלַחְנָה | תִּשָּׁלַחְנָה | תְּשַׁלַּחְנָה |
| 2.*m.* | תִּשְׁלְחוּ | תִּשָּׁלְחוּ | תְּשַׁלְּחוּ |
| 2.*f.* | תִּשְׁלַחְנָה | תִּשָּׁלַחְנָה | תְּשַׁלַּחְנָה |
| 1.*c.* | נִשְׁלַח | נִשָּׁלַח | נְשַׁלַּח |
|  |  |  |  |
| *Imp. Sing.* 2.*m.* | שְׁלַח | הִשָּׁלַח | שַׁלַּח |
| 2.*f.* | שִׁלְחִי | הִשָּׁלְחִי | שַׁלְּחִי |
| *Plur.* 2.*m.* | שִׁלְחוּ | הִשָּׁלְחוּ | שַׁלְּחוּ |
| 2.*f.* | שְׁלַחְנָה | הִשָּׁלַחְנָה | שַׁלַּחְנָה |
| *Jussive 3 sing.* | יִשְׁלַח | יִשָּׁלַח | יְשַׁלַּח |
| *vāv cons. impf.* | וַיִּשְׁלַח | וַיִּשָּׁלַח | וַיְשַׁלַּח |
| *Impf with suff.* | יִשְׁלָחֵנִי | &c. |  |
|  |  |  |  |
| *Inf. cstr.* | שְׁלֹחַ | הִשָּׁלֵחַ | שַׁלַּח |
| *absol.* | שָׁלוֹחַ | נִשְׁלֹחַ | שַׁלֵּחַ |
| *Part. act.* | שֹׁלֵחַ |  | מְשַׁלֵּחַ |
| *pass.* | שָׁלוּחַ | נִשְׁלָח |  |

- 182 -

| Pual | Hitp. | Hiph. | Hoph. |
|------|-------|-------|-------|
| שֻׁלַּח | הִשְׁתַּלַּח | הִשְׁלִיחַ | הֻשְׁלַח |
| שֻׁלְּחָה | הִשְׁתַּלְּחָה | הִשְׁלִיחָה | הֻשְׁלְחָה |
| שֻׁלַּחְתָּ | הִשְׁתַּלַּחְתָּ | הִשְׁלַחְתָּ | הֻשְׁלַחְתָּ |
| שֻׁלַּחַתְּ | הִשְׁתַּלַּחַתְּ | הִשְׁלַחַתְּ | הֻשְׁלַחַתְּ |
| שֻׁלַּחְתִּי | הִשְׁתַּלַּחְתִּי | הִשְׁלַחְתִּי | הֻשְׁלַחְתִּי |
| שֻׁלְּחוּ | הִשְׁתַּלְּחוּ | הִשְׁלִיחוּ | הֻשְׁלְחוּ |
| שֻׁלַּחְתֶּם | הִשְׁתַּלַּחְתֶּם | הִשְׁלַחְתֶּם | הֻשְׁלַחְתֶּם |
| שֻׁלַּחְתֶּן | הִשְׁתַּלַּחְתֶּן | הִשְׁלַחְתֶּן | הֻשְׁלַחְתֶּן |
| שֻׁלַּחְנוּ | הִשְׁתַּלַּחְנוּ | הִשְׁלַחְנוּ | הֻשְׁלַחְנוּ |
| | | | |
| יְשֻׁלַּח | יִשְׁתַּלַּח | יַשְׁלִיחַ | יֻשְׁלַח |
| תְּשֻׁלַּח | תִּשְׁתַּלַּח | תַּשְׁלִיחַ | תֻּשְׁלַח |
| תְּשֻׁלַּח | תִּשְׁתַּלַּח | תַּשְׁלִיחַ | תֻּשְׁלַח |
| תְּשֻׁלְּחִי | תִּשְׁתַּלְּחִי | תַּשְׁלִיחִי | תֻּשְׁלְחִי |
| אֲשֻׁלַּח | אֶשְׁתַּלַּח | אַשְׁלִיחַ | אֻשְׁלַח |
| יְשֻׁלְּחוּ | יִשְׁתַּלְּחוּ | יַשְׁלִיחוּ | יֻשְׁלְחוּ |
| תְּשֻׁלַּחְנָה | תִּשְׁתַּלַּחְנָה | תַּשְׁלַחְנָה | תֻּשְׁלַחְנָה |
| תְּשֻׁלְּחוּ | תִּשְׁתַּלְּחוּ | תַּשְׁלִיחוּ | תֻּשְׁלְחוּ |
| תְּשֻׁלַּחְנָה | תִּשְׁתַּלַּחְנָה | תַּשְׁלַחְנָה | תֻּשְׁלַחְנָה |
| נְשֻׁלַּח | נִשְׁתַּלַּח | נַשְׁלִיחַ | נֻשְׁלַח |
| | | | |
| — | הִשְׁתַּלַּח | הַשְׁלַח | — |
| — | הִשְׁתַּלְּחִי | הַשְׁלִיחִי | — |
| — | הִשְׁתַּלְּחוּ | הַשְׁלִיחוּ | — |
| — | הִשְׁתַּלַּחְנָה | הַשְׁלַחְנָה | — |
| — | יִשְׁתַּלַּח | יַשְׁלַח | — |
| — | וַיִּשְׁתַּלַּח | וַיַּשְׁלַח | — |
| | | | |
| | הִשְׁתַּלַּח | הַשְׁלִיחַ | |
| | | הַשְׁלֵחַ | הֻשְׁלֵחַ |
| | מִשְׁתַּלֵּחַ | מַשְׁלִיחַ | |
| מְשֻׁלָּח | | | מֻשְׁלָח |

|  | Qal | | Niph. |
|---|---|---|---|
| *Perf. Sing.* 3.*m.* | מָצָא | מָלֵא | נִמְצָא |
| 3.*f.* | מָצְאָה | מָלְאָה | נִמְצְאָה |
| 2.*m.* | מָצָאתָ | מָלֵאתָ | נִמְצֵאתָ |
| 2.*f.* | מָצָאת | מָלֵאת | נִמְצֵאת |
| 1.*c.* | מָצָאתִי | מָלֵאתִי | נִמְצֵאתִי |
| *Plur.* 3.*c.* | מָצְאוּ | מָלְאוּ | נִמְצְאוּ |
| 2.*m.* | מְצָאתֶם | מְלֵאתֶם | נִמְצֵאתֶם |
| 2.*f.* | מְצָאתֶן | מְלֵאתֶן | נִמְצֵאתֶן |
| 1.*c.* | מָצָאנוּ | מָלֵאנוּ | נִמְצֵאנוּ |
|  |  |  |  |
| *Impf. Sing.* 3.*m.* | יִמְצָא | יִמְלָא | יִמָּצֵא |
| 3.*f.* | תִּמְצָא | תִּמְלָא | תִּמָּצֵא |
| 2.*m.* | תִּמְצָא | תִּמְלָא | תִּמָּצֵא |
| 2.*f.* | תִּמְצְאִי | תִּמְלְאִי | תִּמָּצְאִי |
| 1.*c.* | אֶמְצָא | אֶמְלָא | אֶמָּצֵא |
| *Plur.* 3.*m.* | יִמְצְאוּ | יִמְלְאוּ | יִמָּצְאוּ |
| 3.*f.* | תִּמְצֶאנָה | תִּמְלֶאנָה | תִּמָּצֶאנָה |
| 2.*m.* | תִּמְצְאוּ | תִּמְלְאוּ | תִּמָּצְאוּ |
| 2.*f.* | תִּמְצֶאנָה | תִּמְלֶאנָה | תִּמָּצֶאנָה |
| 1.*c.* | נִמְצָא | נִמְלָא | נִמָּצֵא |
|  |  |  |  |
| *Imp. Sing.* 2.*m.* | מְצָא | מְלָא | הִמָּצֵא |
| 2.*f.* | מִצְאִי | מִלְאִי | הִמָּצְאִי |
| *Plur.* 2.*m.* | מִצְאוּ | מִלְאוּ | הִמָּצְאוּ |
| 2.*f.* | מְצֶאנָה | מְלֶאנָה | הִמָּצֶאנָה |
| *Jussive* 3 *sing.* | יִמְצָא | יִמְלָא | יִמָּצֵא |
| *vāv cons. impf.* | וַיִּמְצָא | וַיִּמְלָא | וַיִּמָּצֵא |
| *vāv cons. perf.* | וּמָצָאתָ | וּמָלֵאתָ | וְנִמְצֵאתָ |
| *Impf. with suff.* | יִמְצָאֵנִי | יִמְלָאֵנִי |  |
|  |  |  |  |
| *Inf. cstr.* | מְצֹא | מְלֹא | הִמָּצֵא |
| *absol.* | מָצוֹא | מָלוֹא | נִמְצֹא |
| *Part. act.* | מֹצֵא | מָלֵא | נִמְצָא |
| *pass.* | מָצוּא |  | נִמְצָא |

| Piēl | Pual | Hitp. | Hiph. | Hoph. |
|---|---|---|---|---|
| מִצֵּא | מֻצָּא | הִתְמַצֵּא | הִמְצִיא | הֻמְצָא |
| מִצְּאָה | מֻצְּאָה | as | הִמְצִיאָה | הֻמְצְאָה |
| מִצֵּאתָ | מֻצֵּאתָ | Pi. | הִמְצֵאתָ | הֻמְצֵאתָ |
| מִצֵּאת | מֻצֵּאת | | הִמְצֵאת | as |
| מִצֵּאתִי | מֻצֵּאתִי | | הִמְצֵאתִי | Pu. |
| מִצְּאוּ | מֻצְּאוּ | | הִמְצִיאוּ | |
| מִצֵּאתֶם | מֻצֵּאתֶם | | הִמְצֵאתֶם | |
| מִצֵּאתֶן | מֻצֵּאתֶן | | הִמְצֵאתֶן | |
| מִצֵּאנוּ | מֻצֵּאנוּ | | הִמְצֵאנוּ | |
| | | | | |
| יְמַצֵּא | יְמֻצָּא | יִתְמַצֵּא | יַמְצִיא | יֻמְצָא |
| תְּמַצֵּא | as | as | תַּמְצִיא | as |
| תְּמַצֵּא | Qal | Pi. | תַּמְצִיא | Qal |
| תְּמַצְּאִי | | | תַּמְצִיאִי | |
| אֲמַצֵּא | | | אַמְצִיא | |
| יְמַצְּאוּ | | | יַמְצִיאוּ | |
| תְּמַצֶּאנָה | | | תַּמְצֶאנָה | |
| תְּמַצְּאוּ | | | תַּמְצִיאוּ | |
| תְּמַצֶּאנָה | | | תַּמְצֶאנָה | |
| נְמַצֵּא | | | נַמְצִיא | |
| | | | | |
| מַצֵּא | — | הִתְמַצֵּא | הַמְצֵא | — |
| מַצְּאִי | — | | הַמְצִיאִי | — |
| מַצְּאוּ | — | | הַמְצִיאוּ | — |
| מַצֶּאנָה | — | | הַמְצֶאנָה | — |
| | | | יַמְצֵא | |
| | | | וַיַּמְצֵא | |
| | | | | |
| וּמְצֵאתָ | | | | |
| יְמַצְּאֵנִי | | | יַמְצִיאֵנִי | |
| | | | | |
| מַצֵּא | | הִתְמַצֵּא | הַמְצִיא | הֻמְצָא |
| מַצֹּא | | | הַמְצֵא | |
| מְמַצֵּא | | מִתְמַצֵּא | מַמְצִיא | |
| | מְמֻצָּא | | | מֻמְצָא |

Verbs פ״ו

|  |  | Qal | | | Niph. |
|---|---|---|---|---|---|
| Perf. Sing. 3.m. | יָשַׁב | יָרֵא | יָרַשׁ | נוֹשַׁב |
| 3.f. | as | יָרְאָה | as | נוֹשְׁבָה |
| 2.m. | קָטַל | יָרֵאתָ | קָטַל | נוֹשַׁבְתָּ |
| 2.f. |  | יָרֵאת |  | &c. |
| 1.c. |  | יָרֵאתִי |  |  |
| Plur. 3.c. |  | יָרְאוּ |  |  |
| 2.m. |  | יְרֵאתֶם |  |  |
| 2.f. |  | יְרֵאתֶן |  |  |
| 1.c. |  | יָרֵאנוּ |  |  |
| Impf. Sing. 3.m. | יֵשֵׁב | יִירָא | יִירַשׁ | יִוָּשֵׁב |
| 3.f. | תֵּשֵׁב | תִּירָא | תִּירַשׁ | תִּוָּשֵׁב |
| 2.m. | תֵּשֵׁב | תִּירָא | תִּירַשׁ | תִּוָּשֵׁב |
| 2.f. | תֵּשְׁבִי | תִּירְאִי | תִּירְשִׁי | תִּוָּשְׁבִי |
| 1.c. | אֵשֵׁב | אִירָא | אִירַשׁ | אִוָּשֵׁב |
| Plur. 3.m. | יֵשְׁבוּ | יִירְאוּ | יִירְשׁוּ | יִוָּשְׁבוּ |
| 3.f. | תֵּשַׁבְנָה | תִּירֶאנָה | תִּירַשְׁנָה | תִּוָּשַׁבְנָה |
| 2.m. | תֵּשְׁבוּ | תִּירְאוּ | תִּירְשׁוּ | תִּוָּשְׁבוּ |
| 2.f. | תֵּשַׁבְנָה | תִּירֶאנָה | תִּירַשְׁנָה | תִּוָּשַׁבְנָה |
| 1.c. | נֵשֵׁב | נִירָא | נִירַשׁ | נִוָּשֵׁב |
| Imp. Sing. 2.m. | שֵׁב (שְׁבָה) | יְרָא | רַשׁ (רֵשׁ) | הִוָּשֵׁב |
| 2.f. | שְׁבִי | יְרְאִי | רְשִׁי | הִוָּשְׁבִי |
| Plur. 2.m. | שְׁבוּ | יְרְאוּ | רְשׁוּ | הִוָּשְׁבוּ |
| 2.f. | שֵׁבְנָה | יְרֶאנָה | רַשְׁנָה | הִוָּשַׁבְנָה |
| Jussive 3 sing. |  |  |  |  |
| vāv cons. impf. | וַיֵּשֶׁב |  | וַיִּרַשׁ |  |
| Cohort. 1 sing. | אֵשְׁבָה |  | אִירְשָׁה |  |
| Impf. in a with suff. | יָדְעֵנִי | Imper. | דָּעֵהוּ |  |
| Inf. cstr. | שֶׁבֶת | יִרְאָה | רֶשֶׁת | הִוָּשֵׁב |
| absol. | יָשׁוֹב |  | יָרוֹשׁ |  |
| Part. act. | יֹשֵׁב | יָרֵא | יֹרֵשׁ |  |
| pass. | יָשׁוּב |  | יָרוּשׁ | נוֹשָׁב |

## PĒ VAV VERBS

| | | Verbs פ״י | | Verbs assimilating | | |
|---|---|---|---|---|---|---|
| Hiph. | Hoph. | Qal | Hiph. | Qal | Niph. | Hiph. |
| הוֹשִׁיב | הוּשַׁב | יָנַק | הֵינִיק | יָצַת | נִצַּת | הִצִּית |
| הוֹשִׁיבָה | הוּשְׁבָה | as | הֵינִיקָה | יָצַק | | |
| הוֹשַׁבְתָּ | הוּשַׁבְתָּ | קָטַל | הֵינַקְתָּ | | | |
| הוֹשַׁבְתְּ | &c. | | הֵינַקְתְּ | | | |
| הוֹשַׁבְתִּי | | | הֵינַקְתִּי | | | |
| הוֹשִׁיבוּ | | | הֵינִיקוּ | | | |
| הוֹשַׁבְתֶּם | | | הֵינַקְתֶּם | | | |
| הוֹשַׁבְתֶּן | | | הֵינַקְתֶּן | | | |
| הוֹשַׁבְנוּ | | | הֵינַקְנוּ | | | |
| יוֹשִׁיב | יוּשַׁב | יִינַק | יֵינִיק | יֵצַת | | יַצִּית |
| תּוֹשִׁיב | תּוּשַׁב | תִּינַק | תֵּינִיק | יֵצַק | | |
| תּוֹשִׁיב | תּוּשַׁב | תִּינַק | תֵּינִיק | | | |
| תּוֹשִׁיבִי | תּוּשְׁבִי | תִּינְקִי | תֵּינִיקִי | | | |
| אוֹשִׁיב | &c. | אִינַק | אֵינִיק | | | |
| יוֹשִׁיבוּ | | יִינְקוּ | יֵינִיקוּ | | | |
| תּוֹשֵׁבְנָה | | תִּינַקְנָה | תֵּינַקְנָה | | | |
| תּוֹשִׁיבוּ | | תִּינְקוּ | תֵּינִיקוּ | | | |
| תּוֹשֵׁבְנָה | | תִּינַקְנָה | תֵּינַקְנָה | | | |
| נוֹשִׁיב | | נִינַק | נֵינִיק | | | |
| הוֹשֵׁב | | | הֵינַק | | | |
| הוֹשִׁיבִי | | | הֵינִיקִי | | | |
| הוֹשִׁיבוּ | | | הֵינִיקוּ | | | |
| הוֹשֵׁבְנָה | | | הֵינַקְנָה | | | |
| יוֹשֵׁב | | | יֵינַק | | | יֵצֵת |
| וַיֹּושֶׁב | | | וַיֵּינַק | | | |
| הוֹשִׁיב | הוּשֵׁב | | הֵינִיק | | | |
| הוֹשֵׁב | | | הֵינַק | | | |
| מוֹשִׁיב | | יוֹנֵק | מֵינִיק | | | מַצִּית |
| | מוּשָׁב | יָנוּק | יָנוּק | | | |

## Qal

| | act. | stat. | stat. | |
|---|---|---|---|---|
| Perf. Sing. 3.m. | קָם | מֵת | בּוֹשׁ | בָּן |
| 3.f. | קָמָה | מֵתָה | בּוֹשָׁה | בָּנָה |
| 2.m. | קַמְתָּ | מַתָּה | בֹּשְׁתָּ | בָּנְתָּ |
| 2.f. | קַמְתְּ | מַתְּ | בֹּשְׁתְּ | בָּנְתְּ |
| 1.c. | קַמְתִּי | מַתִּי | בֹּשְׁתִּי | בָּנְתִּי |
| Plur. 3.c. | קָמוּ | מֵתוּ | בּוֹשׁוּ | בָּנוּ |
| 2.m. | קַמְתֶּם | מַתֶּם | בָּשְׁתֶּם | בָּנְתֶּם |
| 2.f. | קַמְתֶּן | מַתֶּן | בָּשְׁתֶּן | בָּנְתֶּן |
| 1.c. | קַמְנוּ | מַתְנוּ | בֹּשְׁנוּ | בָּנוּ |
| | | | | |
| Impf. Sing. 3.m. | יָקוּם | יָמוּת | יֵבוֹשׁ | יָבִין |
| 3.f. | תָּקוּם | תָּמוּת | תֵּבוֹשׁ | תָּבִין |
| 2.m. | תָּקוּם | תָּמוּת | תֵּבוֹשׁ | תָּבִין |
| 2.f. | תָּקוּמִי | תָּמוּתִי | תֵּבוֹשִׁי | תָּבִינִי |
| 1.c. | אָקוּם | אָמוּת | אֵבוֹשׁ | אָבִין |
| Plur. 3.m. | יָקוּמוּ | יָמוּתוּ | יֵבוֹשׁוּ | יָבִינוּ |
| 3.f. | תְּקוּמֶינָה | תְּמוּתֶינָה | תֵּבֹשְׁנָה | תְּבִינֶינָה |
| 2.m. | תָּקוּמוּ | תָּמוּתוּ | תֵּבוֹשׁוּ | תָּבִינוּ |
| 2.f. | תְּקוּמֶינָה | תְּמוּתֶינָה | תֵּבֹשְׁנָה | תְּבִינֶינָה |
| 1.c. | נָקוּם | נָמוּת | נֵבוֹשׁ | נָבִין |
| | | | | |
| Imp. Sing. 2.m. | קוּמָה קוּם | מוּת | בּוֹשׁ | בִּין |
| 2.f. | קוּמִי | מוּתִי | בּוֹשִׁי | בִּינִי |
| Plur. 2.m. | קוּמוּ | מוּתוּ | בֹּשׁוּ | בִּינוּ |
| 2.f. | קֹמְנָה | מֹתְנָה | בֹּשְׁנָה | |
| Jussive 3 sing. | יָקֹם | יָמֹת | | יָבֵן |
| vāv cons. impf. | וַיָּקָם | וַיָּמָת | | וַיָּבֶן |
| Cohort. 1 sing. | אָקוּמָה | אָמוּתָה | | אָבִינָה |
| vāv cons. perf. | וְקַמְתָּ | וּמַתָּה | | וּבָנְתָּ |
| | | | | |
| Inf. cstr. | קוּם | מוּת | בּוֹשׁ | בִּין |
| absol. | קוֹם | מוֹת | בּוֹשׁ | בּוֹן |
| Part. act. | קָמָה קָם | מֵת | בּוֹשׁ | בָּן |
| pass. | קוּמָה קוּם | | | (בּוּן בִּין) |

| Niph. | Hiph. | Hoph. | Forms of Intens. | | |
|---|---|---|---|---|---|
| | | | Act. | Pass. | Reflex. |
| נָקוֹם | הֵקִים | הוּקַם | קַיֵּם | | הִתְקַיֵּם |
| נָקֹומָה | הֵקִימָה | הוּקְמָה | קוֹמֵם | קוֹמַם | הִתְקוֹמֵם |
| נְקוּמֹת | הֲקִימֹת | הוּקַמְתְּ | קָמְקֵם | קָמְקַם | הִתְקַמְקֵם |
| נְקוּמֹת | הֲקִימֹות | הוּקַמְתְּ | like Piēl &c. of the | | |
| נְקוּמֹתִי | הֲקִימֹותִי | הוּקַמְתִּי | Regular Verb | | |
| נָקֹומוּ | הֵקִימוּ | הוּקְמוּ | | | |
| נְקוּמֹתֶם | הֲקִימֹותֶם | הוּקַמְתֶּם | | | |
| נְקוּמֹתֶן | הֲקִימֹותֶן | הוּקַמְתֶּן | | | |
| נְקֹומוּנוּ | הֲקִימֹונוּ | הוּקַמְנוּ | | | |
| | | | | | |
| יִקּוֹם | יָקִים | יוּקַם | | | |
| תִּקּוֹם | תָּקִים | תּוּקַם | | | |
| תִּקּוֹם | תָּקִים | תּוּקַם | | | |
| תִּקֹּומִי | תָּקִימִי | תּוּקְמִי | | | |
| אֶקּוֹם | אָקִים | אוּקַם | | | |
| יִקֹּומוּ | יָקִימוּ | יוּקְמוּ | | | |
| תִּקּוֹמֶינָה/תָּקֵמְנָה | | תּוּקַמְנָה | | | |
| תִּקֹּומוּ | תָּקִימוּ | תּוּקְמוּ | | | |
| | תָּקֵמְנָה | תּוּקַמְנָה | | | |
| נִקּוֹם | נָקִים | נוּקַם | | | |
| | | | | | |
| הִקֹּום הָקֵם/הָקִימָה | | | | | |
| הִקֹּומִי | הָקִימִי | | | | |
| הִקֹּומוּ | הָקִימוּ | | | | |
| הִקֹּומְנָה | הָקֵמְנָה | | | | |
| | יָקֵם | | | | |
| | וַיָּקֶם | | | | |
| | אָקִימָה | | | | |
| | וַהֲקִימֹותָ | | | | |
| | | | | | |
| הִקּוֹם | הָקִים | הוּקַם | | | |
| הִקּוֹם , נָקוֹם | הָקֵם | | | | |
| | מֵקִים/מְקִימָה f. | | | | |
| נָקוֹם נְקוּמָה f. | | מוּקָם | | | |

| | Qal | Niph. | Piēl | Pual |
|---|---|---|---|---|
| *Perf. Sing.* 3.*m.* | גָּלָה | נִגְלָה | גִּלָּה | גֻּלָּה |
| 3.*f.* | גָּלְתָה | נִגְלְתָה | גִּלְּתָה | גֻּלְּתָה |
| 2.*m.* | גָּלִיתָ | נִגְלֵיתָ | גִּלִּיתָ/-ֵיתָ | גֻּלֵּיתָ |
| 2.*f.* | גָּלִית | נִגְלֵית | גִּלִּית | גֻּלֵּית |
| 1.*c.* | גָּלִיתִי | נִגְלֵיתִי | גִּלִּיתִי/-ֵיתִי | גֻּלֵּיתִי |
| *Plur.* 3.*c.* | גָּלוּ | נִגְלוּ | גִּלּוּ | גֻּלּוּ |
| 2.*m.* | גְּלִיתֶם | נִגְלֵיתֶם | גִּלִּיתֶם | גֻּלֵּיתֶם |
| 2.*f.* | גְּלִיתֶן | נִגְלֵיתֶן | גִּלִּיתֶן | גֻּלֵּיתֶן |
| 1.*c.* | גָּלִינוּ | נִגְלֵינוּ | גִּלִּינוּ | גֻּלֵּינוּ |
| | | | | |
| *Impf. Sing.* 3.*m.* | יִגְלֶה | יִגָּלֶה | יְגַלֶּה | יְגֻלֶּה |
| 3.*f.* | תִּגְלֶה | תִּגָּלֶה | תְּגַלֶּה | תְּגֻלֶּה |
| 2.*m.* | תִּגְלֶה | תִּגָּלֶה | תְּגַלֶּה | תְּגֻלֶּה |
| 2.*f.* | תִּגְלִי | תִּגָּלִי | תְּגַלִּי | תְּגֻלִּי |
| 1.*c.* | אֶגְלֶה | אֶגָּלֶה/אִגָּלֶה | אֲגַלֶּה | אֲגֻלֶּה |
| *Plur.* 3.*m.* | יִגְלוּ | יִגָּלוּ | יְגַלּוּ | יְגֻלּוּ |
| 3.*f.* | תִּגְלֶינָה | תִּגָּלֶינָה | תְּגַלֶּינָה | תְּגֻלֶּינָה |
| 2.*m* | תִּגְלוּ | תִּגָּלוּ | תְּגַלּוּ | תְּגֻלּוּ |
| 2.*f.* | תִּגְלֶינָה | תִּגָּלֶינָה | תְּגַלֶּינָה | תְּגֻלֶּינָה |
| 1.*c.* | נִגְלֶה | נִגָּלֶה | נְגַלֶּה | נְגֻלֶּה |
| | | | | |
| *Imp. Sing.* 2.*m.* | גְּלֵה | הִגָּלֵה/הִגָּל | גַּלֵּה/גַּל | |
| 2.*f.* | גְּלִי | הִגָּלִי | גַּלִּי | |
| *Plur.* 2.*m.* | גְּלוּ | הִגָּלוּ | גַּלּוּ | |
| 2.*f.* | גְּלֶינָה | הִגָּלֶינָה | גַּלֶּינָה | |
| *Juss.* 3 *sing. m.* | יִגֶל | יִגָּל | יְגַל | |
| *vāv cons. impf.* | וַיִּגֶל | וַיִּגָּל | וַיְגַל | |
| *vāv cons. perf.* | וְגָלִיתָ | וְנִגְלֵיתָ | וְגִלִּיתָ | |
| | | | | |
| *Inf. cstr.* | גְּלוֹת | הִגָּלוֹת | גַּלּוֹת | גֻּלּוֹת |
| *absol.* | גָּלֹה | נִגְלֹה | גַּלֵּה | גֻּלֹּה |
| *Part. act.* | *f.* גֹּלֶה/-לָה | | מְגַלֶּה | |
| *pass.* | גָּלוּי/גְּלוּיָה | נִגְלֶה | | מְגֻלֶּה |
| *intrans.* | קָשֶׁה/-שָׁה | | | |

| Hitp. | Hiph. | Hoph. | Suffixes | | |
|---|---|---|---|---|---|
| | | | **Suffixes** | | |
| הִתְנַגְּלָה | הִגְלָה | הָגְלָה | *Perf.Qal Sing.* 1 c. | גָּלַנִי / ־ַנִי |
| הִתְנַגַּלְתָה | הִגְלְתָה | הָגְלְתָה | 2 m. | גָּלְךָ |
| הִתְנַגַּלִית/־ֵית | הִגְלִית/־ֵית | הִגְלִית | 2 f. | גָּלֵךְ |
| הִתְנַגַּלִית/־ֵית | הִגְלִית | הָגְלִית | 3 m. | גָּלָהוּ |
| הִתְנַגַּלִיתִי | הִגְלֵיתִי/־ֵיתִי | הִגְלֵיתִי | 3 f. | גָּלָהּ |
| הִתְנַגְּלוּ | הִגְלוּ | הָגְלוּ | *Plur.* 1 c. | גָּלָנוּ |
| הִתְנַגַּלִיתֶם | הִגְלֵיתֶם | הִגְלֵיתֶם | 2 m. | |
| הִתְנַגַּלִיתֶן | הִגְלֵיתֶן | הִגְלֵיתֶן | 2 f. | |
| הִתְנַגַּלִינוּ | הִגְלֵינוּ | הִגְלֵינוּ | 3 m. | גָּלָם |
| | | | 3 f. | |
| הִתְנַגְּלֶה | יַגְלֶה | יָגְלֶה | *Impf. Sing.* 1 c. | יַגְלֵנִי |
| תִּתְנַגְּלֶה | תַּגְלֶה | תָּגְלֶה | 2 m. | יַגְלְךָ |
| תִּתְנַגְּלֶה | תַּגְלֶה | תָּגְלֶה | 2 f. | יַגְלֵךְ |
| תִּתְנַגְּלִי | תַּגְלִי | תָּגְלִי | 3 m. | יַגְלֵהוּ |
| אֶתְנַגְּלֶה | אַגְלֶה | אָגְלֶה | 3 f. | יַגְלֶהָ |
| יִתְנַגְּלוּ | יַגְלוּ | יָגְלוּ | *Plur.* 1 c. | יַגְלֵנוּ |
| תִּתְנַגַּלֶּינָה | תַּגְלֶינָה | תָּגְלֶינָה | 2 m. | |
| תִּתְנַגְּלוּ | תַּגְלוּ | תָּגְלוּ | 2 f. | |
| תִּתְנַגַּלֶּינָה | תַּגְלֶינָה | תָּגְלֶינָה | 3 m. | יַגְלֵם |
| נִתְנַגְּלֶה | נַגְלֶה | נָגְלֶה | 3 f. | |
| הִתְנַגְּלֶה/־גַּל | הַגְלֶה/הֶגֶל | | *Imp. Sing.* 1 c. | גָּלֵנִי |
| הִתְנַגְּלִי | הַגְלִי | | 3 m. | גָּלֵהוּ |
| הִתְנַגְּלוּ | הַגְלוּ | | 3 f. | גָּלֶהָ |
| הִתְנַגַּלֶּינָה | הַגְלֶינָה | | *Plur.* 1 c. | גָּלֵנוּ |
| יִתְנַגַּל | יֶגֶל | | 3 m. | גָּלֵם |
| וַיִּתְנַגַּל | וַיֶּגֶל | | | |
| הִתְנַגְּלוֹת | הַגְלוֹת | הָגְלוֹת | | |
| הִתְנַגְּלֶה | הַגְלֶה | הָגְלֶה | | |
| מִתְנַגְּלֶה | מַגְלֶה | | | |
| | | מָגְלֶה | | |

# PĒ NUN VERBS

| | | Qal | Niph. | Hiph. | Hoph. |
|---|---|---|---|---|---|
| Perf. Sing. 3.m. | (נְגַשׁ) | נָפַל | נִגַּשׁ | הִגִּישׁ | הֻגַּשׁ |
| 3.f. | (נִגְּשָׁה) | נָפְלָה | נִגְּשָׁה | הִגִּישָׁה | הֻגְּשָׁה |
| 2.m. | (נִגַּשְׁתָּ) | נָפַלְתָּ | נִגַּשְׁתָּ | הִגַּשְׁתָּ | הֻגַּשְׁתָּ |
| | &c. | &c. | &c. | &c. | &c. |
| Impf. Sing. 3.m. | יִגַּשׁ | יִפֹּל | יִנָּגֵשׁ | יַגִּישׁ | יֻגַּשׁ |
| 3.f. | תִּגַּשׁ | תִּפֹּל | תִּנָּגֵשׁ | תַּגִּישׁ | &c. |
| 2.m. | תִּגַּשׁ | תִּפֹּל | תִּנָּגֵשׁ | תַּגִּישׁ | |
| 2.f. | תִּגְּשִׁי | תִּפְּלִי | תִּנָּגְשִׁי | תַּגִּישִׁי | |
| 1.c. | אֶגַּשׁ | אֶפֹּל | אֶנָּגֵשׁ | אַגִּישׁ | |
| Plur. 3.m. | יִגְּשׁוּ | יִפְּלוּ | יִנָּגְשׁוּ | יַגִּישׁוּ | |
| 3.f. | תִּגַּשְׁנָה | תִּפֹּלְנָה | תִּנָּגַשְׁנָה | תַּגֵּשְׁנָה | |
| 2.m. | תִּגְּשׁוּ | תִּפְּלוּ | תִּנָּגְשׁוּ | תַּגִּישׁוּ | |
| 2.f. | תִּגַּשְׁנָה | תִּפֹּלְנָה | תִּנָּגַשְׁנָה | תַּגֵּשְׁנָה | |
| 1.c. | נִגַּשׁ | נִפֹּל | נִנָּגֵשׁ | נַגִּישׁ | |
| Imp. Sing. 2.m. | גַּשׁ/גְּשָׁה | נְפֹל | הִנָּגֵשׁ | הַגֵּשׁ | — |
| 2.f. | גְּשִׁי | נִפְלִי | הִנָּגְשִׁי | הַגִּישִׁי | — |
| Plur. 2.m. | גְּשׁוּ | נִפְלוּ | הִנָּגְשׁוּ | הַגִּישׁוּ | — |
| 2.f. | גַּשְׁנָה | נְפֹלְנָה | הִנָּגַשְׁנָה | הַגֵּשְׁנָה | — |
| Jussive 3 sing. | | יִפֹּל | | יַגֵּשׁ | |
| vāv cons. impf. | | וַיִּפֹּל | | וַיַּגֵּשׁ | |
| Cohort. 1 sing. | אֶגְּשָׁה | אֶפְּלָה | | אַגִּישָׁה | |
| vāv cons. perf. | וְנָגַשְׁתָּ | וְנָפַלְתָּ | | | |
| Inf. cstr. | גֶּשֶׁת | נְפֹל | הִנָּגֵשׁ | הַגִּישׁ | הֻגַּשׁ |
| absol. | נָגוֹשׁ | נָפוֹל | הִנָּגֵשׁ | הַגֵּשׁ | הֻגֵּשׁ |
| Part. act. | נֹגֵשׁ | נֹפֵל | | מַגִּישׁ | |
| pass. | נָגוּשׁ | — | נִגָּשׁ | | מֻגָּשׁ |

&c.

- 192 -

# PĒ NUN VERBS

| | Qal | | Niph. | | Pass. Qal |
|---|---|---|---|---|---|
| **Perf. Sing.** 3.m. | נָתַן | לָקַח | נִתַּן | נִלְקַח | לֻקַּח |
| 3.f. | נָתְנָה | לָקְחָה | נִתְּחָה | נִלְקְחָה | לֻקְּחָה |
| 2.m. | נָתַתָּ-/תָּה | לָקַחְתָּ | נִתַּתָּ | נִלְקַחְתָּ | לֻקַּחְתָּ |
| 2.f. | נָתַתְּ | &c. | נִתַּתְּ | נִלְקַחְתְּ | לֻקַּחְתְּ |
| 1.c. | נָתַתִּי | | נִתַּתִּי | נִלְקַחְתִּי | לֻקַּחְתִּי |
| **Plur.** 3.c. | נָתְנוּ | | נִתְּנוּ | נִלְקְחוּ | לֻקְּחוּ |
| 2.m. | נְתַתֶּם | | נִתַּתֶּם | נִלְקַחְתֶּם | לֻקַּחְתֶּם |
| 2.f. | | | | | |
| 1.c. | נָתַנּוּ | | נִתַּנּוּ | נִלְקַחְנוּ | לֻקַּחְנוּ |
| **Impf. Sing.** 3.m. | יִתֵּן | יִקַּח | יִנָּתֵן | יִלָּקַח | יֻקַּח יֻתַּן |
| 3.f. | תִּתֵּן | תִּקַּח | תִּנָּתֵן | תִּלָּקַח | תֻּקַּח תֻּתַּן |
| 2.m. | תִּתֵּן | תִּקַּח | תִּנָּתֵן | תִּלָּקַח | תֻּקַּח תֻּתַּן |
| 2.f. | תִּתְּנִי | תִּקְחִי | תִּנָּתְנִי | תִּלָּקְחִי | תֻּקְחִי תֻּתְּנִי |
| 1.c. | אֶתֵּן-/תְּנָה | אֶקַּח | אֶנָּתֵן | אֶלָּקַח | אֻקַּח אֻתַּן |
| **Plur.** 3.m. | יִתְּנוּ | יִקְחוּ | יִנָּתְנוּ | יִלָּקְחוּ | יֻקְחוּ יִתְּנוּ |
| 3.f. | | | | | |
| 2.m. | תִּתְּנוּ | תִּקְחוּ | תִּנָּתְנוּ | תִּלָּקְחוּ | תֻּקְחוּ תִּתְּנוּ |
| 2.f. | | | | | |
| 1.c. | נִתֵּן | נִקַּח | נִנָּתֵן | נִלָּקַח | נֻקַּח נָתַן |
| **Imp. Sing.** 2.m. | תֵּן/תְּנָה | קַח/קְחָה | הִנָּתֵן | הִלָּקַח | — |
| 2.f. | תְּנִי | קְחִי | הִנָּתְנִי | הִלָּקְחִי | — |
| **Plur.** 2.m. | תְּנוּ | קְחוּ | הִנָּתְנוּ | הִלָּקְחוּ | — |
| 2.f. | | | | | |
| **Jussive 3 sing.** | יִתֵּן | יִקַּח | | | |
| **vāv cons. impf.** | וַיִּתֵּן | וַיִּקַּח | | | |
| **Inf. cstr.** | תֵּת/תִּתִּי (נְתֹן) | קַחַת/קַחְתִּי | הִנָּתֵן | הִלָּקַח | |
| absol. | נָתוֹן | לָקוֹחַ | הִנָּתֹן | | |
| **Part. act.** | נֹתֵן | לֹקֵחַ | | | |
| pass. | נָתוּן | לָקוּחַ | נִתָּן | נִלְקָח | |

## Qal

| | act. | | stat. | |
|---|---|---|---|---|
| Perf. Sing. 3.m. | (סַב) סָבַב | | קַל | מַל |
| 3.f. | (סָבָה) סָבְבָה | | קַלָּה | &c. |
| 2.m. | סַבֹּ֫תָ | | קַלּ֫וֹתָ | |
| 2.f. | סַבּוֹת | | קַלּוֹת | |
| 1.c. | סַבֹּ֫תִי | | קַלּ֫וֹתִי | |
| Plur. 3.c. | (סַבּוּ) סָבְבוּ | | קַלּוּ | |
| 2.m. | סַבּוֹתֶם | | קַלּוֹתֶם | |
| 2.f. | סַבּוֹתֶן | | קַלּוֹתֶן | |
| 1.c. | סַבֹּ֫ונוּ | | קַלּ֫וֹנוּ | |
| | | | | |
| Impf. Sing. 3.m. | יָסֹב | יִסֹב | יֵקַל | יִמַּל |
| 3.f. | תָּסֹב | תִּסֹב | תֵּקַל | תִּמַּל |
| 2.m. | תָּסֹב | תִּסֹב | תֵּקַל | תִּמַּל |
| 2.f. | תָּסֹ֫בִּי | תִּסְבִי | תֵּקַלִּי | תִּמְּלִי |
| 1.c. | אָסֹב | אֶסֹב | אֵקַל | אֶמַּל |
| Plur. 3.m. | יָסֹ֫בּוּ | יִסְבוּ | יֵקַלּוּ | יִמְּלוּ |
| 3.f. | תְּסֻבֶּ֫ינָה | תִּסֹבְנָה | תִּקַלֶּ֫ינָה | תִּמַּלְנָה |
| 2.m. | תָּסֹ֫בּוּ | תִּסְבוּ | תִּקַלּוּ | תִּמְּלוּ |
| 2.f. | תְּסֻבֶּ֫ינָה | תִּסֹבְנָה | תִּקַלֶּ֫ינָה | תִּמַּלְנָה |
| 1.c. | נָסֹב | נִסֹב | נֵקַל | נִמַּל |
| | | | | |
| Imp. Sing. 2.m. | סֹב | | | |
| 2.f. | סֹ֫בִּי | | | |
| Plur. 2.m. | סֹ֫בּוּ | | | |
| 2.f. | סֻבֶּ֫ינָה | | | |
| Jussive 3 sing. | יָסֹב | יִסֹב | יֵקַל | יִמַּל |
| vāv cons. impf. | וַיָּ֫סָב | וַיִּסֹב | וַיֵּקַל | וַיִּמַּל |
| Cohort. 1 sing. | אָסֹ֫בָּה | אֶסְבָה | אֶקַּ֫לָּה | אֶמְּלָה |
| vāv cons. perf. | וְסַבֹּתָ | | | |
| | | | | |
| Inf. cstr. | סֹב | | קֹל קַל | |
| absol. | סָבוֹב | | קָלוֹל | |
| Part. act. | סוֹבֵב | | קַל קָלֶה | |
| pass. | סָבוּב | | | |

# VERBS

| Niph. | Hiph. | Hoph. | Forms of Intens. | | |
|---|---|---|---|---|---|
| | | | Act. | Pass. | Reflex. |
| נָסֵב | הֵסֵב | הוּסַב | קֹלֵל | קֹלַל | הִתְקַלֵל |
| נָסֵבָּה | הֵסַבָּה | הוּסַבָּה | קוֹלֵל | קוֹלַל | הִתְקוֹלֵל |
| נְסַבּוֹת | הֲסַבּוֹת | הוּסַבּוֹת | קַלְקֵל | קָלְקַל | הִתְקַלְקֵל |
| נְסַבּוֹת | הֲסַבּוֹת | &c. | like Piel &c. in the | | |
| נְסַבּוֹתִי | הֲסִבּוֹתִי | | Regular Verb | | |
| נָסַבּוּ | הֵסַבּוּ | | | | |
| נְסַבּוֹתֶם | הֲסַבּוֹתֶם | | | | |
| נְסַבּוֹתֶן | הֲסַבּוֹתֶן | | | | |
| נְסַבּוֹנוּ | הֲסִבּוֹנוּ | | | | |
| | | | | | |
| יִסַּב | יָסֵב/יַסֵב | יוּסַב/יֻסַּב | | | |
| תִּסַּב | תָּסֵב | &c. | | | |
| תִּסַּב | תָּסֵב | | | | |
| תִּסַּבִּי | תָּסֵבִּי | | | | |
| אֶסַּב | אָסֵב | | | | |
| יִסַּבּוּ | יָסֵבּוּ | | | | |
| תִּסַּבֶּינָה | תְּסִבֶּינָה | | | | |
| תִּסַּבּוּ | תָּסֵבּוּ | | | | |
| תִּסַּבֶּינָה | תְּסִבֶּינָה | | | | |
| | נָסֵב | | | | |
| | | | | | |
| הִסַּב | הָסֵב | | | | |
| הִסַּבִּי | הָסֵבִּי | | | | |
| הִסַּבּוּ | הָסֵבּוּ | | | | |
| הִסַּבֶּינָה | הֲסִבֶּינָה | | | | |
| | יָסֵב | | | | |
| | וַיָּסֵב | | | | |
| | | | | | |
| הִסַּב | הָסֵב | הוּסַב | | | |
| הִסּוֹב | הָסֵב | | | | |
| | מֵסֵב/מְסִבָּה | | | | |
| נָסָב/נְסַבָּה | | מוּסָב | | | |

See also suffixes to

## Qal

| Perf. | | 3 s. m. | 3 s. f. | 2 s. m. | 2 s. f. |
|---|---|---|---|---|---|
| Suff. s. | כָּבֵד[1] | קָטַל | קָטְלָה | קָטַלְתָּ | קָטַלְתְּ |
| 1 c. | כְּבֵדַֽנִי | קְטָלַֽנִי | קְטָלַתְנִי/כְּבֵד׳ | קְטַלְתַּֽנִי | קְטַלְתִּֽינִי[1] |
| 2 m. | כְּבֵדְךָ | קְטָלְךָ | קְטָלַתְךָ | — | — |
| 2 f. | קְטָלָךְ/כְּבֵדֵךְ | קְטָלֵךְ | קְטָלָתֶךְ | — | — |
| 3 m. | כְּבֵדוֹ | קְטָלוֹ | קְטָלַתְהוּ/‑תּוּ | קְטַלְתּוֹ/‑תָּהוּ | קְטַלְתִּֽיהוּ |
| 3 f. | כְּבֵדָהּ | קְטָלָהּ | קְטָלַתָּה | קְטַלְתָּהּ | קְטַלְתִּֽיהָ |
| pl. | | | | | |
| 1 c. | כְּבֵדָֽנוּ | קְטָלָֽנוּ | קְטָלַתְנוּ | קְטַלְתָּֽנוּ | קְטַלְתִּֽינוּ |
| 2 m. | כְּבֶדְכֶם | קְטַלְכֶם | — | — | — |
| 2 f. | כְּבֶדְכֶן | קְטַלְכֶן | — | — | — |
| 3 m. | כְּבֵדָם | קְטָלָם | קְטָלַתַם | קְטַלְתָּם | קְטַלְתִּים |
| 3 f. | כְּבֵדָן | קְטָלָן | קְטָלַתַן | קְטַלְתָּן | קְטַלְתִּין |

| Impf. | | 3 s. m. | 3 pl. m. | Imper. s. | pl. |
|---|---|---|---|---|---|
| Suff. s. | יִכְבַּד | יִקְטֹל | יִקְטְלוּ | קְטֹל/כְּבַד | קִטְלוּ |
| 1 c. | יִכְבָּדֵֽנִי | יִקְטְלֵֽנִי | יִקְטְלֽוּנִי/יִכְבַּד׳ | קָטְלֵֽנִי/כְּבַד׳[2] | קִטְלֽוּנִי/כְּבַד׳ |
| 2 m. | יִכְבָּדְךָ | יִקְטָלְךָ | יִקְטְלֽוּךָ | — | — |
| 2 f. | &c. | יִקְטְלֵךְ | יִקְטְלֽוּךְ | — | — |
| 3 m. | | יִקְטְלֵהוּ | יִקְטְלֽוּהוּ | קָטְלֵֽהוּ | &c. |
| 3 f. | | יִקְטְלֶֽהָ/‑הּ | יִקְטְלֽוּהָ | קָטְלֶֽהָ/‑הּ | as in imperf. |
| pl. | | | | | |
| 1 c. | | יִקְטְלֵֽנוּ | יִקְטְלֽוּנוּ | קָטְלֵֽנוּ | 3rd plural |
| 2 m. | יִכְבַּד׳ | יִקְטָלְכֶם | יִקְטְלֽוּכֶם/יִכְבְּ׳ | — | — |
| 2 f. | | יִקְטָלְכֶן | יִקְטְלֽוּכֶן | — | — |
| 3 m. | | יִקְטְלֵם | יִקְטְלֽוּם | קָטְלֵם | |
| 3 f. | | יִקְטְלֵן | יִקְטְלֽוּן | קָטְלֵן | |

And so all parts of impf. ending in a Consonant.

So 2 pl. m., and 2, 3 pl. f. which becomes תִּקְטְלוּ

[1] This column may be also written defectively, e.g. קְטַלְתֻּֽנִי, &c.

[2] The first syll. throughout Imperative is half-open e.g. כָּתֳבֵֽנִי kotobenī

[1] כָּבֵד, which is used here to illustrate stative, or intransitive verbs, with verbal suffixes, is, in actual fact, never found with such suffixes.

# THE REGULAR VERB

*Lamed Hē* verbs

**Qal**                                    **Piēl**

| 1 s. c. | 3 pl. c. | 2 pl. c. | 1 pl. c. | 3 s. m. |
|---|---|---|---|---|
| קְטַלְתִּי | קְטָלוּ | קְטַלְתֶּם | קְטַלְנוּ | קִטֵּל |
| — | קְטָלוּנִי/כְּבֵד | קְטַלְתּוּנִי | — | קִטְּלַנִי |
| קְטַלְתִּיךָ | קְטָלוּךָ | — | קְטַלְנוּךָ | קִטֶּלְךָ |
| קְטַלְתִּיךְ | קְטָלוּךְ | — | &c. | קִטְּלֵךְ |
| קְטַלְתִּיהוּ/־יו | קְטָלוּהוּ | &c. | as 3 pl. | קִטְּלוֹ |
| קְטַלְתִּיהָ | קְטָלוּהָ | as 3 pl. | | קִטְּלָהּ |
| — | קְטָלֻנוּ | | — | קִטְּלָנוּ |
| קְטַלְתִּיכֶם | — | — | | קִטֶּלְכֶם |
| קְטַלְתִּיכֶן | — | — | | קִטֶּלְכֶן |
| קְטַלְתִּים | קְטָלוּם | | | קִטְּלָם |
| קְטַלְתִּין | קְטָלוּן | | | קִטְּלָן |

**Impf. and imper. with nūn energ.**

Infin. cstr.

| | | | | |
|---|---|---|---|---|
| | | כְּבֹד | קְטֹל | יְקַטֵּל |
| יִקְטְלֵנִי/יִכְבְּ | קְטָלֵנִי/כְּבׇ | כׇּבְדִי | קׇטְלִי/־נִי | יְקַטְּלֵנִי |
| יִקְטְלֶךָ | | כׇּבְדְּךָ | קׇטְלְךָ/קׇטׇלְךָ | יְקַטֶּלְךָ |
| | | כׇּבְדֵךְ | קׇטְלֵךְ | יְקַטְּלֵךְ |
| יִקְטְלֶנּוּ | קְטָלֶנּוּ | &c. | קׇטְלוֹ/־ֵהוּ | יְקַטְּלֶהוּ |
| יִקְטְלֶנָּה | קְטָלֶנָּה | | קׇטְלָהּ | יְקַטְּלָהּ |
| | | | קׇטְלֵנוּ | יְקַטְּלֵנוּ |
| | | כׇּבְדְּכֶם | קׇטׇלְכֶם[1] | יְקַטֶּלְכֶם |
| | | | קׇטׇלְכֶן[1] | יְקַטֶּלְכֶן |
| | | | קׇטְלָם | יְקַטְּלָם |
| | | | קׇטְלָן | יְקַטְּלָן |

[1] Or קְטׇלְכֶם, קְטׇלְכֶן

For the use and meaning of these suff. see pp. 148 f.
The first syll. is half-open: e.g. כׇּתְבוֹ except before
דְ and כֶם, where it is closed, e.g. כׇּבְדְּךָ, כׇּתְבְּךָ.

# THE NUMERALS

|   | With the Masculine | | With the Feminine | |
|---|---|---|---|---|
|   | Absol. | Cstr. | Absol. | Cstr. |
| 1 | אֶחָד | אַחַד | אַחַת | אַחַת |
| 2 | שְׁנַיִם | שְׁנֵי | שְׁתַּיִם | שְׁתֵּי |
| 3 | שְׁלֹשָׁה | שְׁלֹשֶׁת | שָׁלֹשׁ | שְׁלֹשׁ |
| 4 | אַרְבָּעָה | אַרְבַּעַת | אַרְבַּע | אַרְבַּע |
| 5 | חֲמִשָּׁה | חֲמֵשֶׁת | חָמֵשׁ | חֲמֵשׁ |
| 6 | שִׁשָּׁה | שֵׁשֶׁת | שֵׁשׁ | שֵׁשׁ |
| 7 | שִׁבְעָה | שִׁבְעַת | שֶׁבַע | שְׁבַע |
| 8 | שְׁמֹנָה | שְׁמֹנַת | שְׁמֹנֶה | שְׁמֹנֶה |
| 9 | תִּשְׁעָה | תִּשְׁעַת | תֵּשַׁע | תְּשַׁע |
| 10 | עֲשָׂרָה | עֲשֶׂרֶת | עֶשֶׂר | עֶשֶׂר |

| 11 | אַחַד עָשָׂר | אַחַת עֶשְׂרֵה |
|---|---|---|
|  | עַשְׁתֵּי עָשָׂר | עַשְׁתֵּי עֶשְׂרֵה |
| 12 | שְׁנֵי עָשָׂר | שְׁתֵּים עֶשְׂרֵה |
|  | שְׁנֵים עָשָׂר | שְׁתֵּי עֶשְׂרֵה |
| 13 | שְׁלֹשָׁה עָשָׂר | שְׁלֹשׁ עֶשְׂרֵה |
| 14 | אַרְבָּעָה עָשָׂר | אַרְבַּע עֶשְׂרֵה |
| 15 | חֲמִשָּׁה עָשָׂר | חֲמֵשׁ עֶשְׂרֵה |
| 16 | שִׁשָּׁה עָשָׂר | שֵׁשׁ עֶשְׂרֵה |
| 17 | שִׁבְעָה עָשָׂר | שְׁבַע עֶשְׂרֵה |
| 18 | שְׁמֹנָה עָשָׂר | שְׁמֹנֶה עֶשְׂרֵה |
| 19 | תִּשְׁעָה עָשָׂר | תְּשַׁע עֶשְׂרֵה |

| 20 | עֶשְׂרִים | 60 | שִׁשִּׁים |
|---|---|---|---|
| 30 | שְׁלֹשִׁים | 70 | שִׁבְעִים |
| 40 | אַרְבָּעִים | 80 | שְׁמֹנִים |
| 50 | חֲמִשִּׁים | 90 | תִּשְׁעִים |

| | |
|---|---|
| 100 | מֵאָה *fem.*, *cstr* מְאַת, *plur.* מֵאוֹת *hundreds.* |
| 200 | מָאתַיִם *dual* (for מְאָתַיִם). |
| 300 | שְׁלֹשׁ מֵאוֹת,   400 אַרְבַּע מֵאוֹת, &c. |
| 1,000 | אֶלֶף *masc.* |
| 2,000 | אַלְפַּיִם *dual.* |
| 3,000 | שְׁלֹשֶׁת אֲלָפִים,   4,000 אַרְבַּעַת אֲלָפִים, &c. |
| 10,000 | רְבָבָה   *pl.* regular,  רְבָבוֹת. <br> רִבּוֹא רִבּוֹ   *pl.* רִבֹּאוֹת and רִבּוֹת (later forms). |
| 20,000 | רִבּוֹתַיִם *dual.* |

# HEBREW - ENGLISH WORD LIST

א

אָב      (77/100) father [cstr. אֲבִי; pl. אָבוֹת]

אָבַד      (95) to perish

אָבָה      (95) to wish

אֶבֶן      (100) ƒ stone

אַבְרָם      (106) Abram

אֱדוֹם      (51) Edom

אָדוֹן      (64/127f.) lord, master

אָדָם      (38) man, mankind

אֲדָמָה      (97) ƒ ground, soil

אַדְמֹנִי      (122) red-cheeked, ruddy

אָהֵב      (96) to love

אֹהֵב      (150) |pt.| friend, lover

אוֹ      (126) or; אוֹ...אוֹ either...or

אוּלָם      (126) but [i.e. for a very strong contrast]

אוֹר      (29) light

אָז      (126) then

אֹזֶן      (68/91) ƒ ear; [du. אָזְנַיִם]

אָח      (100) brother [cstr. אֲחִי; pl. אַחִים]

אֶחָד      (108) one

אַחֲרוֹן      (153) last

אַחֲרֵי      (72) after

אָיַב      (82) to be hostile

אֹיֵב      (60/82) |pt.| enemy [pl. אֹיְבִים]

אַיֵּה      (124) where?

אִיזֶבֶל      (42) Jezebel

אֵיכָה / אֵיךְ      (124) how?, how!

אַיֶּלֶת / אַיָּלָה      (92) ƒ female deer, hind

אֵי־מִזֶּה      (124) from where?  whence?

אַיִן      [cstr. אֵין] (51/65/71) |abs.| non-existence; |in cstr. relationship| there is/was not

אִישׁ      (27/100) man, husband [pl. אֲנָשִׁים]

אָכַל      (51/95) to eat

| | |
|---|---|
| אָכְלָה | (91/97) f food |
| אַל | (76) not |
| אֶל | (50) to, towards |
| אֵל | (121) God; |with a superlative sense| mighty, high, etc. |
| אֵלֶּה | pl. of זֶה/זאת |
| אֱלֹהִים | (52/121) God; gods |
| אֶלֶף | (153) thousand |
| אִם | (97/126) if, when |
| אֵם | (100) f mother |
| אָמַן | (145) to confirm, support; [Hiph. הֶאֱמִין] to believe, trust; stand firm |
| אָמַץ | (139) to be strong; [Pi. אִמֵּץ] to make strong, make courageous, (150) strengthen |
| אָמַר | (56/95f.) to say; (112) to promise |
| אֱמֶת | (134) f truth |
| אָנָה | (118/124) to where?, whither? |
| אֱנוֹשׁ | (39) man, mankind |
| אֲנִי / אָנֹכִי ‖ אֲנַחְנוּ | (37) |1st per. s/pl pron. c| I ‖ we |
| אָסַף | (132) to gather, take away; [Niph. נֶאֱסַף] to be gathered, taken away; (134) to assemble |
| אַף | (125) also, moreover |
| אָפָה | (95) to bake |
| אֶפְרַיִם | (83) Ephraim |
| אָצִיל | (150) extremity, remote corner |
| אֲרוֹן | (107) chest, ark (of the covenant) |
| אֲרִי | (51) lion |
| אֹרֶךְ | (118) length |
| אֶרֶץ | (28) f land, earth [+ def. art. הָאָרֶץ] |
| אֵשׁ | (52) f fire |
| אִשָּׁה | (28/100) f woman; wife [pl. נָשִׁים] |
| אֲשֶׁר | (47) |rel. pro.| who, whom, whose, which |
| אֵת | (46) untranslatable direct object marker [אֶת־] |
| אֵת | (50/72) with [אֶת־] |
| אַתָּה / אַתְּ ‖ אַתֶּם / אַתֶּן | (37) |2nd per. s/pl pron. m/f| you |

| | |
|---|---|
| בְּ | (51) in; with; (109) on; among, by |
| בַּאֲשֶׁר | (112) because |
| בדל | (114/146) [Hiph.] to divide, separate |
| בֹּהוּ | (113) emptiness |
| בּוֹא | (57/83) to come; go; enter [pf. and pt. בָּא] |
| בּוֹר | (146) pit |
| בָּזָה | (122) to despise |
| בָּחַר | (55/60) to choose [+ בְּ] |
| בָּטַח | (96) to trust in (someone) [+ בְּ] |
| בֵּין | (50) between |
| בַּיִת | (51/100) house [pl. בָּתִּים] |
| בֵּית־אֵל | (83) Bethel |
| בֵּית לֶחֶם | (65) Bethlehem |
| בַּמָּה | (108) how? |
| בֵּן | (65/100) son; [pl. בָּנִים] |
| בָּעַל | (127) to own, possess |
| בַּעַל | (97/125) lord, master, owner; husband; Baal |
| בֹּקֶר | (29/90) morning |
| בָּרָא | (48) to create; (141) [Niph.] to be created |
| בָּרוּךְ | (54) Baruch |
| ברך | (138) [Pi.: pf. בֵּרֵךְ, impf. וַיְבָרֶךְ] to bless |
| בָּרַח | (134) to flee |
| בְּרִית | (71) f covenant |
| בַּת | (33/100) f daughter [(69) pl. בָּנוֹת] |
| בְּתוֹךְ | (141) in the middle of |

| | |
|---|---|
| גְּבוּרָה | (134) f strength |
| גָּדוֹל | (30) great |
| גָּדַל | (120) to be great; to grow; (140) [Pi.] to bring up (a child); magnify |
| גִּדְעוֹן | (77) Gideon |
| גּוֹי | (127) nation, people |
| גּוּר | (127) to sojourn, take up temporary residence |
| גָּלָה | (58/105) to uncover, reveal; (154) to depart, go into exile; [Hiph.] to carry into exile, deport |

| | |
|---|---|
| גׇּלְיׇת | (53) Goliath |
| גִּלְעׇד | (134) Gilead |
| גַּם | (72) also, even; (125 f.) גַּם...גַּם both...and; גַּם לֹא...וְגַם לֹא neither...nor |
| גַּן | (141) garden [+ art. הַגַּן] |
| גׇּנַב | (76) to steal |
| גַּנׇּב | (155) thief |
| גְּרׇר | (127) Gerar |
| גׇּרַשׁ | (134) to drive out; [Niph.] to be driven out |

ד

| | |
|---|---|
| דְּבוֹרׇה | (39) Deborah |
| דבר | (140) [Pi.: pf. דִּבֶּר , impf. וַיְדַבֵּר] to speak |
| דׇּבׇר | (33) word; (48) thing, matter, affair |
| דְּבַשׁ | (54) honey |
| דׇּג | (90) fish |
| דׇּוִד | (50) David |
| דׇּם | (52) blood |
| דַּעַת | (141) ƒ knowledge |
| דֶּרֶךְ | (83) way, road; journey [pl. דְּרׇכִים] |
| דׇּרַשׁ | (126) to make a request [אֶל־ = to] |

ה

| | |
|---|---|
| ה | (27) Idef. art.I the |
| הֲ | (123 f.) untranslatable interrogative particle; (124) הֲ...אִם Whether...or? Is...or? |
| הֵמׇּה (הֵם) / הֵנׇּה ǁ הִיא / הוּא | (37) I3rd per. pron. s/pl m/f I he/it, she/it ǁ they; (40) Idemo. pron. of further reference s/pl ǁ m/fI that ǁ those |
| הׇיׇה | (93/105 f.) to be [impf. יִהְיֶה; V.C. Impf. וַיְהִי] |
| הֵיכׇל | (27/71) temple; palace |
| הׇלַךְ | (50) to go, walk, [(103) impf. יֵלֵךְ]; (140) [Hitp.] to walk to and fro |
| הלל | (138/140) [Pi.: pf. הִלֵּל, impf. וַיְהַלֵּל] to praise |
| הִנֵּה | (72/124) behold, lo, see |
| הַר | (27) mountain, hill, hill-country [+ def. art. הׇהׇר] |
| הׇרַג | (48) to kill, slay |

ו

ו          (27) and;  (32) but

ז

זָבַח      (155) to slaughter (for  sacrifice)
זֶה / זֹאת ‖ אֵלֶּה   (40) Idemo. pron. of nearer reference s/pl
          ‖ m/f I this ‖ these
זָהָב      (28) gold
זָכַר      (48) to remember
זָעַק      (96) to cry out
זָקֵן      (45) Ivb.I to be old;  (82)  Iadj.I old; In.I elder
זֶרַע      (92/146) seed,  descendants, offspring

ח

חבא       (143) Hiph. [הֶחְבִּיא] to hide, keep hidden; withdraw
חֶבֶל מִדָּה   (118) measuring line
חָדַל      (79) to cease, leave off,  stop, come to an end
חָדָשׁ     (36) new
חוה       (140) Pi. [impf. יְחַוֶּה] to make known, tell, declare
חוֹל      (65) sand
חוּץ      (146) outside, out-of-doors
חָזַק      (95) to be strong;  (150) [Hiph.] to seize, grasp
חָזָק      (124) strong
חָטָא      (118) to sin
חֵטְא      (93) sin [pl. חֲטָאִים]
חָיָה      (139) to live; Pi. [חִיָּה] to preserve alive;  bring to
          life
חַיִּים    (88) Ipl.I life
חָכַם      (46/74) to be wise
חָכָם      (27) Iadj.I wise, shrewd, skillful; In.I wise man;
חָכְמָה    (23) ƒ wisdom, skill,  shrewdness, prudence
חֲלוֹם     (127) a dream
חָלוּק     (122) smooth
חָמָס      (134) violence
חֲמִשָּׁה    (122) five
חֵן       (124) grace

חָנָה     (134) to encamp

חִנָּם     (124) |adv.| for nothing, in vain

חֵץ     (99) arrow

חֹק     (99) statute

חֶרֶב     (27) sword

חרשׁ     (145) Hiph. [הֶחֱרִישׁ] to be silent, speechless; be deaf

חָשַׁב     (132) to think, reckon; Niph. [ נֶחְשַׁב ] to be accounted

חֹשֶׁךְ     (29) darkness

## ט

טָבַח     (155) to slaughter (for food, not for sacrifice)

טַבָּח     (154) cook; |pl.| guardsmen, bodyguard

טוֹב     (30) good

טָהֵר     (137) to be clean, pure; Hitp. [הִטַּהֵר] to purify oneself

## י

יָד     (34) ƒ hand [du. יָדַיִם]

יָדַע     (103) to know [impf. יֵדַע]

יְהוּדָה     (51) Judah

יְהוּדִי     (119) Judean [ ƒ = יְהוּדִית]

יהוה     (64) Yahweh [read as אֲדֹנָי]

יוֹם     (28) day [(88) pl. abs. יָמִים, pl. cstr. יְמֵי]

יוֹמָם     (124) |adv.| by day, in the daytime

יוֹנָה     ƒ (107) dove; m Jonah

יטב     (146) to be well; Hiph. [הֵיטִיב] to do (something) well, deal well (with someone)

יָכֹל     (45/103) to be able; [impf. יוּכַל]

יָלַד     (85) to bear (a child), give birth; (103) [impf. יֵלֵד]; (133) Niph. [pf. נוֹלַד, impf. יִוָּלֵד] to be born; (143) Hiph. [pf. הוֹלִיד, impf. יוֹלִיד] to cause to bring forth children; (144) [Hoph. הוּלַד ]

יֶלֶד     (41) boy, lad; child

יַלְקוּט     (122) container, wallet

יָם     (65) sea

יָמִין    (150) right hand

יָנַק    (57) to suck; (143) Hiph. [pf. הֵינִיק, impf. יֵינִיק] to suckle

יָפֶה    (93) beautiful, fair [(106) ƒ יָפָה]

יָצָא    (103) to go out [impf. יֵצֵא] (146) [Hiph.] to send out, bring out

יָרֵא    (102) to be afraid [impf. יִירָא]

יָרַד    (50/103) to go down [impf. יֵרֵד]

יַרְדֵּן    (97) Jordan

יְרוּשָׁלַיִם    (51) Jerusalem

יָרֵךְ    (134) ƒ thigh [cstr. יֶרֶךְ]

יָרַשׁ    (102) to inherit [impf. יִירַשׁ]

יִשְׂרָאֵל    (51) Israel

יֵשׁ [יֶשׁ־]    (65/71) there is/was

יָשַׁב    (50/57) to sit; dwell; remain; (71) to settle; (103) [impf. יֵשֵׁב]

ישֵׁב    (77/82) lpt.l inhabitant, dweller [pl. יֹשְׁבִים]

## כ

כ    (51) as, like

כַּאֲשֶׁר    (79) when; (112) as

כָּבֵד    (32) ladj.l heavy, serious; (45) lvb.l to be heavy; (120) to be difficult; (140) [Pi.] to make heavy, harden

כָּבוֹד    (141) glory

כִּבְשָׂה    (91) ƒ ewe lamb

כֹּה    (72/125) thus

כֹּהֵן    (28) priest

כּוֹכָב    (65) star

כול    (138) [Hiph.] to contain, include, hold in, endure; Pi. [pf. כִּלְכֵּל, impf. יְכַלְכֵּל] to include; supply

כון    (133) Niph. [pf. נָכוֹן impf. יִכּוֹן] to be set, established

כּוֹס    (34) ƒ cup [pl. כּוֹסוֹת]

כִּי    (54/126) for, because; that

כִּי אִם    (126) but [for a strong contrast after a negative]

כֹּל [כָּל־]    (65/118) totality, all

כֶּלֶב      (122) dog

כְּלִי      (122) utensil, receptacle

כַּמָּה      (118) (according to) what?

כְּמוֹ      (109) [poetic form of כְּ to which suffixes are added] like, as

כֵּן      (125) thus, so

כְּנַעַן      (65) Canaan

כִּסֵּא      (50/97) throne

כֶּסֶף      (28) silver

כַּף      (107) *f* palm (of hand); sole (of foot)

כְּרוּב      (146) cherub

כָּרַת      (71) to cut; |+ בְּרִית| make a covenant

כָּתַב      (48) to write


### ל

ל      (51) to, at, for

לֹא      (31/76) not, no; (134) לֹא...עוֹד no longer

לֵבָב/לֵב      (89/97/141) heart

לוֹט      (82) Lot

לחם      (134) [Niph.] to fight, fight with one another, do battle

לֶחֶם      (65) bread, food

לַיְלָה      (28/88) night

לָמַד      (139) to learn; Pi. [לִמֵּד] to teach

לָמָּה      (60) why?

לְמַעַן      (97/146) in order that, so that; (112) for the sake of

לִפְנֵי      (72) before

לָקַח      (69/107/116) to take, [impf. יִקַּח]


### מ

מְאֹד      (65/125) very; (121) exceedingly [follows the adj. it qualifies]

מֵאָה      (153) *f* hundred [du. מָאתַיִם]

מֵאַיִן      (124) from where?, whence?

מאן      (138) Pi. [pf. מֵאֵן impf. יְמָאֵן] to refuse

מָאַס      (150) to reject

מִדְבָּר      (71) desert, wilderness

מָדַד (118) to measure

מָה (39) what?; (40) |+ adj.| how!

מוּת (118) to die [pf. and (90) pt. מֵת]

מִזְבֵּחַ (46) altar

מטר (145) [Hiph.] to rain; send rain

מָטָר (145) rain

מִי (38f.) who?

מַיִם (36) water

מָכַר (77) to sell

מָלֵא (134) to be full, to fill; [Niph.] to be filled; (138) Pi. [pf. מִלֵּא , impf. יְמַלֵּא] to fill

מַלְאָךְ (50/65) angel, messenger

מִלְחָמָה (118) ƒ war, battle

מלט (134) [Niph.] to escape, slip away, save oneself

מָלַךְ (85) to rule; (146) to be king/queen, reign; [Hiph.] to make king

מֶלֶךְ (27/90) king

מַלְכָּה (63/91) ƒ queen

מִלִּפְנֵי (111) away from [ = לִפְנֵי + מִן ]

מַמְלָכָה (91) ƒ kingdom [cstr. מַמְלֶכֶת]

מִן (53) from, away from

מָנוֹחַ (107) resting place

מִסְפֵּד (98) mourning

מְעַט (124) little, few, some

מֵעִם (111) from, away from [ = עִם + מִן ]

מָצָא (56/96) to find; (143) [Hiph.] to cause to find

מִצְוָה (97) ƒ commandment

מִצְפָּה (134) Mizpah

מִצְרִי (106/119) Egyptian [ƒ מִצְרִית]

מִצְרַיִם (50) Egypt

מָקוֹם (60) place

מַקֵּל (100) rod, staff

מַרְאֶה (122) appearance

מֹשֶׁה (16) Moses

מָשַׁל (77) to rule ( + בְּ = over)

מֹשֵׁל (82) |pt.| ruler

מִשְׁפָּט (83) judgement; right; (91) justice

מָחוֹק (54) sweet

נ

נָא־ (75) |particle of entreaty| please! I/we pray, I/we beseech you

נבא (126/140) Niph. [נִבָּא] to prophesy; Hitp.[הִתְנַבָּא] to act like a prophet, rave; to prophesy

נְבוּזַרְאֲדָן (155) Nebuzaradan

נְבוּכַדְרֶאצַּר (155) Nebuchadrezzar

נבט (122/146) Hiph. [הִבִּיט] to look

נָבִיא (36) prophet

נְבִיאָה (42) f prophetess

נֶגֶב (118) Negeb; South; South-country

נגד (144) Hiph. [pf. הִגִּיד, impf. יַגִּיד] to tell, declare, report, show; Hoph. [pf. הֻגַּד, impf. יֻגַּד]

נָכָה (117) to smite, strike;
(133) Niph. [pf. נִכָּה , pt. נִכֶּה] to be smitten

נגשׁ (115/146) to draw near, come near; Hiph. [הִגִּישׁ] to bring near, cause to approach

נָהָר (93) stream, river

נוּחַ (107) to rest

נֹחַ (107) Noah

נָחַל (145) to inherit; [Hiph.] to cause (someone) to in-herit (something)

נַחַל (100) stream, wady

נחם (137f.) Niph. [pf. נִחַם, impf. יִנָּחֵם] to repent, be sorry; pity; be comforted; Pi. [pf. נִחַם, impf. יְנַחֵם] to comfort, console

נָסַע (117) to set out (on a journey); [lit.] to pull up (tent pegs)

נַעַר (92) lad, young man

נָפַל (58/115) to fall

נֶפֶשׁ (97) f breath; life force, soul

נצל (146) Hiph. [הִצִּיל] to save, deliver

נָקַם (140) to take vengeance; [Hitp.] to show oneself vengeful

נָשָׂא (117) to lift up, raise; bear, carry

נָתַן     (58 f./116) to give [impf. יִתֵּן]

ס

סָבַב     (59) to turn, turn away; go around, surround; (116 f.) [impf. יָסֹב and יִּסֹב]; (133) Niph. [ pf. נָסַב, impf. יִּסַב] to turn around; (139) Pi. [pf. סֹבֵב, impf. יְסֹבֵב] to encompass, enclose; (144) Hiph. [pf. הֵסֵב, impf. יָסֵב] to turn

סְדֹם     (82) Sodom

סוּס     (33) horse

סוּסָה     (34) ƒ mare

סָפַר     (65) to count; (140) [Pi.] to recount, declare

סֵפֶר     (48/90) book

סָתַר     (131/134) to hide; [Niph.] to hide oneself, be hidden; (140) Hitp. [הִסְתַּתֵּר] to hide oneself

ע

עָבַד     (85) to serve, labour; be a slave; (96) worship

עֶבֶד     (27) slave, servant

עֲבֹדָה     (54) ƒ work, service; worship

עָבַר     (96) to cross

עַד     (50) until, as far as

עֵדֶן     (146) Eden

עוֹד     (125) still, yet; (134) לֹא ... עוֹד no longer

עוֹלָם     (88) eternity, age; [+ עַד־ forever]

עַז     (54) strong, mighty, fierce

עָזַב     (96) to leave, forsake, abandon

עָזַר     (150) to help

עֶזְרָא     (86) Ezra

עַיִן     (65) ƒ eye [du. עֵינַיִם]

עִיר     (29) ƒ city, town, [(100) pl. עָרִים]

עַל     (50) upon, beside, on account of, against

עָלֶה     (93) leaf, [collectively] leaves

עֵלִי     (118) Eli

עַל־כֵּן     (126) therefore

עַם     (32/99) people [+ def. art. הָעָם; pl. עַמִּים]

עִם     (50/108) with

עָמַד     (50/55) to stand
עַמּוֹן     (134) Ammon
עָמָל     (27) trouble
עָנָה     (118) to answer, reply
עֵץ     (50) tree; (141) [collectively] trees
עָצוּם     (32) powerful
עֶרֶב     (29) evening
עֵשֶׂב     (97) grass, plants, herbage
עָשָׂה     (40/60) to do, make
עָשַׁר     (140) to become rich; [Hitp.] to pretend to be rich
עֵת     (83) f time, season
עַתָּה     (72/125) now

פ

פַּחַד     (92) fear, dread
פְּלִשְׁתִּי     (122) Philistine
פֶּן     (126) lest, so that not
פָּנִים     (110) |pl.| face
פָּעַל     (55/130) to do, make
פָּקַד     (144f.) to oversee, inspect, review; (149) visit; [Hiph.] to cause someone to oversee, appoint as overseer, put in charge of
פַּר     (36) ox [+ def. art. הַפָּר]
פָּרָה     (36) f cow
פַּרְעֹה     (141) Pharaoh
פָּשַׁע     (140) to rebel [+ בְּ = against]
פִּתְאוֹם     (124) |adv.| suddenly
פָּתַח     (86) to open

צ

צָבָא     (93) army, host [pl. צְבָאוֹת]
צַדִּיק     (31) righteous
צָדַק     (137) to be righteous, just, in the right; [Hitp. הִצְטַדֵּק] to justify oneself; (145) [Hiph.] to declare someone in the right, to acquit
צֶדֶק     (150) righteousness

| | |
|---|---|
| צְדָקָה | (63) *f* righteousness |
| צִוָה | (141) [Pi.] to order, command |
| צִנָּה | (122) *f* shield |
| צָעַק | (134) to cry, call out; summon; [Niph.] to be called out, be summoned |

ק

| | |
|---|---|
| קָבַר | (77) to bury; (131) [Niph.] to be buried |
| קֶבֶר | (77) grave |
| קֶדֶם | (146) East [לְ מִקֶּדֶם  – to the East of] |
| קָדַשׁ | (139) to be holy; [Pi.] to make holy, sanctify; [Hitp.] to sanctify oneself; (145) [Hiph.] to sanctify |
| קָדֵשׁ | (127) Kadesh |
| קֹדֶשׁ | (64) holiness |
| קָדוֹשׁ | (32) holy |
| קוֹל | (71) voice, sound [pl. קוֹלוֹת] |
| קוּם | (57/104) to arise, stand [pf. and pt. קָם]; (144) [Hiph. pf. הֵקִים, impf. יָקִים] to raise; [Hoph. pf. הוּקַם, impf. יוּקַם] |
| קָטַל | (73/129f.) to kill, slay |
| קָטֹן | (45) |vb.| to be small, little; (53) |adj.| small, little, young |
| קַל | (129) |adj.| light |
| קִלֵּל | (122) [Pi.] to curse |
| קֶלַע | (122) sling |
| קָצֶה | (150) *f* end, extremity |
| קָרָא | (48/88) to call, call out, cry, proclaim; read; (88) [+ לְ] to name |
| קָרַב | (127) to approach, draw near; [euphemism for 'to have sexual intercourse with'] |
| קָרֵב | (122) |pt.| approaching |

ר

| | |
|---|---|
| רָאָה | (60) to see |
| רְאוּבֵן | (146) Reuben |
| רֹאשׁ | (27) head |

| רִאשׁוֹן | (153) first |
| רֵאשִׁית | (48/113) f beginning |
| רַב | (65) ladj.l many, numerous; ln.l (154) chief [pl. רַבִּים] |
| רָבַב | (153) to be many |
| רֶגֶל | (91) f foot |
| רָדַף | (77) to pursue |
| רוּחַ | (121) f spirit, breath, wind |
| רוּם | (138) to be high, exalted; rise up; Pi. [pf. רוֹמֵם, impf. יְרוֹמֵם] to exalt; Pu [pf. רוֹמַם, impf. יְרוֹמַם] to be exalted |
| רֹחַב | (118) breadth |
| רָחוֹק | (107) far, distant |
| רָחַף | (113) [Pi.] to hover |
| רֵיק | (124) empty |
| רֵיקָם | (124) ladv.l in vain, empty handed |
| רָם | (36) high, lofty |
| רָמָה | (83) Ramah |
| רֹמַח | (92) spear |
| רַע | (32) bad, evil |
| רָעָב | (32) famine |
| רָעָה | (99) f an evil; lf adj.l evil |
| רֹעֶה | (122) lpt.l shepherd |
| רָעַע | (144) to be evil; [Hiph. הֵרַע] to do harm, treat wickedly |
| רָשַׁע | (144) to be guilty; Hiph. [הִרְשִׁיעַ] to declare someone guilty, condemn, convict |
| רָשָׁע | (83) wicked |

שׂ

| שִׂים | (57/104) to put, place [pf. and pt. שָׂם] |
| שָׂמֵחַ | (90) joyful |
| שָׂנֵא | (100) to hate |
| שָׂפָה | (34) f lip [du. שְׂפָתַיִם]; (65) f edge, bank, shore |
| שַׂר | (36) prince, officer [ + def. art. הַשַּׂר] |
| שָׂרָה | (36) f princess; Sarah |
| שָׂרַף | (52) to burn |

שׁ

| שָׁאוּל | (51) Saul |
| שָׁאַל | (100) to ask, request; (139) Pi. [שִׁאֵל] to enquire carefully, practise beggary |
| שְׁאֵלָה | (118) f request |
| שְׁבִיעִי | (52) seventh |
| שׁבע | (133/134) [Niph.] to swear, take an oath |
| שָׁבַר | (131) to break; [Niph.] to be broken; (136/139) [Pi.] to shatter, smash to pieces |
| שָׁבַת | (52) to rest |
| שַׁבָּת | (80) Sabbath |
| שׁוב | (118) to return, come back [pf. and pt. שָׁב]; (146) Hiph. [הֵשִׁיב] to restore |
| שׁוּר | (127) Shur |
| שָׁחַט | (94) to slaughter |
| שׁחת | (134) [Niph.] to be destroyed, corrupted, spoiled |
| שִׁיר | (36) song |
| שָׁכַן | (59) to dwell; (146) [Hiph.] to place |
| שָׁלוֹם | (79) peace, wholeness, soundness, security, health |
| שָׁלַח | (55/77/95) to send; stretch out; (138) Pi. [pf. שִׁלַּח, impf. יְשַׁלַּח] to set free; (143) Hiph. to let loose |
| שׁלך | (146) [Hiph.] to cast, throw, fling |
| שְׁלֹמֹה | (39) Solomon |
| שָׁם | (77/125) there |
| שֵׁם | (98/141) name |
| שָׁמָּה | (125) to there, thither |
| שָׁמַע | (71) to pay heed to [+בְּ]; (86) to hear, listen |
| שְׁמוּאֵל | (28) Samuel |
| שָׁמַיִם | (36) lpl.l heaven(s), sky |
| שָׁמַר | (43/79) to guard, watch; to keep, protect; (131) [Niph.] to guard oneself, beware; (137) Hitp. [הִשְׁתַּמֵּר] to take heed to oneself, be on one's guard |
| שֹׁמֵר | (82) lpt.l watchman |
| שָׁנָה | (152/154) year |

שָׁעָה      (150) to gaze; Hitp. [pf. הִשְׁתָּעָה, impf. יִשְׁתָּעָה] to gaze about (in anxiety)

שׁעַן      (134) [Niph.] to lean on, rest on

שַׁעַר      (82) gate

שָׁפַט      (48) to judge

שֹׁפֵט      (82) |pt.| judge

שָׁפַךְ      (52/77) to pour out, spill; shed (blood)

שָׁקַל      (134) to weigh; Niph. to be weighed

שָׁתָה      (125) to drink

### ת

תֵּבָה      (107) ƒ (Noah's) ark;   basket

תֹּהוּ      (113) formlessness

תְּהוֹם      (113) the 'deep', the   primaeval ocean

תָּוֶךְ      (141) middle [cstr. תּוֹךְ ]

תּוֹרָה      (48) ƒ instruction; law; Law; Torah

תַּחַת      (50) beneath, under; in place of, instead of

תָּמַךְ      (150) to grasp, lay hold of

תֹּמֶר      (83) palm tree

תְּפִלָּה      (71) ƒ prayer

# GENERAL INDEX